Learning

to Love

Africa

Monique Maddy

Learning
to Love
Africa

My Journey from Africa to

Harvard Business School and Back

HarperBusiness

An Imprint of HarperCollins*Publishers*

HarperCollins books may be purchased for educational, business, or sales promotional use. For information, please write to: Special Markets Department, Harper-Collins Publishers Inc., 10 East 53rd Street, New York, New York 10022.

DESIGN BY SARAH MAYA GUBKIN

Library of Congress Cataloging-in-Publication Data
Maddy, Monique
Learning to love Africa : my journey from Africa to Harvard Business School and back / by Monique Maddy.
p. cm.
Includes index.
ISBN 0-06-621110-7
1. Maddy, Monique. 2. Businesswomen--Tanzania--Biography. 3. New business enterprises--Tanzania. 4. Enterpreneurship--Tanzania. I. Title.
HD6072.6.T34M33 2004
384.535'092--dc22   2003065276
[B]

04 05 06 07 08 ❖/RRD 10 9 8 7 6 5 4 3 2 1

This book is dedicated in loving memory and with thanks to Pappi, Ma Kema, Mamma Ade, and Pappa Larry, to Mummy and to the people of Africa, whose voices are too seldom heard.

For always roaming with a hungry heart
Much have I seen and known; cities of men
And manners, climates, councils, governments,
Myself not least, but honor'd of them all;
And drunk delight of battle with my peers,
Far on the ringing plains of windy Troy.
I am a part of all that I have met;
Yet all experience is an arch wherethrough
Gleams that untravel'd world whose margin fades
For ever and for ever when I move.
How dull it is to pause, to make an end,
To rust unburnish'd, not to shine in use!

—*Ulysses,* Alfred, Lord Tennyson

Contents

Prologue

September 1993. As I boarded the flight in Dar es Salaam to London and then on to the United States, I was confident about my new venture. I had just a few more sections of the business plan to beef up, and a final report to send to each of my sponsors. Thanks to the timely intervention of a friend, the Nightmare Summer of the Interns was almost forgotten. I had only one major problem to contend with now.

When I graduated from Harvard Business School in June I had relinquished my student immigration status, and so now I was returning to the United States on a tourist visa that had been issued to me in Dar es Salaam. I only had a one-way ticket and a Liberian passport, which was almost worse than not having any passport at all. As a foreigner, I could not stay in Tanzania, and for reasons of safety I could not go back to Liberia even if I wanted to. Boston was where I had friends, connections, and couches to sleep on. But if denied entry I would be shipped to Liberia, where I had no family, no home, to a country still in the midst of a protracted civil war in which almost half of the country's population of three million had been displaced internally or fled to neighboring countries. Within ten years close to a quarter of a million Liberians would be slaughtered, including members of my own family, simply for having been born into the "wrong" tribe or practicing the "wrong" religion, and the country's president, Charles Taylor, would be indicted by an international court for war crimes and crimes against humanity.

I had a one-day layover in London, where I was spending the night at the house of Shannon Fergusson, a classmate from HBS. I took a bus to the city center, then hailed a cab to her place. As I got in, I realized that something was missing. "Oh my God!" I cried out. "I left my purse in the airport shuttle bus; it has everything in there—my money, my ticket, my passport, everything." I was like the cautionary tale in the American Express traveler's checks commercial. I was almost in tears. Unlike a U.S. citizen, I could not simply visit my embassy in London and ask for a new passport and assistance in getting home. I had absolutely no proof that I was Liberian (although I do not know who in her right mind would lie about being Liberian in order to secure a Liberian passport), even if there were a functioning Liberian Embassy in London—and there was not. I had once dealt with a Liberian consulate in Sweden that was literally a guy in his Volkswagen van doling out passports in return for hefty fees paid in cash (diplomatic ones cost extra), no proof of citizenship necessary.

This suddenly made me a stateless, homeless refugee in England, at the mercy of Shannon and a cabdriver whom I had met no more than two minutes before.

"Don't worry, Ma'am," he said, turning to look at me through the glass divider. "We're going to get your bag back." He was a short, middle-aged man with graying hair and crooked teeth; he certainly did not seem like the James Bond type. But he had what it took to save me; "The Knowledge," as they call it, of London's complicated street layout and transportation system. Like MI5 agents we raced through the narrow city streets, weaving in and out of traffic in an attempt to catch the bus. We turned a corner and it came into sight, and I jumped out of the taxi, waving my hands frantically in the air as the cabbie beeped the horn insistently. I bounded up the stairs of the bus and . . . the purse was still there! So were many of the passengers who had remained on the bus when I got off. They actually gave me an ovation. I wanted to thank each and every one of them for being kind enough to not steal it.

Shannon, outside her apartment waiting for me, was a sight for sore eyes. Barely had we sat down for a drink when the doorbell rang. It was my taxi driver—standing there with my PDA. In my frazzled, frantic rushing about I had left it in his cab. My state of mind was showing. On that day I was more flipped out about how to get back into the United States than about how to get my new Tanzania business venture off the ground, because without the one, the other was impossible.

The next day, during the entire seven-hour flight to Boston, I obsessed over the story I was going to tell if challenged at immigration. Would it sound suspicious if I said that I was coming back to Boston to work on a business plan? Was it better to say that I was just visiting friends, former HBS classmates? What would I put as my contact address on the immigration form? What if the agent asked me to show him my return ticket, which typically was required by persons holding tourist visas?

We all disembarked and headed through the Logan airport terminal to the immigration point, where I dutifully entered the queue marked ALIENS. I could hardly think of a better word to describe myself in that moment. My first move was to decide which officer to aim for. I looked for a sympathetic-looking male rather than a female, as the men had always been easier on me in the past.

Soon it was my turn to show my passport and my heart began pounding. I could not believe my bad luck. When he looked up, I realized that I had seen the officer before, one year earlier, when I had applied to U.S. immigration for temporary protection status, a special permit given to Liberian nationals who had entered the States during a specific period after the civil war broke out in 1989. It was intended to allow Liberians to stay in the country for as long as the political situation in Liberia remained dangerous and unstable. I had been denied the permit because I had missed the cutoff period by a couple of months. But I remembered the officer with whom I had dealt—his name was Mario, and he was Puerto Rican. Should I indicate that I recognized him? If I did, would I have to reveal under what conditions we had met? Surely that would only exacerbate my already tenuous situation. So I pretended to not know him and just prayed that he did not remember me. He looked at my passport. He looked at my visitor's visa. He asked me why I was coming to America. I told him that I had friends here that I wanted to see.

"Where is your return ticket?" he asked. I told him that I did not have one and that I would buy it later, when I was certain of my return date. And, I thought to myself, where the hell I am going.

He had the right and the authority to turn me back right then and there. People were sometimes turned away for far less—even having the wrong appearance. He hesitated and gave me a long hard look, which lasted an eternity. He seemed to sense that something was amiss. But he decided not to act on his suspicions. "You're like me," he said, pointing to his skin. "I'll let you go." I was in.

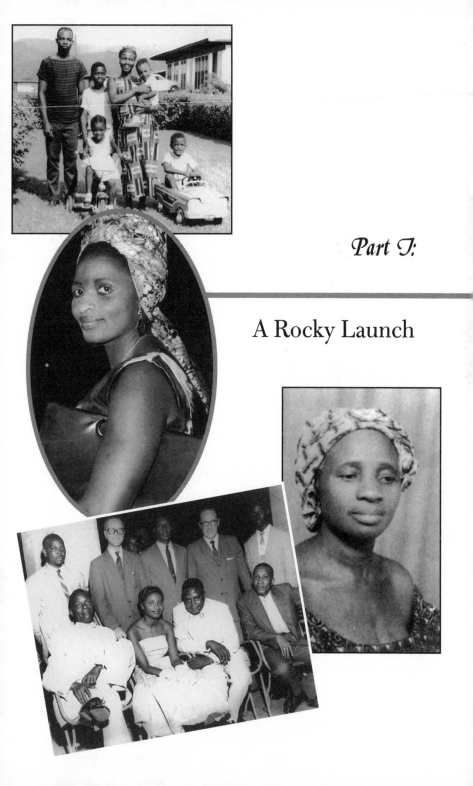

Part I:

A Rocky Launch

1

Mutiny in Dar es Salaam

June 1993. The British Airways Boeing 747 began her gradual descent through the thick layer of clouds, bringing into full view the majestic snow-capped Mount Kilimanjaro. After more than 24 hours of travel, the six of us all looked and felt pretty ragged. But I could feel the sense of adventure rising in the others. Unbeknownst to me at the time, they had already achieved their primary objective for the summer, even before we had done a day of work. They were in Africa.

Barely a week earlier I had been attending commencement exercises at Harvard. Now here I was, a freshly minted MBA, seizing a second chance at realizing my dream of giving back to Africa, the continent where I was born. I had tried once before, going through the United Nations, and had been disillusioned horribly by the experience. But now I was a little older (thirty), a little wiser, and armed with the knowledge, skills, and valuable contacts that I had acquired during my two years in Cambridge.

General Colin Powell, then the Chairman of the Joint Chiefs of Staff, had urged us in his commencement speech to "take from Harvard not just knowledge, but wisdom; not just intelligence, but also humanity; not just a drive for self-fulfillment, but as well a sense of service and a taste for hard work." I was leading the charge, accompanied by what I presumed was a battalion of like-minded troops: five eager and idealistic first-year HBS students. They had chosen to intern for me and my shell of a start-up rather than for one of the well-established and lucrative consulting firms such as Bain or McKinsey, or for the prestigious investment banks like Goldman Sachs and Morgan Stanley, all of which were eager to snap up fresh HBS talent. These firms were professional meccas for most HBS students; in 1993 a job offer from one of them was validation that you had arrived, that your $100,000 investment in higher education had paid off, and that you were set to achieve greater and greater things in life. During the spectacle of "hell week," a frenetic five-day period of intense interviews, an overwhelming majority of otherwise smart and rational human beings at HBS subject themselves to humiliating boot-licking sessions that masquerade as interviews, typically conducted by HBS alumni who come seeking new Harvard blood for their companies. This cycle guarantees that many of the best and brightest are processed efficiently, like blue-chip cogs in the corporate top-executive manufacturing process. These firms are not for everybody; they certainly were not for me. Even at the best of them, differentiation is a liability, and I was different—and had no desire to conform.

I was certain that my five interns were different too, that they shared my vision to change the world: to build Africa's first transcontinental communications company. I had spent my entire second year at business school obsessed with pursuing this goal. I launched the effort in earnest in September 1992. As part of the elective second-year MBA program, HBS students can opt to conduct field studies, usually in teams of three to six students, that allow them to study a particular area of interest and apply some of the basic management and analytical tools that are learned in the first year. Some of these studies are funded by major corporations, which have particular projects they want an MBA team to work on. Other studies are sponsored by smaller companies, and yet others, such as my own, are initiated by students, who either absorb the costs of the field study themselves or, if they are particularly industrious, raise funds from anyone who will back them. I sent letters to six major U.S. communications companies seeking money for my study, and whenever possible, I addressed my correspondence to someone with a connection to the business school, usually an alumnus in a top management position. For example, one such person was Henry Schacht, then the CEO of Cummins Engine Co., a graduate of the business school, and a close friend of John McArthur, the HBS dean at the time. Henry was also a member of the board of directors of AT&T, then the largest long-distance carrier in the United States.

Through Henry, my proposal eventually found its way to an executive who headed up AT&T Submarine Systems, a division that was working on a proposal to build a fiber-optic cable around the continent of Africa. But I soon learned that AT&T did not care how many people had access to basic telephone service in Africa. What the company needed was political influence with the governments of the African countries to ensure that what little telecommunications had already penetrated the continent would benefit AT&T. Thus, the division head informed me, my field study was not the right fit for AT&T.

Even so, I received a total of almost $50,000 from sponsors including Sprint International, the Lockheed Co., General Electric, and Motorola. I needed $100,000 to conduct the full study, however, and time was running out to submit my proposal for faculty approval. I had to find another $50,000 fast.

Having worked for the UN for five interminable years before I went to Harvard, I knew that UN money was always available for new ideas, as most of the old ones had failed. The organization was reinventing itself constantly to become relevant to poverty reduction—or merely to stay alive. I knew exactly what made a successful proposal in the eyes of the UN and similar development organizations. Certain topical buzzwords had to be included: poverty alleviation, small-business promotion, environmental protection, and empowerment of women in developing countries. These were the ones most in vogue in the early 1990s. For me, applying for a grant from the UN was like shooting fish in a barrel.

After some to-ing and fro-ing, including an afternoon of mostly idle and irrelevant chitchat at the midtown Manhattan apartment of the Moroccan heading the division I had applied to, the UN agreed to match the $50,000. This entire fund-raising experience was my first real sign of the cachet of the HBS name, and of the power and value of its alumni network. Time and again, as I built my company, which I decided to call African Communications Group (ACG), I would experience the feeling of membership in a highly exclusive club.

By the end of the academic year my field study team had narrowed the communications services we wanted to offer to telecommunications as the need in this area was greatest, as was the opportunity, and the economics of the business looked promising. We finally selected Tanzania to be our transcontinental launchpad.

My next move was to choose Dar es Salaam, Tanzania, to host the pilot project in the summer of 1993. Dar es Salaam translated literally means "port of peace." The metaphor can be extended to embrace the whole of Tanzania, which has often been a refuge from the political and social upheavals of neighboring Uganda, Rwanda, and the Congo, all of which have endured brutal ethnic conflicts. I knew that from a foreign investor's perspective, Tanzania's political and social stability were its greatest assets. The other variables—operating licenses, currency risks, market risks—were dicey enough.

Tanzania might seem an unusual choice for a new business venture. After securing its independence from Great Britain in 1961, Tanzania (then called Tanganyika) had followed a socialist path to development, led until 1985 by the charismatic and idealistic Julius Nyerere. As an undergraduate at Georgetown University, I had done a report on Nyerere's Ujamaa ideology and had admired him, if only for his optimism on a continent plagued with self-aggrandizing despots like Uganda's Idi Amin, Zaire's Mobutu Sese Seko, and the Central African Republic's Emperor Jean-Bédel Bokassa, to name a few. Yet, his well-meaning socialist economic policies had failed abysmally and plunged the population into ever deeper levels of poverty. Under new leadership and, more important, with mounting international pressure and the promise of financial assistance from the World Bank and the International Monetary Fund, Tanzania was being wooed into the loving embrace of capitalism. This development duo confidently proclaimed that such an ideological shift was fixing the world's most intractable economies—in Asia, Latin America, Eastern Europe, and elsewhere in Africa. It was guaranteed to do the same for Tanzania.

From my vantage point at the HBS campus on the banks of the Charles River I bet on Tanzania because it was an oasis of peace in a continent fraught with at best instability, and at worst full-scale warfare. I also relied on my discussions with officials of the Tanzanian government, the U.S. government, and international organizations, all eager to increase the flow of foreign investments to the East African country. To hear them tell it, Tanzania was destined to be the Singapore of Africa. That sounded reasonable enough. After all, Singapore hadn't been much more developed than Tanzania in 1965, when it first became a republic, and Tanzania was endowed with many more natural resources.

But my overall choice to focus on Africa, rather than another emerging market region, had deep personal resonance. Africa is the continent of my birth. No matter where I go or what I do, it is at the core of who I am, and it is from Africa that I draw my strength, my identity, and my essence. Africa is the epic of a people fighting a daily and seemingly futile battle, and doing so with strength, pride, dignity, and even humor—all traits that I admire. It is a place that has always fascinated and invigorated me, especially now that I can put it into perspective with the much more comfortable and stable life that I lead in the United States. Even for the privileged in Africa, life can be a constant struggle, not of course for basic survival, but merely to keep from sinking into total frustration: Will we have water today? When will the electric power shut down and for how long? If the car breaks down, how long will it take to get the spare part shipped in from London or Frankfurt? Will my meeting be canceled? Without a phone how can I find out? Perhaps I can send a message, if the driver comes. In Africa there are too many headwinds and too few tailwinds, like sandstorms, the clouds of dust spiraling ferociously across the Sahara desert, constantly blurring one's vision and obstructing the path to the nearest oasis. But you know that the water is out there, somewhere, so you just keep going.

As we descended into Dar es Salaam, I glanced over at Linda and Mike Katz. They were the first two students I had signed on to the team, husband and wife, a package deal. They were both engineers from the Midwest. Linda was short and stocky, with dark brown curly hair, and gregarious. She never shied away from giving her opinion, which she always presented as fact. From the moment I hired the two of them she called me incessantly, providing daily reports on all that she was doing to prepare for our trip—"Don't worry, Monique," she would say, "I am in charge"—and reminding me that I was giving her and Mike the opportunity of a lifetime. Mike was equally enthusiastic, but it was clear to me from the outset that in that marriage, Linda was indeed in charge.

I appreciated their excitement, so much so that I delegated to them the responsibility of recruiting the three other summer interns required for the postacademic portion of the field study: the reality check. I was still preoccupied with completing and defending our preliminary findings, which were based on my team's early research and analysis; these had included a visit to the International Telecommunications Union in Geneva, Switzerland, at the beginning of the semester, and meetings all over the United States with our corporate sponsors. Our supervising professor was Howard Stevenson, HBS's entrepreneurial guru at the time. When Howard selected and supervised a field study, it gave it instant credibility and increased the venture's likelihood of success. My other major priority was ensuring that the UN office in Tanzania, our local host, took all the necessary logistic measures we needed, such as providing us with accommodations and transport, and scheduling our initial meetings with government officials.

I realize in retrospect that Linda and Mike seemed as interested in choosing people with whom they felt they were likely to have a good time, as in choosing those best suited to the complex task of starting a new business in a developing country. Admittedly, I had not established demanding eligibility criteria. The job description, had I done my duty and written one, would have required only of the candidate a willingness to spend up to three months in the tropics working on a business plan for an exciting new venture. I could pay each intern about $600 a week plus housing, as the UN was providing us with lodging free of charge. While I did interview each candidate the Katzes presented to me, it was more a formality than a rigorous screening of their qualifications. In hiring them I unwittingly assembled the elements of a Let's Go Africa holiday tour group.

After the Katzes, the first two interns I signed on were Patrick Donahue and Paul Gormley. Patrick was extremely skinny, about five-foot-eight, with deep, piercing eyes. He was the couple's good friend, their third wheel. Paul, who prior to HBS had worked as a consultant for McKinsey, was witty and had a quiet confidence about him and a sense of wanting to do the responsible thing. He was also an avid in-line skater, which appealed to me as a fellow jock—I was an avid runner and very much into sports. The last intern I took on board was Rick Bolander. Tall and model handsome, Rick was at 33 the oldest member of our group. Although he went to great lengths to impress me with his technical expertise—he had worked for AT&T before he entered business school—I had the feeling that Rick relied heavily on his looks in his life and career. I am not sure what it was, but right from the start I suspected that he had his own agenda in Africa. I interviewed him several times before offering him the job, but with only a few weeks to go before the end of the semester and most first-years already committed to summer internships, no other candidates emerged. Anyway, I reassured myself, he had the Katzes' seal of approval.

I was grateful to the members of the team for the work they did prior to the trip. Under limited supervision they put together schedules, work plans, surveys, and questionnaires, all of which were to be used during our summer in Tanzania. They seemed even more eager than I was to get to Africa. I advised them that it would probably be wise if, before leaving for Africa, we waited until the last installment of our funding had been transferred into the account that I had set up. My team had already spent most of the money from the corporate sponsors during the academic phase. The UN had not yet sent its $50,000, and our cash balance was low. But Linda managed to persuade one of the interns to buy five round-trip tickets on his own credit card in advance, and assured me that they all would have sufficient cash to get them through the first couple of weeks in Tanzania. They pleaded with me to let them leave at the earliest possible date, even volunteering to go without me. That I could not let them do. It was a ludicrous idea—what credibility would they have if they showed up without me and my connections? Brilliant though I assumed they were, ACG was my baby, and I was not about to let a bunch of novices screw it up. Moreover, I did not think that any one of them could last a day in

Africa without a chaperon. So only four days after commencement we boarded the jet for Tanzania.

Upon arrival at Dar es Salaam International Airport we collected our bags and headed outside the terminal, where we were greeted by a junior-level UN representative named Eric Boateng, a quiet and reserved Ghanaian who had been assigned to assist us. He wore a simple gray short-sleeved cotton suit, common business attire for the country and climate, and appeared relieved that we had made it out of the terminal with no significant mishaps. Eric helped us load our suitcases into the waiting chauffeur-driven vehicles and confirmed that two houses had been assigned to us—I envisioned two small villas of the type typically inhabited by the average expatriate in Dar es Salaam—and that all the meetings we had requested with government authorities, including the head of the national telecommunications carrier, the Tanzania Posts and Telecommunications Co., had been arranged. He smiled gently at the six of us, the young Turks from HBS who were coming to build the first transcontinental telecommunications company in Africa, a goal that only the naive or the most ambitious and invincible could believe in. I was ambitious and felt invincible.

On the ride from the airport to our home in the mostly expatriate residential area of the city, we passed first through Dar es Salaam's industrial zone, concrete buildings that housed light-manufacturing facilities, car dealerships, and sprawling, brightly lit, gaudy home furniture and fixings showrooms. Most of these businesses were owned by Tanzanians of Indian descent. We next drove through the center of town, along heavily congested streets, full of vehicles, pedestrians, and traders eager to sell their numerous wares (fresh cashew nuts, plastic cell phones, clothes hangers, soap, bug spray, newspapers) with full service delivered to the driver's or passenger's seat. The vendors, mostly raggedly clad young teenage boys working on commission, ran up to the cars as soon as they stopped at a traffic light.

Those hawking newspapers and magazines for expatriate consumption made sure that the most scintillating titles were revealed. In their view, this strategy made it almost irresistible for expatriate motorists to move on without buying a copy. Many of the stories in the tabloid news those days were recycled stories about Princess Diana from the London broadsheets and were targeted at homesick Brits. Tanzanians themselves had little interest in the comings and goings at Buckingham and Kensington palaces, and would certainly not pay good money to find out. I, however, was not immune, having done much of my early education at a boarding school in Kent, England, and early on I mastered the skill of gleaning just enough information to satisfy my thirst for gossip without having to actually purchase the paper. The fundamental flaw in the peddlers' marketing strategy was that they kept the publications in front of the motorists for too long. While I had no qualms about taking advantage of reading-without-paying in the checkout line at Stop-N-Shop in Boston, for these young boys the stakes were much higher, so I would frequently succumb to a purchase.

In the center of town were modern office buildings that housed embassies, major international airlines (such as British Airways, KLM, and Lufthansa), and banks, currency exchange offices, hotels, private businesses, and other commercial signs that Tanzania was in the early phases of its transition to capitalism. Dilapidated government buildings were also part of the architectural fabric. It was in these buildings that we were to meet with government officials in the subsequent days, weeks, and months to lay out our strategy for our telecommunications revolution. Juxtaposed to and randomly interspersed with these concrete office blocks were shanty kiosks lining the streets, out of which everything from canned foods, to fake hair from China, to clothes and electronics, were sold in an open-air market that was part 7-Eleven, part Wal-Mart, part flea market.

This gave way to vendors operating out of rickety wood or corrugated-iron shacks. These shelters performed both advertising and sales functions, with either the Coca-Cola or Pepsi logo painted prominently on the front and sides, a low-cost and localized expression of their fierce global rivalry. My favorite of these open-air joints were the corn vendors, who stood or sat over their charcoal broilers roasting fresh African corn for immediate consumption.

We left the central business district and approached the wealthy residential areas, where expatriates and prominent government officials live in white multistoried mansions with manicured gardens filled with beautiful bougainvillea, hibiscus, and African violets. The homes have private electricity and water supplies, and satellite dishes perched upon almost every roof linking their occupants either to the world they left behind or the one they aspired to. The most prominent and impressive houses are located along Msasani Road, a winding strip that hugs the coast of the mesmerizing deep-blue hue of the Indian Ocean. Among them is the American ambassador's residence, Old Glory waving prominently above it, permanently defended by U.S. Marines. It lies only blocks away from the embassy bombed by al-Qaeda in 1998. Msasani Road affords a spectacular view of the ocean and generates a profound sense of tranquillity utterly at odds with the hustle and bustle that lies just minutes away in the central business district.

When the vehicles pulled up to our residences, the elation that I felt at being back in Africa quickly evaporated. What had temporarily been a lawn had reverted to thick African bush. The houses' once yellow paint had been faded by the sun into a pale white, and the bright red dust found just about everywhere in sub-Saharan Africa, particularly during the dry season, served as a second coating. Eric had neglected to mention that the houses assigned to us had not been inhabited for several years and were categorized by the UN as "abandoned" or "condemned" properties. I tried not to betray the shock that I felt because I did not want to appear rude or hurt his feelings; I also figured that there was precious little that he could do to improve the situation even if he wanted to, which he clearly did, as I could see from the sympathetic expression on his face.

Inside skittered ants, mosquitoes, cockroaches, giant spiders, and lizards. And those were only the creatures that I could both see and identify; God only knows what else was lurking in there. The bedrooms, with neither window screens nor bed nets, were holiday resorts for mosquitoes. Bad as all of this was, it was far better than the domestic conditions in which the average Tanzanian struggles to survive every day. In Africa, the malaria parasite kills about 3,000 children a day, because its victims cannot afford even basic forms of protection, such as bed nets and antimalarial tablets (which the physicians at Harvard had supplied us with in abundance, for about $5 a pill).

The mattresses were soiled well beyond hygiene, much less decency. But all that I have described pales in comparison to what we discovered next in the bathroom. The once white sink was now a rusty brown color laced with long dark streaks extending from the drain to the rim. The toilet was filled with brown water and barely flushed, and the drain of the shower stall was filled with human feces, which may well have seeped in from the toilet. I was horrified and ashamed. I had imagined that our accommodations would at the least be clean and equipped with modest but functional furnishings. What had I led us into?

Oddly enough, with the exception of Linda, frightened out of her wits by the spiders (luckily Mike was there to chase and kill them for her—the one area in which he took charge), the team took our new surroundings in stride. The guys assured me that they had lived in conditions far worse as undergraduates. They viewed this as part of the overall African experience and were grateful that there was a real house, a toilet, and a shower, rather than the mud hut that they had probably both fantasized about and feared. Right about then a simple mud hut seemed infinitely more appealing to me than the appalling concrete structure with its so-called modern amenities that we were standing in. Eric invited me to come and stay with his family. Tempted as I was by the offer—I was certain that he would have a far better setup—I knew it wouldn't be right from a team-building perspective for me to break ranks. Besides, in some perverse way, the squalor made my cause seem all the more noble. We divided ourselves into two groups. Mike, Linda, and I stayed in the house I just described. Patrick, Paul, and Rick were assigned to the second, marginally better one.

The next morning a delegation of UN wives came to welcome the Harvard MBAs. We were minicelebrities, or at least a novelty. They were women from Europe and Asia; the latter typically had worked as secretaries for the UN in Asian posts before landing their functionary husbands. Like some multinational welcome wagon, the wives graciously had come to induct us into their world with their white man's survival guide and kit for Africa. In their goodie bags were household supplies that they had assembled from their own private stocks: assorted cups, plates, knives, forks, pots, pans, and other basics to get us started. They then accompanied us to the stores as we purchased food, cleaning supplies, and the other sundries needed to bring the houses to minimum levels of habitation. In my bedroom alone, I discharged an entire can of highly toxic mosquito repellent that advertised itself with KILLS WADOUDOU DEAD. I wondered if the chemicals would kill me before wadoudou did, but decided to take my chances. The wives warned us to be careful when walking along the beach, and dutifully proceeded to recount a litany of frightening expatriate run-ins with local thugs, which I suspect had become more embellished with each recounting. The purpose was to frighten us out of our wits and scare us away from all but the most essential contact with the locals.

Unemployment being what it is in Tanzania, word quickly spread that new musungus, Swahili for white people, had occupied the houses. In this context I was considered a musungu, as the word gradually had assumed a more socioeconomic connotation and is applied to Western foreigners in general. Enterprising candidates began appearing on our doorsteps, offering their services as domestic servants (or houseboys, as they are called, as political correctness is a luxury not affordable in nuts-and-bolts Tanzania) and gardeners. The aspirants arrived clutching worn and tattered sheets of paper that contained personal references from Europeans and Americans that testified to the honesty, integrity, loyalty, and good services of the bearer. The letters had been written by white men and women, and we were therefore expected to take them at face value. Indeed, when we asked if the authors of these testimonials were available for us to speak with, we were invariably told that the people had since left Tanzania "for good," as they say when an expatriate leaves the country to return home or, more often, to take on a new assignment elsewhere in the developing world. Some of the reference letters were of impressive vintage, over a decade old.

From my upbringing in Liberia and other periods of living in Africa I had years of experience with hiring and working with domestic help, and almost instinctively knew whom to trust. In countries like Tanzania even the best domestic, if he is lucky enough to find a job, makes the equivalent of only $30 to $50 a month. With those meager earnings he is expected to provide for his family, which often includes at least one wife, children, brothers, sisters, cousins, and others of his extended family who live in his home village far away from the capital city and depend on him to send them financial support to supplement their mainly subsistence-level agricultural existence on the farm. So the highest degree of personal discipline and integrity are required of him to resist the daily temptations that arise in the house of a wealthy Tanzanian or expatriate. Without a vigilant employer the domestic help is exposed constantly to and tantalized by household and personal items of high market value that can easily be converted into cash.

To this I should add that, as in similar variations on the theme that I have witnessed in every country and region I have visited around the world, there is an inherent bias and stereotyping in each country of Africa against certain other African nationals, or among different groups of people of the same nationality. When I lived in Angola I was told by expatriates, and even some Angolans, to hire only Cape Verdeans, not Angolans, and definitely not Zaireans. "They," it was claimed, were the worst thieves of all. In the Central African Republic I was told which tribes were known to be the hardest workers, and again, under no circumstances was I to hire Zaireans. Now in Tanzania I was being advised to hire Malawians, as they were supposed to be conscientious and to fear the wrath and retribution of the Tanzanian police; they were therefore less inclined to steal from their employers. As these myths were handed down from one generation of expats to the next, they gained currency through sheer repetition and persistence.

Linda immediately fell for a Malawian candidate named Robert. Robert, about fifty, had excellent credentials and an avuncular-looking face. Linda pronounced him "sweet and adorable." What made me uneasy were his quickly shifting eyes. There was something elusive in his demeanor that just did not sit right with me. I recommended that we review more candidates. But in the end, hire Robert we did. I confess that his eighteen-year-old son, an avid distance runner, was my tipping point; I could pay him to run miles with me every morning.

The interns immediately adopted Robert as their protégé and marketing project, giving him their old Reebok sneakers, HBS T-shirts, and various other heavily emblazoned U.S.A.-themed sweatshirts. They also were determined to treat him as an equal, a buddy, the American way, including giving him liberal access to their personal belongings. I, however, kept my bedroom door locked when I wasn't around and warned the others about the importance of being cautious with their valuables. I am sure they thought I was a snob, or worse.

After a couple days of intense scrubbing and scouring, most of it done by Robert, we had a clean house, and we soon established a relatively comfortable domestic routine, including communal dinners, which I preferred not to participate in because I tend to like my private time and am particular about my diet—I preferred cheese and crackers, yogurt and fruit at dinner and was not into spending day and night with the group. They liked to convene in the kitchen after the workday and boil a big pot of spaghetti with meat sauce and just hang out. I tried to fit in for the first week or so, but then I found myself coming up with excuses not to join them at dinner, preferring to retire with a good book. Their conversations about "the natives" and the other "oddities" of Tanzanian life gave me, an African in Africa, the peculiar feeling of being an outsider.

Eric had scheduled back-to-back meetings for us for the first couple of weeks as we began the serious task of developing the business plan for my telecommunications company. I would need this to raise money for ACG when I returned to the States in the fall; I would have to persuade sophisticated venture capitalists and other potential investors in America to part with their money in exchange for shares in the company and its future returns.

In Tanzania we met mostly with government officials who had decision-making authority in matters pertaining to foreign investments (we needed to import equipment) and telecommunications (licenses to operate and provide various telecommunications services), and we drove to see them in a beat-up old white Suzuki Jeep Samuri that the UN had assigned to us. The vehicle had no air conditioning and seats so low and worn out that we had the impression we were sitting on the floor of the Jeep itself, and the roads were distressingly visible through the holes that had been punctured in the bottom of the car's carcass. By noon, with the temperature approaching 100 degrees, the guys, who wore long-sleeved shirts and ties (jackets were completely discarded after the first couple of days and sleeves rolled up), were drenched in sweat as we arrived to meet with the Tanzanian authorities who were going to help clear the path for ACG to blaze the telecommunications trail. Despite our sometimes disheveled appearances, we were always received by our host with a tremendous amount of enthusiasm—we were the whiz kids from Harvard, and if nothing else we were a welcome respite from the endless stream of European, Japanese, and American salesmen trying to sell the Tanzanian government everything from telecommunications towers and switches to heavy-duty construction equipment to useless and redundant consulting services.

The most telling sign of our important status was the service of tea and savories. These refreshments were so good that we eventually reached the point where some of us, myself included, looked forward more to the service than to the substance of the meetings, because it soon became clear to us that it was almost impossible to accomplish anything through these contacts. We had no cash with which to personally enrich our hosts, and anyhow, ACG was small potatoes compared to companies such as Alcatel, AT&T, Deutsche Telekom, or British Telecom, which also were knocking at their doors.

The UN's $50,000 still had not come through, and I was beginning to curse myself for caving in to the interns' insistence that we come to Tanzania sooner rather than later. I began and ended each workday at the UN's head office in Dar es Salaam, desperate for a telex in response to those that I was sending out almost daily to New York requesting the urgent transfer of our funds. Night after night I came home empty-handed, and after dinner met with the group to summarize the day's meetings and work on the business opportunities that were emerging from our meetings. One such opportunity involved public pay phones; another was cellular service, which in 1993 was not yet available in Tanzania. Yet another was a contract to provide data communications to Tanzania's largest bank. These were the types of ventures that my corporate sponsors were interested in learning more about. They were also the type of projects upon which the foundation of my transcontinental empire would be built.

Within two weeks of our arrival, I noticed that Linda had turned her planning resourcefulness and enthusiasm in addition to ACG business to other pursuits: weekend retreats to nearby game parks and to the exotic island of Zanzibar. Rick already had signed up for scuba-diving lessons, although he immediately regretted it when during one of his maiden dives his ear was injured severely in a heavy blast from an underwater explosion. Fishermen were using dynamite to catch a large number of fish at once. Patrick soon discovered that once a week the marines hosted "movie night." On these evenings, Americans and a few Europeans got together at the U.S. embassy for movies, hamburgers, beer, and popcorn. It became a regular haunt of the interns—it was the closest they could come to being "home" while 8,000 miles away. The marines' dedicated service to country not withstanding, I had no desire to spend my spare time in Tanzania drinking beers and eating popcorn with a bunch of 20-year-old American servicemen and -women.

Three weeks after our arrival, the Katzes, Rick, and Patrick notified me that they would be taking two weeks off for vacation prior to the scheduled end of their assignment. While I was surprised that they had waited until we were ensconced in Tanzania before revealing their intentions to me, their objectives sounded reasonable enough—so long as the work that we had come to do was completed prior to their departure, and that is what I told them. Because the interns had used the services of the local UN travel office to plan portions of their vacation, I soon discovered that everyone except Paul had from the beginning been planning early departure dates, giving them several weeks of African safari time, whether or not the work of ACG was completed. With this new revelation, tension between the interns and me started to build. For me it centered on the work, which I felt they were not doing; for them it was on money they felt I was not paying. Despite repeated telexes from both the local UN managing director and from me, the money was still not there. Salary and safari, definitely not start-up, had become the interns' mantra. When I reminded them that I had warned of the risk of our coming to Tanzania before the money was in ACG's bank account, the Katzes indignantly accused me of bringing the group over under false pretenses and of having no intention of paying them for their work. I responded equally indignantly that this was untrue, but I also knew in my heart that I had made a rookie management mistake by not properly handling their expectations. Having worked for the UN I was well aware of the bureaucratic delays inherent in that organization. I had only myself to blame for coming to Tanzania before we had the money, and for not putting up a stronger resistance to the interns by following my early intuition to wait until all financial matters had been resolved satisfactorily.

Over the next few days the tension continued to mount. Their communal dinners shifted from the house that Linda, Mike, and I shared to the one occupied by Patrick, Paul, and Rick. Even though I knew by then that I did not fit in with the group, the shift hurt, but at least it gave me the place all to myself each evening until Linda and Mike returned to go to bed. Meanwhile, I was meeting Tanzanians and developing a small social network of my own, a crowd of Africans and expatriates alike who were quite well informed about the merits and demerits of investing in Tanzania, and who could give me advice and pointers based on their own experiences. Admittedly, I am a workaholic, and once I focus on something it consumes me. ACG consumed me; I wanted to soak up every bit of information and knowledge that I could during my summer in Tanzania. Why could my interns not do the same, I wondered. Every time they went off to movie night with the marines, or on some three-day holiday escapade, I felt a little more betrayed. Of course they were fixated on the idea that they had been duped, because their money had not yet come through, and that therefore they owed me nothing.

After we'd been in Dar for almost a month, the UN office in New York finally sent the local office the authorization to disburse the funds. This was the outcome of numerous strings being pulled and all sorts of bureaucratic hoops being jumped through to accommodate us. Rather than rejoice when I gave them the good news, however, the interns insisted that I pay them immediately for the entire three months, even though they had yet to do most of the work that we had come to do, and most of them already had declared that they were leaving early to go on safari in the north of the country. In other words, they did not trust me, but they expected me to trust them. I insisted that the payments would be disbursed periodically, and only after the work was done. They then threatened to leave if I did not concede. But I did not.

One evening as we were preparing to attend the annual Saba Saba fair, Linda came into my room to ask me if I had seen her missing stockings. The way she said it sounded more to me like "Monique, what did you do with my stockings?"

I asked her if she had spoken to Robert about it. She said yes, and again asked whether I had seen them, even though I had already gone through my entire closet in front of her, thinking that Robert quite possibly could have mixed up our clothes.

I replied defiantly, and I admit a trifle petulantly: "I have not seen your stupid stockings. Moreover, I have had it up to here with you and your stupid insinuations and innuendos." I was of course referring to her suspicions regarding the payment of salaries.

From then on it was open warfare. With Mike's protective arm around her, a sobbing Linda said that she was no longer interested in attending the opening night of the Saba Saba fair. As a result, the rest of the team decided to stand by her and refused to attend the fair. I went alone. After my departure they convened a tribal meeting to plot my overthrow. It was almost midnight when I returned, and mutiny in Dar es Salaam had begun.

The good news for me was that Linda had decided that she

would no longer speak directly to me. In solidarity, Mike and Patrick would talk to me only on an as-needed basis. Paul was the group's designated spokesman, and he informed me that everyone had agreed that they would henceforth report directly to the head of the local UN office in Dar es Salaam rather than to me. I told him that this was unacceptable and that under these conditions they were all free to leave Tanzania. I secretly hoped that Paul would stay. I liked him and I needed him: I still had to produce reports for the companies that had sponsored us, and there was no way that I could do it on my own in the allotted time.

By noon the next day the intern rebellion was already fresh fodder on the local UN grapevine, because that morning the four of them had stormed into the office of the UN general manager, Antonius Vissers, demanding a meeting to voice their grievances against me. I hadn't seen Toon, as he was called, for almost six years; he'd been one of the people who had recruited me in 1986 to work for the UN.

He was a redheaded, sunburned Dutchman, a typical worn-out UN bureaucrat who had spent too much time in the tropics, having begun his development service in his early twenties. Now well into his fifties, his options for getting a comparable job for comparable pay elsewhere were limited. Seeing Toon reminded me of why I had left the UN. An acting managing director in Dar es Salaam, shuffling meaningless papers and proposals and attending equally meaningless meetings with members of the Tanzanian government, he was near the pinnacle of his career. He was the consummate diplomat, but the honorable type, trying to please everyone even when it was clearly impossible to do so. He was determined to be impartial and objective about our plight. Certainly I felt embarrassed to have handed him this bowl of mixed nuts. Weren't we supposed to be responsible, Harvard-educated adults with lofty goals? I doubted that this is what Colin Powell had had in mind when speaking to us. After listening to the interns' gripes against me, Toon invited me to join them in his office. I walked in and found them all sensing victory. Suddenly Linda was speaking to me again. She informed me, on behalf of the team, that I did not know how to treat people properly and that I had devalued their work and misled them about the payment terms. She accused me of being temperamental and dictatorial, and stated that under no conditions would they report directly to me. She then spelled out the terms under which I was to communicate with them. Paul would be the intermediary and the team would determine its own assignments for the remainder of their stay. Mike and Pat chimed in with their own aspersions.

In vain I tried to reconcile these people with the Linda, Mike, and Pat that I had known during the recruiting period at Harvard Business School. All I knew was that under no circumstances was I willing to accept their terms, and I told them so. That they thought I would have gone along with their ludicrous proposal showed how little they really knew or understood me. After almost half an hour of unproductive discussion that must only have served to confirm for Toon the group's collective dysfunction, he pronounced our situation hopeless and irreconcilable and declared that, while it was unfortunate, it was clearly impossible for us to continue with our assignment, as he did not have the time to manage us, nor did he want to interfere with our objectives. It would be best if the group disbanded; he would notify the UN in New York, and the organization would assist us with our return travel arrangements. After the interns exited, Toon asked me to remain.

He looked at me quizzically. "Monique," he said, "I don't see how you did that. I take my hat off to you."

I smiled ruefully at him. "What else could I have done?" I thought. I certainly was not going to give them the satisfaction of seeing me break down. Toon's reaction, however, inspired me. If he believed that I was nonplussed in the face of such a vicious attack on my character, the team must have believed I was non-plussed as well.

Paul asked me to give them a couple of days to weigh their options. Not surprisingly, I was soon informed that Linda and Mike had decided to leave. That was the best news I had heard all summer. First they were going on a lengthy safari to northern Tanzania, and then they were heading south to Victoria Falls in Zimbabwe, prior to returning to the States and their second year at business school.

So I had subsidized their safari. It was a small price to pay for their imminent departure. But leave it to the Katzes to make a dramatic exit. A couple of days before they were scheduled to leave, they discovered that they had been robbed of almost all the cash that they had counted upon for their vacation. Mike and Linda had never locked their bedroom door, and Mike came home in the middle of the day to pack and caught Robert red-handed. He had manufactured a key, or perhaps even used a safety pin, to open the suitcase in which they had kept their cash. Slowly and surreptitiously he had been pilfering their stash until he had established an Individual Retirement Account of more than $500 for himself, a small fortune for your average houseboy in Tanzania. He had doubtlessly stolen the infamous stockings as well, and other personal items from the Katzes, and probably had given them as gifts to his family and friends or sold them on the thriving local market for Western goods.

Despite all that had transpired between us, I felt genuinely sorry for the Katzes. When I arrived on the scene Robert's eyes were darting madly as he explained to us what a God-fearing person he was and how he would never steal anything from anybody. He looked to me for reassurance, thinking that given my feelings for Linda and Mike, I might side with him. He was wrong. I was sure he had done what he was being accused of. In Tanzania, innocent until proven guilty did not apply. I also knew that they would never see their money again. Mike seemed utterly defeated and unable to deal with the situation. But Linda felt otherwise. She decided then and there to take on Tanzanian law enforcement. She managed to convince Mike and Pat to accompany her to the police station to report the theft. The police station consisted of a few scruffily uniformed officers lounging around in a dark and musty little room; an out-of-order, old, black rotary phone; and a tattered notepad in which to record the occasional incident. The pen, they would have to borrow from the alleged victims. The spectacle of three musungus approaching in distress must have been enticing; like ravenous lions roaming the Serengeti, they could smell a killing. What Linda and her cohorts failed to realize was that law enforcement in Tanzania operated differently from the Cambridge police force. There were few guidelines, and those that existed were hardly ever enforced. Moreover, the police did not have an iota of sympathy for these rich American kids, who were truly delusional if they thought that the police would capture and imprison one of their own on their behalf, even if he were from Malawi. By reporting the incident, the Katzes unwittingly had given the officers a lead on their next revenue source, as third-party theft was how the police subsidized their measly incomes. The best that Linda and Mike could hope for was that the police would find Robert at his home, bring him to the station for questioning, convince him to give them a portion of his take—a finder's fee, if you will—after which he would serve the symbolic one or two nights in prison to give the Katzes the impression that something had been done, and that in Tanzania law enforcement is taken seriously. Had I been Robert's victim, the reaction would have been no different. After several hours at the station, during which time I am sure the policemen spoke to each other in Swahili, laughing in the faces of the musungus, the trio finally realized that justice would not be served. The police, of course, felt it had.

The Katzes were crushed. All they had left were the few traveler's checks that Robert had been kind enough to leave behind—funny money, in his mind. The students of HBS had been outsmarted by the illiterate and undercapitalized Robert, Inc.

Once the Katzes were gone, I turned my attention to Pat, Rick, and Paul, who all agreed to complete their assignments. Not that it was a festival of love and forgiveness: I needed them to finish the business plan as much as they needed me to pay them to finance their tropical expedition. Moreover, it was too late for them to return to the United States and find other summer jobs. I apportioned the work among them so that within four weeks, ACG would have at least three concrete business proposals, each describing the business, the market opportunity, the competition, the technology, capital requirements, and the return on investment. I knew that I could no longer count on their full cooperation and goodwill; henceforth they would probably work like indentured servants, doing only the minimum amount required to fulfill their obligations. That put me in a major predicament. The UN expected me to demonstrate that as a result of its investment in my study, private foreign investments into the Tanzanian telecommunications sector would increase, and that there would be a corresponding transfer of knowledge to the high-tech sector. The corporate sponsors expected me to identify opportunities for them to sell their services and equipment. I expected myself to come up with a business plan that would make both these things happen and enable me to raise funds to launch my new business, ACG, Inc. Once the intern salaries had been taken care of, the sponsorship money was dwindling, and by the end of the summer it was almost zero; now I was using my credit cards. I had no other source of capital. The best I could do was salvage, and build on, the work that had already been done. I slept on it for a night, thought, and even prayed for divine inspiration and intervention. The next morning I had both. It would take a miracle to make it happen, but I would try to get Côme Laguë to come to Tanzania.

2

Côme to the Rescue

During the first year the 800 or so students of the Harvard Business School are divided into groups of about 90 each called sections. Each section is assigned to a classroom in one building. On the first day of classes students choose their seats, with some obsessives, me among them, getting up before the crack of dawn to have the first picks. The seat one gets that day determines where one sits for the entire year; hence it was an important strategic choice.[1] The classroom was structured like an enclosed Roman amphitheater, and the most coveted seats were those in what we referred to as the "sky deck," the last tier of seats in the classroom, farthest away from the purview and proximity of the professors, who remained center stage at the base of the room. This highly coveted nosebleed region had serious attitude and personality. Shannon Fergusson and I were the only women up there. At the other extreme, the bottom tier, closest to the professors, was the "worm deck," so named because it was where the brownnosers and nerds self-segregated, and where those who had not gotten up early enough on the first day were stuck.

That is the way it worked during the first year at HBS. We remained in our seats and it was the professors who came in and out to teach their courses. It is an efficient system and also serves another important function: bonding. Sitting in the same room day after day for an entire year, we developed a bunker mentality. We got to know the 89 people around us well, so that after a few months we could predict what each would say, how he or she thought, and his or her general philosophy on life. Love them or hate them, we were family and we stuck together. At least that is how it was with the Slammin' Section D, Class of 1993. Ten years later I can still pick up the phone and call any one of my section mates and casually resume where we left off, even if it has been as many years since we last spoke.

We also got to know who was at HBS by stroke of genius, who was somewhere in the middle, and who was there by stroke of luck or connections. I considered myself for the most part in the middle category. At 29, and with one master's degree and five years of work with the United Nations already under my belt, I no longer suffered under the illusion that graduating in the top 5 percent of my class would guarantee me success in life. But there were those at HBS who felt that by working hard they could earn, upon graduation, Baker Scholar status. Being a Baker Scholar meant being in the top 5 percent of the graduating class—graduating with high distinction. It was a big deal at HBS. Many students led miserable lives to achieve Bakerdom. Unfortunately, for most it just was not in the cards.

Then there were those I called the naturals, the "genetically encoded." These were the people who, even if they had spent the entire two years absent from class and merely showed up for exams, could have been Baker Scholars. Côme Laguë was one such student.

At HBS the Socratic method is used; the professors teach by asking the students probing questions, rather than by lecturing. The entire section is required to read the case beforehand, and at the beginning of class an unlucky section mate is targeted by the professor, without prior warning, to open the case. The dreaded "cold call," as it is euphemistically known, is a ten-minute torture session during which the victim is expected to intelligently extrapolate the most salient information from the case and draw meaningful conclusions—only to have them ripped apart mercilessly by those of us who feel inclined to weigh in to receive high marks for our diligent class participation or to enlighten our benighted classmates. If the cold-called student cannot come up with any brilliant insights, he can always resort to firing off a barrage of "case facts," which means that at least he has done the minimum amount of work required; that is, he's read the case but done no analysis. Sometimes, under the direst circumstances, the cold-called student will read the case for the first time while he is actually doing the opening. To successfully execute this option requires both chutzpah and oratorical dexterity. I watched Shannon pull this off on more than one occasion, with admirable panache. But most important, this option is one significant step above the dreaded "pass."

"Pass" means that you are totally unprepared and cannot pull it off extemporaneously. It also means the professor has to call on another student to do the job, or essentially, take the fall for you. In the eyes of the class, this makes you a schmuck. In the eyes of the professor, you are an almost certain fail. It was such a blemish on one's record and the blow to the pride that on one memorable occasion one section mate who would have been better served by exercising her pass option defiantly chose to brave it instead. A few minutes into her excruciatingly painful delivery she fell apart completely and broke down in tears. It was not pretty.

Soon after observing this debacle I decided that offense would be the best form of defense. I developed my own strategy to avoid being cold-called, one that was so successful that I may be the only student in the history of the Harvard Business School to have survived the entire two years without ever being asked to open a case. My strategy involved the laws of probability and a willingness to keep meticulous class-participation records similar to those kept by the professors for grading purposes. For each class I would note who had spoken and for roughly how long. I would keep track of who the professor had called upon to open the case. I noted that it was rare that a person was called upon twice, except in the case of one elderly professor, who rather horrifyingly called upon my section mate Grant Winfrey three times in one semester. Grant should have been given an honorary Baker status just for that.

Those who did not participate in classroom discussion were the most vulnerable to being called upon to open, because classroom participation accounted for 50 percent of our grades. I referred to my well-calculated immunization strategy as my Cold Call Strategic Defense Initiative (CCSDI). I learned after a few weeks that by weighing in from time to time with a substantive comment that offered a new perspective on the subject under discussion, or, as was more often the case, simply hailed from way out of left field, I could successfully stave off the dreaded cold call. This ploy had multiple payoffs. It gave one of my Baker-aspiring section mates the stage to strut his stuff; provided a good jolt to the classroom discussion just when it was needed; and guaranteed that I got credit for class participation. Most important, though, these well-timed interventions reduced the probability of my being cold-called to almost zero, especially when I knew and could document almost as accurately as the professor could that there were at least 20 other people in the room from whom we had not heard in weeks. They were the ones whose names I blissfully encircled in my tiny little crimson ledger and filed under the category "Sitting Ducks."[2]

On the day that I discovered the pure genius of Côme, the opening was particularly brutal; moreover, it was during the first couple of months of our HBS experience, arguably the most stressful period of the entire two-year experience. During that time two people from our section alone checked out of the program: one, a sky-deck resident, a former investment banker from the firm Wasserstein Perella, who decided that HBS had nothing new to teach him and that he was wasting his time there; the other, a worm decker, graduate of Stanford University, brilliant mechanical engineer, and veteran of the U.S. armed forces who rather belatedly discovered that he was petrified at the prospect of public speaking and woke up every morning sick to his stomach, with the real and looming threat that this could be the day that he would be cold-called. It was like the "sword of Socrates" dangling ominously over his head.

We were studying a case in Technology and Operations Management class that was called the "Aggregate Production Planning Game." It was an exercise in production process analysis, including statistical forecasting, marginal product costs, inventory management, and production resource matching. Had I been the one cold-called that day, I would have cried. Fortunately I was not, and the student asked to open took the case facts route. It seemed that none of us had been able to crack the case. After about 15 minutes of circuitous discussion, with poor Professor Marco Iansiti becoming visibly frustrated that the class would end without his being able to impart the "case takeaways" via the sacrosanct Socratic method, Côme raised his hand. He has bright red hair and matching freckles all over his face. When he smiles he looks just like the happy six-year-old version of him in a picture hanging on the wall at his parents' house in Montreal. He has an electrical engineering degree from McGill University, and prior to coming to HBS worked at the Monitor Co., the consulting firm founded by the renowned Michael Porter, who is also a professor on the faculty at HBS. Côme is shy and reserved, and as a consequence he rarely spoke in class. Yet on that particular day, he was on fire, and he and Marco engaged in a love fest for 15 minutes as Côme proceeded to deliver the most brilliant analysis of a case that I have ever heard. The class was stunned, not because he was so smart—we already knew that—but because of the ease with which he analyzed and then solved the problem, complete with a computer simulation and multiyear forecast. I was totally blown away.

From that day on he was my hero, not just on account of his brilliance, but because of the way he managed his gift with total modesty. I often sought out Côme after that. I used the fact that we both spoke French to break the ice. I approached him if I needed help in understanding a particular problem, especially where heavy-duty numbers were involved; he is a mathematical genius. Half of the time what he patiently tried to explain to me sounded like Greek, but I would go away, spend the next few hours alone studying what he had said, and it eventually always made sense. During our second year Côme and I both enrolled in Howard Stevenson's entrepreneurial class and, like me, Côme pursued his own, independent, field study, also with Howard as his supervisor. In Howard's class we sat next to each other and frequently had lunch together. At these lunches we exchanged ideas and updated each other on our projects and respective field-study team dynamics. Mine of course were always tumultuous, his always serene.

By the end of the academic year, Côme had concluded from his field study that the company he envisioned was not financially viable and that he would go back to work for Monitor after graduation. I still had no idea if my telecommunications idea was financially viable or not; nevertheless, I was determined to persevere. He agreed to serve on my future board of directors, in exchange for which I promised him a lifetime and unlimited supply of my African mahogany statues, which I knew he admired. I knew that I was the one getting the better deal. By the time Côme discovered the bargain basement prices he could negotiate for himself on the streets of Dar es Salaam for these handsome carvings, it was way too late. He was already in, hook, line, and statues.

So there in Dar es Salaam, in my darkest moment, I opened up my class directory, which luckily I had brought with me. I knew that Côme was on holiday in Europe and was then going to Southern Africa. He had listed his parents' address in Canada; surely he would be in contact with his family during his two-month trip. I gave an enticing postcard of Zanzibar Matemwe Beach to a Canadian I had befriended in Tanzania who was returning home that week. She promised to mail the card as soon as she arrived in Toronto. On the back I had written the following:

> *Côme,*
> *I need to talk to you. If you can, please call or fax me here in Tanzania. Telephone 255.514.6716 (w) 255.514.6718 (fax) 255.516.6529 (home). Things are going well but I am going to need your help and that of others. Hope your holiday is going well. Please contact if and when you can. Best regards, MM.*

Meanwhile, I had assigned Patrick to work on a project with a local entrepreneur named F. Tingitana. Tingi, as he was known, was one of the first local entrepreneurs of the new capitalist Tanzania, which for him was both a blessing (first-mover advantage) and a curse, because the free market frontiers of Tanzania were littered with bureaucratic land mines. Our goal was to help him develop a business plan to expand his existing public pay phone operation, Resources Consulting Group (RCG), throughout the city of Dar es Salaam. A couple of years earlier, on a government-sponsored trip to Malaysia, Tingi had noticed that the public pay phones in Malaysia were being used heavily. He concluded that he could do good business by installing similar pay phones in Tanzania, where fewer than 100,000 phones served a population of 26 million. He went to great lengths to source the technology from a manufacturer in Switzerland, Landys & Gyr, and had begun with an installed base of six pay phones, which constituted his entire operation when we met him in the summer of 1993. He faced serious technical, political, and financial constraints.

The first set of challenges centered on the fact that his technology was heavily reliant on the physical network infrastructure of the national phone carrier, Tanzania Posts and Telecommunications Co. (TPTC), and that company, accustomed to its monopoly status, was not cooperating with him. They viewed RCG as a potential threat to their own meager pay phone operations. Another major obstacle RCG faced was political. In Tanzania, as in most developing countries, who you know counts much more than what you know. Tingi neither knew, nor did he have access to, the right "whos." His final constraint was access to capital. There was little venture capital available to entrepreneurs like him in those days, and for RCG to scale up to a large company, which it had to do to successfully compete with TPTC, outside financing was indispensable.

Patrick had struck up a good working relationship with Tingi, who was grateful to see his vision taking shape in the form of a business plan, which we had agreed I would then take with me to the States to raise funds for a joint venture, in which ACG would be the majority partner. I concluded that modest though it was in scale, because Tingi's business was already operational and generating revenue, it represented our best chance for getting funded.

Shortly after the Katzes left I had moved into the apartment of a Swedish friend who was away on holiday. Compared to the UN house that we had been assigned, this was luxury living: everything was clean; the furniture was from Ikea; and it even had a telephone, which rang early one morning about two weeks after I had sent the postcard to Côme's parents. The line crackled loudly and irritatingly. I could not hear the voice at the other end. It sounded like an international call, but my hopes were dashed when there was silence at the other end of the line. At this point all I could think about was Côme coming to my rescue, and each time the phone rang, I jumped, hoping it was finally him.

One evening, about a week later, the phone rang. On the line was Côme. He was calling from a small hotel in Bulawayo, in southwest Zimbabwe.

"Monique, what's going on?" he said cheerfully. "My parents said that it was urgent that I call you. I tried to reach you earlier this week, because we had a layover at the airport in Dar es Salaam, but the pay phone was not working." Such was the state of telecommunications in Tanzania that Côme had had to travel close to a thousand miles out of the country to reach me.

I wasn't sure what to say. Should I tell him the full extent of the disaster, or should I sugarcoat it? If I really described how bad my plight was, it might scare him off. I could not blame everything on my disbanded team. I had to take some of the blame—even Côme wouldn't cut me that much slack. I had lost so much self-confidence that I was afraid of how he would judge me. But then I thought, I have to be completely honest with him; I owe him that much at the least.

"Côme," I began hesitantly, "my entire team has fallen apart and I am nowhere near the completion of my business plan."

He did not miss a beat. "What happened, exactly? They just up and left? Who's there now? How bad is the situation?"

"They said that I was not a good manager and that they no longer want to work for me, and quite frankly I no longer have faith in the quality of their work. From the beginning they have viewed this as their opportunity for fun in the sun. They could care less if this business takes off or not. I still have reports to deliver to the sponsors, and a business plan to write for my new venture. I have given them assignments to complete, but I really need someone to take a fresh and high-level look at the whole concept, for a sanity check," I said. "Côme, I really need you to come and help me pull this thing together."

I knew that he was traveling with Charlene Li, another class-mate, though not section mate, of ours. They and a group of other graduates had gone off on holiday together shortly after graduation in June.

"Monique, I don't have any power suits or anything, just khaki shorts and a pair of jeans, so I won't be able to accompany you to any meetings. But if you just want me to come up and sit in your place and write reports and run numbers, I can do that, no prob-lem—it will probably help me expense part of my vacation for tax purposes, anyway. I am kind of tired of doing this safari thing. Vic-toria Falls was great, though, oh man, and Charlene and I are hav-ing a great time. Africa is amazing." From the way he spoke about Charlene, I knew that the two of them were no longer "just friends." But the call was costing Côme about $10 a minute, and I did not think he wanted to spend it talking about his love life.

Then he said the words I was praying for: "I will just fly up and spend the week with you working on the business plan. Charlene will understand." It turned out that their return flight from Harare, Zimbabwe, to Europe had a stopover in Dar, and Côme figured that they could reunite then.

With the assurance that he was arriving in ten days, my confi-dence skyrocketed. Happily and, admittedly a tad smugly, I announced to Paul, Patrick, and Rick that my section mate, by implication, a family member, was coming, and that he and I would finish the remaining work together.

This had a sobering and motivating impact on them. Given their competitive natures, the interns did not want to leave behind work that did not meet at least minimum standards. A couple of days before Côme arrived, Patrick went off on his safari and Paul returned to Boston. For his part, Rick suddenly began telling me that he would be willing to keep working on the ACG business plan in the future, and would I therefore help him secure a local-resident permit? It would definitely benefit the project, he said, and ease his future trips to Tanzania if he had local-resident status, and, he conveniently failed to mention, entitled him to a 90 percent discount on an outfitted climb up Kilimanjaro, complements of the Tanzanian people.

I cannot help but wonder what we would have accomplished that summer if my interns had applied the same industriousness to the ACG business plan as they did to their vacation planning.

I met Côme at the Dar es Salaam airport with a UN representative who helped whisk him through immigration. Soon we were at work, hashing out the sponsor report and the business plan. I told him that of the three projects I thought the pay phone opportunity offered the brightest fund-raising and return prospects and suggested that we focus our efforts on that one. Côme spent the first day reviewing the work that had been done by the interns. "This is total crap," he said. "I can't believe you paid these guys to do this. The financials need to be started from scratch." I have the feeling that even if Einstein had developed the model, Côme would have crashed it—he would not have been able to resist the challenge. He rolled up his sleeves, took a deep breath, and soon he was in a place that I have never been to: (NC), numbers-crunching nirvana.

After hours of detailed spreadsheet analysis, I suggested to Côme that we go around the city to see the TPTC public pay phones and compare them with RCG's. The TPTC pay phone stations looked more like dilapidated mud-splattered shacks than functional booths. Most of the phones had long since ceased to function, some of them irreparably dismembered by angry and frustrated users. The enclosures, many of them repeatedly rammed into by overly zealous or intoxicated drivers, served as garbage bins and urinals. We decided right then and there that enclosed booths were out for ACG. The few phones that actually worked took only coins, which were barely in circulation in the Tanzanian economy anymore, due to rampant inflation; a caller would have had to use a truckful to place just one long-distance or international call. Côme could not resist the urge to produce a few exhibits for potential investors to demonstrate to them the weakness of the competition. He pulled out his camera and began photographing Tanzania's government-owned public pay phones. Within seconds a policeman came running toward us, brandishing his baton.

"What are you doing? This is illegal!" he yelled furiously. "You are not allowed to do this. Show me your passports. You must come with me to the station."

By this time I had spent over two months in Tanzania and had made some high-level contacts, including Paul Rupia, one of Tanzania's most prominent and influential politicians, who, it turned out, had studied in the country of my birth, Liberia. We had a mutual friend, and Paul had promised to help me in any way that he could because he was convinced that Tanzania needed private foreign investments to help the country develop.

"We are here with the UN," I protested to the police in the most authoritative voice that I could muster. "The gentleman here is a tourist and we are recording some of the local scenery. My name is Monique Maddy, and I am a friend of His Excellency Paul Rupia. You may contact him. I can assure you that we do not intend to misuse these photographs." Rupia was the magic word; we were free to go. Again, "who" you know.

Later that day we compared the national pay phones that we had visited to Tingi's RCG phones. The RCG phones were cleaner, card-operated, and had much longer lines of callers at each of them. The customers purchased the cards from attendants standing at the booths, which were manned 24 hours a day—an inefficient system even factoring in the low cost of labor in Tanzania, but Tingi had not yet figured out a distribution network to market and sell his cards. As we moved from location to location, Côme would station himself in front of the RCG phone booths with his stopwatch, monitoring phone usage and calculating how much money was being made per minute, per hour, and per day on each phone, all of which he would later plug into our brand-new and significantly improved financial model. "This is like a gold mine," he said, eyes wide. When Côme looked at Tanzania's seriously dilapidated infrastructure, like me, all he saw was opportunity.

"Monique, how many other places in the world do you think there are where you can just go in and start from zero like this?" When I told him that there are at least another forty-some countries in Africa alone, he said, "Man, this is amazing."

I knew that Côme had signed up to return to Monitor after the summer; the company had paid part of his tuition at Harvard, so I did not want to get my hopes up. But he was undergoing a transformation before my eyes. On his third day in Tanzania I took him to meet various government officials. For me this was a welcome excuse to get him out of the house and a brief escape from his spreadsheet trance. One of the people I took him to meet was Paul Rupia. Paul's offices were in the presidential palace. As we drove up to the palace, escorted by heavily armed security guards, Côme could sense the power and authority emanating from the building. Paul welcomed us into his office. It felt like driving up to the White House and getting an official reception from Dick Cheney.

"So, you Harvard people are going to help us develop our country, are you?" he said with a smile and a hint of healthy skepticism.

We explained our public pay phone project and I informed Paul that our local partner, Tingi, was incurring problems in securing additional technical facilities from the TPTC and that it would help us tremendously if he would draft a letter that would serve as the government's endorsement of our proposed pay phone joint venture with Tingi. He agreed to do so, and promised that it would be copied to all the relevant authorities in Tanzania, and sealed with the stamp of approval of the President's Office, the highest authority in the land.

To celebrate this major coup I took Côme to the Oyster Bay Hotel restaurant on Msasani Road. We sat on the balcony, overlooking the Indian Ocean as the sun sank into the sea, a gentle breeze wafting through and the candle flickering on the table. We both ordered the restaurant's specialty, lobster thermidor, a succulent delicacy consisting of a Tanzanian lobster baked to a golden brown in a rich béchamel sauce and served on the half shell. Côme became the first in a long chain of individuals who would succumb to my lobster trap. Anyone who tastes Oyster Bay's lobster thermidor finds an excuse to return to Tanzania.

We spent the last couple of days of his visit working until two or three in the morning on the business plan. Tingi was often with us, pulling out reams of crumpled papers that he kept stuffed in the European-style grip purse he carried everywhere. These documents provided the information that Côme needed to complete his financial model. Meanwhile, I was focusing on the text of the document, my forte. Côme and I agreed that we would not leave a copy of the plan with Tingi because by now it was in such good shape that he might well use it to raise money elsewhere and cut us out of the deal. We also signed a memorandum of understanding with him, according to which he would give us exclusivity for six months to raise $400,000 in exchange for 75 percent of the company (an implied postmoney valuation of $533,000), which would be renamed ACG Tanzania and would form the cornerstone of our transcontinental network. If we failed to secure the funding in the allotted time, Tingi was free to approach other potential investors.

Côme may have come to Tanzania to get me out of a jam, but by the end of the week he had found another calling. From a shy and reserved young man who had never traveled out of North America he had blossomed into a global entrepreneur, intoxicated by the challenge and the potential impact his knowledge and skills could have on a country like Tanzania. The routine consulting work to which he was returning paled in comparison. His world had changed.

I left Tanzania about a week after he did, in the beginning of September 1993. I was in love with our business plan and I had spent every night of that final week reviewing it and finding ways in which Tingi and I could tweak it even more to maximize our chances for raising the start-up capital. On the eve of my departure, Tingi arrived clutching the ubiquitous purse. He worked with me until two in the morning. We shook hands, and I assured him that I would not let him down, and that I would be in constant contact with him. His interim assignment was to attempt to secure more technical concessions from TPTC for us to expand our network, and I provided him with a copy of Rupia's letter to assist him with this process. "Monique, I assure you that I will do everything to make sure that this business takes off. You have renewed my hope," he said.

Côme, in turn, had renewed my hope. I had a gut feeling that if I could raise $400,000, he would quit Monitor and join me to take ACG to the next level.

Now all I had to do to make my dream come true was get back into the United States, no easy task. In Tanzania, I was an important expat, a musungu, a graduate of the Harvard Business School, a Western elite. But to the U.S. immigration officials standing between me and my future I was just another foreigner, an alien with a Liberian passport, no less, and a lapsed student visa. I was what is unofficially known in developed countries as an "undesirable," one of the millions of third world vagabonds or drifters, from Africa, Asia, Latin America, and Eastern Europe, desperately seeking to escape our miserable lot and cash in on the American dream. Their goal was to keep out of America as many of us as possible, to prevent the dream from becoming a collective nightmare.

3

A Modest Proposal

LIBERIAN SOLDIERS FLEE REBEL ADVANCE BY COMMANDEERING TIMBER-COMPANY VESSEL AT GUNPOINT 1.5 MILLION ALREADY DISPLACED BY THE LONG-RUNNING CIVIL WAR . . . U.S. STATE DEPARTMENT URGES AMERICANS TO LEAVE . . . REBELS IN THE CENTRAL AFRICAN REPUBLIC CAPTURE BANGUI AND LEADER DECLARES HIMSELF PRESIDENT . . . U.S. STATE DEPARTMENT URGES CITIZENS TO LEAVE . . . IN CONGO-BRAZZAVILLE FLEEING CIVILIANS JAM ROADS BY THE TENS OF THOUSANDS, TRYING TO ESCAPE RIVAL ETHNIC MILITIAS BATTLING FOR CONTROL ARMED WITH MORTARS AND MACHETES.

These headlines were taken from news bulletins in 2003, but sadly they could just as easily have been written today or 10 years ago, and they will be written 10 years from now if Africa continues on its current path. Incredible though it may seem, Africa has not always been like this.

Of course one can trace the beginning of the downslide and disintegration of Africa all the way back to the 15th century, when Columbus first discovered America. But that story has been well chronicled already. I am more concerned with the past half-century or so, when what began as an ambitious but temporary and viable program to restore world peace, foster economic growth in Europe, and ensure global financial stability became the permanent blueprint for economic development everywhere, for countries as disparate as Lithuania and Liberia: development off-the-racks, prêt-à-porter. I am of course referring to the Marshall Plan for the Reconstruction and Development of Europe. The Marshall Plan was a targeted economic program designed to help a populace that was already well educated, industrialized, and much a part of the pre–World War II global economy. Its scope was therefore limited to strengthening existing European nations in the aftermath of the war, not to building new ones from the bottom up. Europeans were already well accustomed to the concept of nationhood, even if not always in agreement with the validity of particular national boundaries.

Precisely because of its limited scope, the Marshall Plan was immensely successful; it helped launch Europe along a path that led to increasing levels of political, economic, and cultural integration, even as it continued to broaden its membership.

But they could not leave well enough alone. In the spirit of the times, a small group of mostly American and European politicians, policymakers, and technocrats created additional institutions to help meet other, more global, objectives. One of these institutions was the United Nations, a successor to the failed and defunct League of Nations. The UN was given such a broad mandate—"maintain international peace and security . . . develop friendly relations among nations based on respect for the principle of equal rights and self-determination of peoples . . . cooperate in solving international, economic, social, cultural, and humanitarian problems a—that it could practically be whatever it wanted to be without violating any of its covenants. It could play God.

Then came the International Bank for Reconstruction and Development (later known as the World Bank) and the International Monetary Fund. The IBRD was created to provide capital to countries where private capital was reluctant to go; none of its founders seemed to realize that if private capital did not go somewhere on its own, there were probably good reasons why not. But rather than take the time to figure them out and flush with cash, they determined to send the money to those countries anyway. The IMF's objective was to create an international monetary system that would allow countries to pursue full-employment fiscal policies without the risk of depleting their foreign exchange reserves, thereby ensuring global economic stability. These intergovernmental behemoths, the United Nations, the World Bank, and the IMF, as well as a slew of copycat governmental and nongovernmental organizations, in turn spurred numerous offshoots and programs with everexpanding, overlapping, and competing mandates. What they all had in common was that their survival depended above all else on the careful nurturing and preservation of global poverty.

When I consider the collective and individual damage that these institutions and their flock have wrought on Africa and developing countries all over the world in the name of economic development, I am reminded of a passage by one of my favorite satirists, Jonathan Swift, in *Gulliver's Travels*. Except for the redeeming fact that most Africans seem to somehow find room for humor and hope in a seemingly intractable situation, my impressions of Africa as they relate to the continent's experience with the so-called development "experts" mirror those of Gulliver as he describes the hopeless city of Lagado, the capital of the flying island of Laputa, which sits on the normal island of Bulnibari over which Laputa hovers:

All the buildings were in ruins and the people walked around in rags, with expressions of despair written on their faces. The surrounding countryside was no different, being poorly cultivated, and the people toiling away with no apparent result.

The origin of the misery is that forty years ago the officials had returned from the island of Laputa, full of airy theories and ideas, whereby all practical methods of living were not to be used. An Academy of Projectors was established in every town to think up new ideas. But, so far, none of the projects had worked in practice; and until they do the country waits in waste and misery.

Like their brethren at the Academy of Projectors, the UN, World Bank, and IMF are so obsessed with fancy theories and abstractions that they have completely discarded the value of common sense. The result is delusion and chaos, not to mention the perpetual suffering of hundreds of millions of innocent bystanders. If these so-called experts are the guardians or protectors of the poor, surely it begs the question: *Sed quis custodiet ipsos custodies?* But who will guard the guardians?

The aid industry, the players of which, for the purposes of this memoir, I will refer to collectively as Laputa, Inc., was created ostensibly to reduce global poverty and promote economic growth. But, setting the early success in Western Europe aside, Laputa has done far more to absorb the third-world brain drain and reduce the world's number of free-floating Ph.D.s on the dole than it has to achieve even a semblance of net improvement in the fortunes of its African and other third world wards. Trivial economic theories, once safely relegated to the relatively harmless confines of class-room discussions and research cubicles at top universities, have found new life and vigor in the socioeconomic laboratory that the third world has become at the hands of the United Nations, the Bretton Woods institutions, and countless redundant nongovern-mental organizations vying for a slice of the antipoverty pie.

The leaders of Laputa, Inc., are chameleons who excel at the brilliant art of reinvention, illusion, and self-preservation. If Africa did not exist, they would have invented it. The Eastern Europes, the Russias, the Afghanistans, and the Iraqs are mere distractions, appetizers to them. Africa is their staple. Laputa, Inc., is accountable to few, despite the fact that almost all of its functionaries are directly or indirectly on your payroll and mine. Part Dr. Jekyll, part Mr. Hyde, they have to convince us that there is sufficient poverty and misery in the world that the cash register will keep ringing, while at the same time show just enough progress to give the appearance of positive change. Any pea-brained statistician (of which there are many in Laputa, Inc.) worth the sheepskin his Ph.D. is printed on can accomplish this by skillfully manipulating data such that, unbeknownst to his audience, he is comparing not only apples to oranges, but next Saturday to the moon. Take the following communiqué issued by the World Summit on Sustainable Development, held from August to September 2002 under UN auspices. The summit was held in South Africa at Johannesburg's swanky Sandton Convention Center, conveniently sequestered from the squalor and despair of the numerous shantytowns nearby. If it was anything like the many UN-sponsored events that I attended in my day, the delegates' evenings were filled with rollicking festivities, animated by live music and the generous flow of Dom Perignon, vintage French wines, and Russian caviar. Rice and beans would not have been on the menu.

East Asia's poverty rate has fallen from about 28 per cent in 1990 to 15 per cent in 1998, with the number of people living in poverty declining from 418 million to 267 million [good news].

In sub-Saharan Africa, the poverty rate is about 48 per cent and has remained unchanged over the last decade. However, the number of people living in poverty has grown, from 20 million in 1990 to 300 million in 1998 [bad news].

What the communiqué fails to mention is that none of the successes of "East Asia"—China, Japan, Korea, the Russian far east, and Taiwan—can be attributed to Laputa, Inc., while almost all of Africa's failures can be.[1] Likewise, not long ago the World Bank leadership pointed out that the world spent approximately $800 billion on military expenditures in 2002, compared with $56 billion that was spent in development assistance. Again, what Laputa fails to point out, is that if they had been doing their jobs with even the modicum of effectiveness over the past half century, that is increasing economic prosperity in the countries that they serve, many of the very issues that are the main catalysts to wars in the twenty-first century, poverty, misery, political suppression, lack of prospects and other afflictions suffered by hundreds of millions in the Thrid World, would have been substantially reduced. As a result, the military buildup that we are witnessing today to fight wars in places such as Afghanistan, Iraq, and against global terrorism, would probably have been reduced by several orders of magnitude. Nevertheless, the UN secretary general, Kofi Annan, calls on us to double our investment in the UN to $100 billion a year to meet the summit's goals, which, not surprisingly, are the same as those targeted when the UN was first established almost half a century ago. For its part, the World Bank estimates the cost for the full-time professional global antipoverty squad team to achieve the same goal to be between $40 billion and $60 billion a year, the difference between the two estimates being that between five-star hotels and four-star establishments, first-class versus business class. Laputa makes voodoo economics look like high mass, or high math, as the case may be. Yet widespread guilt, genuine compassion, apathy, and ignorance of their modus operandi continue to ensure that we replenish Laputa's overstuffed coffers on behalf of real or invented causes until, that is, someone brave enough and powerful enough catches on and realizes that they are not eliminating poverty, but exploiting it.

The truth is that there are other paths to development, some even suitable for the poorest countries. I myself was born in as remote a corner of Africa as exists. Yet I managed to find my way from there to the elite halls of an English public school and to the American Ivy League and traveled in the urbane circles of the United Nations, global corporations, and high finance. But none of this would have been possible if it hadn't been for the activities of one private company that totally transformed the dense tropical rain forest in which I was born into a diverse, complex, and multicultural world, where business opportunities were created and entrepreneurs thrived. Happily it was a place that Laputa, Inc., knew nothing about. We were citizens of a corporation that took good care of us, far better care than any of us ever received from our national government. I and many others now scattered across the globe succeeded because the corporation depended on our success, rather than on our dependence, and because its officers were accountable to shareholders who had a better understanding and appreciation of human rights and good governance than most African governments do. Indeed, that world, Yekepa, was a world that I took too much for granted, even as we were surrounded by chaos. For many years the chaos was kept at bay. But eventually it, and other events, conspired to swallow us up.

For a long time I have agonized over the vexing and seemingly intractable problem of Africa. Had I been born anywhere else in the world, I probably would have spared myself the countless sessions of intellectual contortions that have defined my unrelenting quest for an alternative solution to the continent's problems. I might otherwise be a Hindu lying along the banks of the Ganges River contemplating my next life. Or perhaps a Norwegian stockbroker cruising along a fjord, reeling in my salmon with the reassuring knowledge that my stock in the shipping company started by my great-grandfather is enjoying an unprecedented rise on the Oslo Bors. Or maybe I would be an academic, a self-appointed guru of global poverty, reeling in millions of publicly funded dollars to collect and disseminate data and write alarming reports that I know will never be read, much less acted upon; attending global conferences; and basking in the certainty that with my proposed solution to poverty, job security will never be an issue for me, because unlike the tulip craze of the 17th century, or the dot-com bust of the 21st century, the poverty business is not a fad—it is hot, it is growing, and for the industry's biggest players it is a highly lucrative business.

But fortune dealt me the hand of Africa, and even though I am now an American, I care deeply about Africa's future. As the Roman lyricist Horace put it, *Patriae quis exsul se quoque fugit?* What exile from his country has also escaped from himself? So rather than leave Africa in the hands of its current caretakers, a choice that will most certainly lead to further marginalization, human suffering, and impoverishment of the continent, I propose a much more benign and cost-effective solution.

There are about 650 million people in sub-Saharan Africa. Thanks to Mother Nature, Africa is blessed with a particularly harsh and debilitating climate and a full arsenal of hazardous and potentially fatal diseases, including malaria, cholera, yellow fever, diarrhea, and AIDS. All of these afflictions can be perceived as being of incalculable value in my plan, which is to dispose of the continent.

I owe my inspiration in this matter also to Jonathan Swift and his "modest proposal" for making poor Irish children a benefit to the British and not a burden to their parents and country. My plan (from which Laputa, Inc., is permanently barred from profiting in any way) similarly spares Africans from future misery, from being a burden to themselves and to their leaders, and makes them beneficial to the global community.

The benefits of my proposal are many. First, the world will no longer have to bother its conscience with constant compassion for Africa and her people. Second, those who are suffering from AIDS, malaria, hepatitis, cholera, and other afflictions will die a euthanasic death. In this way they will be spared the gruesome prospect of serving out a life sentence of misery, with no health care, no education, no political rights, no free speech, and no economic prosperity. For many of them, death, the ultimate parole, is a more humane form of justice than what they currently live to endure, and far less costly to the global community. Third, unlike the many failed experiments of Laputa, Inc., my plan is specific, has concrete deliverables, and will be executed fully within twenty-five years. Fourth, and most importantly, my plan is entirely self-funded. It follows here:

A Modest Proposal for the Euthanasia of a Continent

Barring the discovery of a miracle cure found to be growing freely and in abundance in the African bushes, for many the HIV/AIDS death sentence is not likely to be commuted, no matter how much money the international organizations raise. This is true for a number of obvious reasons. Given the deplorable state of the African economies, as well as the fact that most of its inhabitants live on less than $1 per day (even the World Bank acknowledges that close to 3 billion people on this planet live on less than $2 a day, most of them in Africa), whether an AIDS drug costs $1,000 per day, $100, or $1 is irrelevant to most Africans; most will be unable to afford it even at the lowest price. Based on current and past trends, this means that AIDS will kill approximately 2 million men, women, and children per year, or close to 50 million in our 25-year time frame. Be that as it may, AIDS in Africa is the crisis du jour, and hardly a self-respecting and enterprising development agency or independent development expert has not latched on to it as their latest meal ticket. Other diseases, such as malaria, cholera, hepatitis, and meningitis, as well as poor hygiene and sanitation, chronic malnutrition, famine, and basic poverty, will kill approximately 150 million people in the same time frame, which leaves us with 450 million people still on the continent.

That is where war comes in. At any given time there are about ten African countries engaged in some form of civil or cross-border conflict. In Angola, a country I lived in for two years, 3.5 million people have been killed since the war started in 1975. Then there are the estimated 6 million to 20 million land mines that pockmark the country, all either death traps or serious mutilating machines. Using the statistics of the Angola conflict to figure an average rate of death by war, we can assume that around 140,000 men, women and children are killed directly or indirectly from war-related causes in each country each year. Multiplying these figures times ten, then again times 25 (our time frame), we can reasonably expect that at least 35 million Africans will die in this fashion. Those who are merely mutilated we will shoot to put them out of their misery and spare the state the medical expense, assuming such medical services are even provided.

We've got our number down to 415 million people. At least a quarter of those are probably under age twelve, illiterate, and unproductive. By the standards of the International Labor Organization, these children should not be working or fighting wars, as many of them are forced to do. They should be in school. But with access to even basic health care and education severely restricted, they face dim prospects in Africa. They can therefore be adopted by those antiglobal, anticorporate protesters in the streets of Seattle, Washington, Prague, Genoa, and Geneva who make an upper-class sport out of demonstrating against almost any international economic measure or major corporation that suits their fancy, regardless of the consequences for the people they claim they are defending. Like the Lost Boys of Sudan, who in 2001 were plucked out of refugee camps in East Africa by church groups for placement in some welcoming and some not so welcoming communities across Middle America to assume positions bagging our groceries in suburban supermarkets, or the more recent U.S. State Department's approval of the resettlement of up to 12,000 Somali Bantu in about 50 U.S. cities, from Chicago, to Phoenix, to Denver, to Buffalo and Syracuse, New York, so too could the 104 million child refugees from Africa find new homes in Europe, Asia, and elsewhere in North America.

This still leaves us with a population of 311 million to dispose of; I propose that we send about 5 million to the "new" expanded Europe to take on menial jobs that Europeans prefer not to do and are already being performed by other legal and illegal Africans, Asians, and East Europeans who have immigrated to what U.S. Secretary of Defense Donald Rumsfeld appropriately referred to as the "Old Europe." If their intentions are sincere, this measure should placate European antiglobalization protesters who argue rightly, although for the wrong reasons, that Africa and Africans are getting a raw deal. I have no doubt that France would favor such an initiative heavily. Jacques Chirac and his dashing foreign minister, Dominique de Villepin, are fond of Africa, particularly when France is in need of friends in high places on the UN Security Council, such as tiny Guinea, a former colony from which the French were unceremoniously ejected in 1958 by the country's first president, Sékou Touré, a radical socialist. (Of course no one mentions how the French were in such a huff at this rebuff that they pulled out the plumbing and the electrical wiring from buildings they had constructed in that impoverished country on their way out.)

It would be fiscally irresponsible to completely depopulate the continent without fully extracting its natural resources within our 25-year time frame. This task will require a significant amount of labor, both skilled and unskilled. In this way perhaps 100 million Africans could be gainfully employed by multinational corporations that have won, through an international competitive bidding process, exclusive rights to an American-style "all you can eat" economic banquet of Africa's commodities, minerals, and precious stones. A portion of the proceeds from the sale of these resources will be set aside to pay off the ruling elite for their compliance with my proposal. We have to give them something in return for relinquishing their power. Another portion of the proceeds will be placed in a trust (let us call it the Seattle Initiative) established to assist the antiglobal activists in feeding, lodging, and educating their new African charges. This will ensure that the young African immigrants will not burden their liberal foster parents, who may even find a small profit to be made from this arrangement.

We are down to 206 million Africans. The overwhelming majority of them are unemployed, frustrated, and ripe for political dissent. The good news is that with so few left on the continent, the GDP per capita in sub-Saharan Africa will have increased significantly even without any additional output. That is what I call productivity, something that has been lacking in much of Africa for decades. But with so much additional wealth to be gained from the accelerated removal of the continent's assets, the rich will still want to be richer, and by force of habit will rebel, spurring further civil unrest that will lead to more civil wars, cross-border and regional wars, and hence even more deaths. If they do not rebel spontaneously, a nongovernmental outfit, of which there are many in Washington, D.C., can be engaged to plant the seeds of democracy, a concept that when applied to Africa, given the extremely high levels of demagoguery and low number of educated voters almost always opens the door to further chaos. Invariably, the ultimate outcome of these democratic initiatives is determined by bazookas rather than by ballots. The survivors will then be free to continue the reckless pilfering of the continent's residual assets, unperturbed by bourgeois notions of democracy and accountability. With their most salient qualifications being corruption, brutality, and incompetence, most of them will be hard-pressed to find refuge anywhere else on this planet and will probably remain in Africa to the bitter end.

Power will be further consolidated, arms dealers will be knocking each other over to trade dynamo for diamonds and any other easily disposable assets. A final wave of wars on the continent will last for just about as long as there remain resources to fight for, and for all intents and purposes we will have completed our mission

within our target time frame of 25 years. Thus, the African continent and most of its population will be happily spared the certainty
of miseries and evils that await them at the hands of Laputa, Inc.,
and the entire world will have profited from its demise.

Obviously, it is not my desire to kill off an entire continent. But I do
not wish to stand idly by witnessing the slow and certain demise of
the place of my birth, the cradle of mankind. For that matter, nor
should any reasonable, compassionate, or business-savvy person on
this planet.

We must therefore acknowledge the obvious: No country has ever
become a success story by relying on institutional handouts. No country ever will. Nations and economies are built and sustained by good
social, economic, political, and judicial governance, by the industriousness of individuals (entrepreneurship) and corporations. The
truth is that the whole world, not a select few, benefits if sub-Saharan
Africa is a major economic power rather than a perpetual basket case;
think how many more copies of Microsoft Windows would be sold,
how many more Fords and Chryslers, IBM computers, and new
Boeing jets would be needed to service close to a billion more middle-
class consumers. Even AT&T would reach out and touch hundreds
of millions of African someones. Instead of applauding and settling for
Luciano Pavarotti and Posh, Scary, Sporty, and Baby Spice singing in
Modena, Italy, to raise money for the poor children in Liberia, as they
did in 1998, why not aspire to a day when the great Italian tenor can
look to his rack and pull his "spice" of the moment and sing to a sold-
out stadium crowd of paying fans in Monrovia, the capital city of
Liberia. That is progress. But as long as Africa remains under the
stewardship of Laputa, Inc., and the bar remains so pathetically low,
misery and marginalization are the only certainties, and sadly the only
opera that the people of Liberia and many other similarly afflicted
countries will ever experience is the tragedy of their own lives.

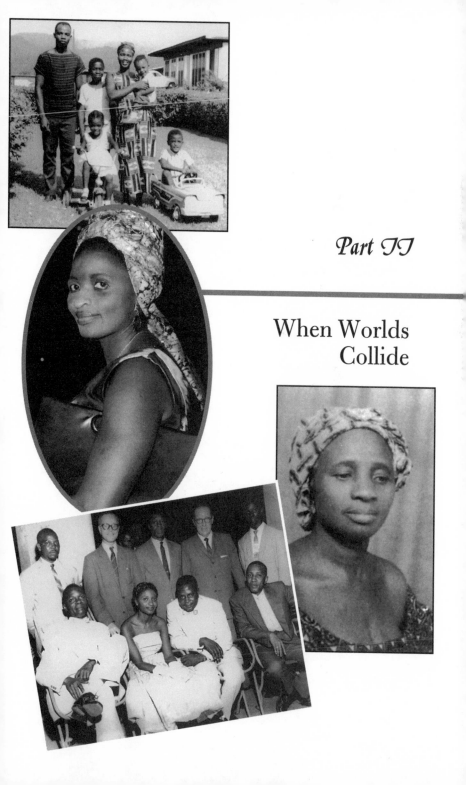

Part II

When Worlds
Collide

4

King of the Road

As I have already said, Africa does not have to be like this, nor should it be. It is a matter of aligning Africa's long-term interests with those of the rest of the world—that is, increasing global wealth and productivity rather than increasing global aid.

I was born on August 14, 1962, deep in the hinterland of Liberia, in a place called Grassfield. I was born in an incubator, although not in the literal sense. This was not the kind of incubator one finds in the neonatal ward of a Western hospital. (Grassfield did not have one, of course.) Instead, this was a conceptual bubble, a zone of relative safety, created by a corporation to protect the newly arriving village inhabitants from the harsh realities of the African jungle. I was born in a company town, a village entirely sponsored by a private enterprise that had penetrated as deep into the heart of Africa as a global business could in those days.

The name Grassfield was our convenient fiction. The truth is that the place was such virgin territory in 1962 that it had not yet been given a proper name. The recently arrived immigrants referred to it as "grass field" because the term aptly and economically described the terrain that had been freshly hacked to accommodate the Western-style housing that was about to be erected in the area.

Grassfield was in the Nimba region of Liberia, which stretches across the length of Liberia's borders with Sierra Leone, Guinea, and the Ivory Coast. It lies approximately 200 miles north of the Liberian capital of Monrovia, which is located on the Atlantic and is the center of all commercial and political activity in the country. South of Grassfield is the dense tropical rain forest, the largest in Africa, which stretches almost to the coast. To the north are a mixture of grassy savanna and forested mountain, including the Nimba Mountain range, the highest peak of which stands at 6,700 feet above sea level, and is the highest point in West Africa. This elevation provided the village and its few indigenous inhabitants with some respite from the harsh tropical heat and humidity of the jungle and the disease-bearing mosquitoes and tsetse flies.

It was in the Nimba Mountain range, the source of many of Liberia's rivers, that in the mid-1950s vast deposits of some of the highest-grade iron ore in the world—by some estimates 500 million tons, worth—were discovered by European and American mining interests. Within ten years of the discovery of the ore, a Swedish mining operation called LAMCO had completely transformed an entire geographic region of Liberia, much of which had been almost impenetrable, sealed off as it was by the rain forest, eventually providing the country with up to 70 percent of its revenue. For those not born there, the area had been a place to be avoided. European and American literature from the time, and even coastal Liberians in the same period, described the region as a perilous zone of primitive tribal cultures, filled with secret societies, witchcraft, and cannibals.

I can only surmise that Grassfield's new arrivals, still weary from their long and tedious journey inland, and perhaps in complete awe of and fascination with the strangeness of their new surroundings, simply could not afford to expend precious energy contemplating fancy place names. In any case, the name was never embellished further, and the "Place of Birth" line on my Liberian passport, which I carried until I became a U.S. citizen in 2003, read "Grassfield, Nimba County."

The community was small, about 400 people. Perhaps three-quarters were indigenous Liberians; at least 95 percent of them were completely illiterate and living the traditional tribal life. Extended families cohabited in mud huts with thatched roofs. There were no schools, no shops, no churches, and no medical facilities. For many of these people, a simple cutlass was the most complex technology available, and it adequately served their needs. Now, in the 1960s, their lives were about to change radically. They would learn to read and write and to operate complicated machinery, working at high speeds, in the continuous industrial process of an iron-ore mine in which a foreign investment of close to $300 million was being made.

Of the remaining 100-odd villagers, about 90 were Europeans, mostly from Sweden, Norway, Germany, England, Ireland, Scotland, and the Netherlands via Indonesia (in other words, Dutch adventurers on the run from one thing or another). The last dozen or so, my father among them, were known as Coasters because they came from neighboring former British colonies along the west coast of Africa—in Pappi's case, from Sierra Leone. As a result of the British colonial influence and the more outward-oriented perspective of the coastal towns, these men had obtained basic but good educations and were accustomed to working with foreigners, which made them attractive hires for international firms in search of skilled local workers.

Pappi was charismatic. He was also handsome and a sharp

dresser, but his was a casual elegance. He preferred to have only the best, even if that meant he could only afford five shirts instead of ten. They were a certain Italian brand, and he would wear them until they were worn out, and then reorder more of the same. His skin was a deep black, almost indigo. Such skin is rarely seen outside of Africa, and whenever I come across it in the West, I can instantly pinpoint the person's origin. The fact that I inherited some of Pappi's color made me the butt of jokes, especially among the Americo-Liberians, the descendants of the freed American slaves who founded Liberia in the early 19th century and who subscribed to the ludicrous notion that lighter skin was a symbol of racial superiority.

Each morning at five o'clock Pappi would turn on the BBC for the world news, and on Saturdays he played the soccer pool, in which he placed bets on who would win in the various European leagues. I am not sure how it worked, but he would have his form with lots of boxes, and a pen, and his glasses on. As the announcer read the scores of the various British sides, "Liverpool: 1, Manchester: nil; Leeds United: 2, Birmingham: nil; Chelsea: 1, Newcastle: 1," and so on, Pappi would check in the boxes tabulating his winnings. Those were the only 15 or so minutes during which he did not want us to disturb him.

Pappi enjoyed being with his family, and was popular among his colleagues. He was a workaholic and a perfectionist. Cooking and gardening were his avocations and his passions, and he had been encouraged and nurtured in these by his mother, my grandmother, Mamma Ade (short for Adesemi), who excelled in both of these fields. But as much as he loved food, he would live on 1,500 calories a day if he felt that he needed to be in top shape. He was also a strict disciplinarian as a result of the Victorian upbringing he had received in Sierra Leone, probably further enhanced by the fact that Mamma Ade had been a prison guard in Freetown.

Mummy, on the other hand, was much more easygoing. She did

all that she could to ensure that he had the support to fulfill his dreams. She was quiet and reserved and also beautiful and elegant. She had long, beautiful hair and a face one remembered, with high cheekbones. She was born Julia Carter, but soon took on the name of her foster family, Richards. At the age of 2 she had been sent by her mother, my grandmother, Ma Kema, to live with Ma Kema's sister, Gertrude, who also had been married into an America-Liberian family, but who, unlike Ma Kema, had converted from Islam to Christianity. Mummy's Aunt Gertrude lived in the Liberian county of Virginia, and she enrolled Mummy in an Episcopal boarding school run by U.S. missionaries. This custom was not uncommon in Liberia. Many people who lived in villages would send their children to live with America-Liberian families, where in exchange for working in the house, they would obtain an education. Unfortunately, in many instances this custom was abused, and the ward would be treated slightly better than a slave by his or her foster parent. But this was not the case with Mummy, perhaps because her father himself was an America-Liberian and her foster mother, who treated her as if she were her own child, was her aunt, rather than a total stranger.

Mummy was eventually sent to live in Monrovia with another aunt, Ellen King, the daughter of the former president of Liberia, C. D. B. King. She received her degree in nursing and worked for the Liberian government until she won a U.S. grant to study nursing at Boston University. After securing her degree, Mummy returned to Liberia to teach at a nursing school. It was during this period that she met Pappi, who by then had already been in Liberia for a few years. Even back then he was fashion conscious, and he and Mummy met in a Monrovia shoe shop one afternoon. Pappi told her he would take her to a store where she would find "the perfect pair of shoes to fit the perfect lady." They used to tell us children that they took an instant liking to each other. Still, they were quite an odd couple, given that Mummy had by then become an integral part of the powerful King family and Pappi was a clerk and taxi driver from Sierra Leone. After several years of scraping by, doing odd construction jobs here and there, and eventually securing permanent work with the Department of Public Works, Pappi had saved enough money to purchase a used car, a Mercedes-Benz, which he converted into a cab that he drove around in the evenings until midnight to earn extra money.

These were the days well before the omnipresence of the four-wheel drive, and the heavy, well-built, and luxurious Mercedes was known locally as the King of the Road. Pappi kept that car for 15 years, and later, during the rainy season in Liberia, whenever we got stuck in the mud during long drives to see my grandmother or to Monrovia, a cheering audience of villagers would soon gather alongside the dirt road, pushing the car and rooting for the King of the Road to extricate itself. It was a little like a sporting match, with onlookers cheering as the car slid dangerously from one side of the road to the other, slipping and swerving as Pappi battled with the steering wheel and the various gears. When the car finally dislodged itself from the mud and lurched forward to freedom, the crowd would break into a round of applause, chanting rhythmically, Mer-say-deez! Mer-say-deez! Mer-say-deez!

Buying that car was a smart move, because it stood out among the Datsuns and Toyotas and attracted the most exclusive clientele, among them the Swedish executives of what would soon be LAMCO, by whom Pappi was hired to ferry to various government offices and to the airport. One of his passengers was Marcus Wallenberg, of the famous Wallenberg family in Sweden. Wallenberg was the driving force behind LAMCO and was so impressed by Pappi that before departing from Liberia he turned to a company official and said, "Hire this man." Soon afterward Pappi took a job as bookkeeper with the accounting department of the new LAMCO office in Monrovia, as the company prepared to commence operations in the Nimba Mountain. Proving that Wallenberg had an eye for talent, Pappi then distinguished himself in a way that tremendously affected the fortunes of LAMCO. At great risk to himself, Pappi thwarted an attempted theft, allegedly backed by the highest authorities in the neighboring country of Guinea. He had caught two agents red-handed in the LAMCO offices, trying to steal some geological maps that the Guineans probably were hoping to use to prove that the concession that the Liberian government had awarded LAMCO was invalid and that the territory covered by the concession was actually on Guinean, not Liberian, territory. The loss of these maps would have made the issue a matter of international jurisdiction, and would have placed the entire LAMCO project in jeopardy. For his efforts Pappi was awarded the Liberian Presidential Medal of Bravery. Not surprisingly, this further cemented Pappi's status within LAMCO.

About a year after that incident, and in the presence of the small LAMCO start-up team, he and Mummy were married. A couple of years later along came my brother Claudius, and shortly thereafter LAMCO was ready to move its workers up to Grassfield. That was where I spent my infancy, but my first real memories are of a town called Yekepa, where we moved when I was two, when LAMCO was more established and had expanded its operations. Yekepa, the village nearest to where iron ore was discovered in December 1956 by a Scottish geologist named Sandy Clark, was named after the village chief. Old Man Yeke, as he was known, liked to declare to any who would listen that the mines and the ore in it belonged to him and his villagers. His claim probably had some validity, but he had no means of enforcing it, and the royalties went to the Liberian government rather than to Old Man Yeke. But he got something much more valuable in the long run—the most thriving and modern town in Liberia, if not in all of West Africa during that time.

Before the mining company arrived, Old Man Yeke's village had fewer than 50 people. Sequestered in the dense tropical forest, it was accessible only by foot and with much hard labor to clear the forest. The villagers rarely ventured beyond their tiny enclave and lived on what they produced or killed. This was fine with the Liberian government, the philosophy of which was to not incorporate the indigenous people in any meaningful way into the political structure or even provide them with a basic education, out of fear that knowledge would lead first to political awareness followed by political discontent and, ultimately, subversion.

Not even LAMCO's physical, social, and economic transformation of Yekepa and its surrounding areas could sway the Liberian government from its belief that opening up the hinterland too quickly would be a license to political anarchy. Had it been left to the government alone, Old Man Yeke and his tiny village, as well as thousands of citizens throughout the Liberian hinterland, would have undoubtedly remained as they were: poor and ignorant, disenfranchised yet tax-paying natives. As was the case in the British and French colonial empires, the ruling class of Liberia believed in taxation without representation.

Indeed, when the government finally granted citizenship to the indigenous people in 1904, it had merely been to establish claim over them and their territory, and to prevent French and British encroachment, not to enfranchise the citizens, which happened almost half a century later, and at that, only measuredly.

You cannot really appreciate or understand the achievement of Yekepa unless you know the sad context in which it existed, which is the story of Liberia.

By the late 18th century there were hundreds of thousands of blacks in the United States. This caused concern among certain white American leaders that their presence in such great numbers might have a negative impact on the general welfare of the nation. Others, mostly southern whites, believed that the existence of an overwhelming number of freed blacks could threaten the very institution of slavery. After America won its independence from Britain, yet another faction of the white community began to question the moral and political justification of slavery in light of America's own newly acquired freedom. To them it was unseemly and hypocritical that certain groups living in America did not share the liberties and legal protections for which the colonialists had fought so valiantly. In an attempt to harmonize these disparate viewpoints, and those of some blacks who believed that they might find freedom and a better life out of America, a number of proposals to deal with the so-called black problem were put forward. One suggested sending blacks to territories in the western hemisphere still under European control, such as Florida, Louisiana, and the West Indies. Another proposal was to send them to Africa.

One of the most ardent American supporters of this idea was Captain Paul Cuffee, a wealthy half-black, half–Native American Quaker from Massachusetts. A successful entrepreneur, Cuffee was convinced that a repatriation project could be self-financing and even highly lucrative for its proponents. It is difficult to understand how he might have come to such a conclusion given that he had done extensive research, and had corresponded with British institutions and members of Parliament who had been responsible for Britain's own earlier, similarly inspired, disastrous Sierra Leone experiment on the west coast of Africa in 1787. Cuffee had even visited Sierra Leone in 1811 on a reconnaissance mission, where he found conditions that could hardly have been described as idyllic. Nevertheless, he reasoned that if black American settlers were transported to Africa, they would live free and prosperous lives by cultivating produce for export and sale in America. Cuffee died in 1817 before he could make his dream a reality, but his cause was taken up by the American Society for Colonizing the Free People of Color in the United States.

That organization, soon renamed the American Colonization Society (ACS), existed to repatriate free blacks to Africa. It was inspired not so much by the economic motives advocated by Cuffee as by whites' desire to rid themselves of large numbers of blacks in America. Its membership included General Andrew Jackson, Henry Clay, James Madison, Francis Scott Key, and Bushrod Washington, the nephew of George Washington, who was elected president of the ACS in 1817. A number of auxiliary societies were also established in Baltimore, Philadelphia, New York, Virginia, and Ohio. Their collective goal was to deport or, as they put it, to "repatriate" freeborn blacks and manumitted slaves to West Africa—repatriate being something of a misnomer given that none of these blacks had ever been to Africa. Other than the color of their skin, they had no more in common with the people of that continent than did the white organizers who wanted to send them there.

Although President James Monroe was supportive of the organization, the U.S. Congress initially voted against providing any federal funding to ACS and the other colonizing societies. After the passage of the Anti-Slave Trade Act in 1819, however, Congress authorized the grant of $100,000 to the ACS for the purchase of suitable land in West Africa for the repatriation effort. Most of the rest of the ACS's funding came from philanthropic contributions. As a result, the funds made available to the society were woefully inadequate relative to their noble ambitions and the obstacles they faced. This shortness of funding turned out to be a blessing in disguise, because it meant that only a limited number of people were sent out on the initial journey in 1820. Aboard the ship *Elizabeth* were the Reverend Samuel Bacon and John P. Bankson, representatives of the U.S. government; Samuel C. Crozer, representing the ACS; and about 80 free blacks. Shortly after their arrival, Bacon, Bankson, Crozer, and about 20 of the new settlers died.

Despite this inauspicious launch, on December 12, 1821, a fresh shipment of settlers was sent over from America aboard the schooner *Alligator*. The ship anchored off Cape Mesurado, on the left bank of the St. Paul River of the Grain Coast, as the area which is now Liberia was then called. The U.S. government agent, Captain R. F. Stockton of the United States Navy (native of New Jersey who would later be elected a U.S. senator from that state), and the ACS representative, Dr. Eli Ayres, disembarked their vessel and demanded to meet with King Peter, the local potentate. Peter kept them waiting unceremoniously for some days before emerging from his dwelling deep within the bushes. While he was happy to accept the would-be settlers' gifts of rum, mirrors, beads, and tobacco, he politely but firmly declined their offer to purchase land. Peter and his constituents feared that the two white men had come to disrupt the lucrative slave trade that they were still actively conducting, particularly to South America, now that slave trafficking had been declared illegal by both Britain and the United States. As far as they were concerned, slavery was a one-way ticket across the Atlantic, and they were at a loss to understand why the whites were proposing to bring the slaves back. They suspected a ruse.

The Americans, having failed to accomplish their objective with diplomacy and open bribery, resorted to plan B. Captain Stockton pulled out his gun and put it to King Peter's head, and within minutes, the Americans had their land. They later called it Liberia, derived from the Latin word *liber*, or "free." For King Peter and his people this marked the beginning of the contrary: *servitium*, Latin for "slavery."

During the 19th century the ACS sent between 15,000 and 30,000 free blacks to Liberia; thousands of others were sent by other U.S. back-to-Africa societies to settlements in the area. The largest out-migration from any one region was from Southampton County, Virginia, in 1831–32. This exodus included many blacks escaping the harsh vigilante and legislative reprisals stemming from the Nat Turner rebellion, one of the most violent slave rebellions in American history, in which many lives, both black and white, were lost. It is estimated that more than a quarter of the free black community in Southampton fled to Liberia.

Other settlers included freed slaves who, as a condition of their release, had promised to immigrate to Liberia, and some who had been bequeathed their freedom upon the death of their owners. Many were illiterate and poor. About a quarter of them died within one year of their arrival in Liberia from numerous causes, including malaria, yellow fever, and dysentery. Most had no sources of nutrition and virtually no medical treatment was available to them.

Another wave of settlers on the Grain Coast were Africans liberated from slave ships on their way to the Americas that had been intercepted by British antislave patrols in the Atlantic. Many of these individuals had been taken from elsewhere on the African continent and were therefore more easily and willingly integrated into the indigenous population than the American immigrants. They were later called the Congo People, and a few of them rose to prominence in the aristocracy that would later emerge in Liberia, dominated by those coming from America.

The Americans had little capital, no prior government experience, and little if any means of engaging in a meaningful level of commerce. It was all they could do to even eke out a subsistence-level existence given their unfamiliarity with the land, the local crops, and the strong opposition they faced from the local inhabitants, upon whom they were completely dependent for vital food supplies. Unable to escape, the overwhelming majority of the settlers were virtual prisoners in this new land. Only a few managed to escape back to America. Many died in the new settlement within a very short period after their arrival because of the extremely perverse and very alien conditions under which they were living.

The Americans were not embraced by the people they had come to enlighten and civilize. America, they knew. But of the great West African empires of Ghana, Mali, Songhay, or the Mende peoples, all of which were part of the history of this region and its people, they knew nothing. To the Americans, these African tribesmen were mere savages. In the eyes of the natives, the former slaves were inferior by virtue of having once been slaves. The stage was therefore set for an enmity that would last over 150 years.

The settlers, while far better armed with American-made weaponry than were their opponents, faced constant threats from the deposed King Peter and other native people, who launched persistent attacks against the American settlers in Cape Mesuardo and other surrounding Americo-Liberian colonies. This led the individual colonies to form a federation for mutual defense. Peter and the other natives were fighting a futile battle against the much better armed Americans, but they were fierce to the bitter end. At one point, while he still had a bit of an upper hand, Peter even threatened to sell the settlers back into slavery.

The Americans had that institution on their minds, as well. Where they had once been the slaves, they were now determined to be the masters. Perhaps the saddest legacy of the founding days of Liberia was the emergence of a class system that included the establishment of slavery. William Nesbit, a businessman who voluntarily immigrated to Liberia and was one of the fortunate few to escape back to America, wrote of his experience:

> *Slavery here is the Slave's Slave. A parallel to the Liberian system of slavery is scarcely to be found on the American continent; certainly no where else but on the least favored plantation. Slavery [in America] is severe servitude, generally with plenty to eat; but in Liberia, they have the same tasks to perform, the same stripes to endure, severer masters to please, without sufficient clothing to deserve the name, nor enough rice and cassado, which are the slaves' only food, to satisfy their appetites. They need not, like Oliver Twist, ask for more; their only chance for a full meal, is to steal it; and in that country, theft would be a poor dependence; and as to meat, the slave must content himself if he can catch a monkey, a snake, a crocodile, lizard, rat, or something of this kind, which they often*

do, and devour it with a gusto, that would astonish and dis-
gust the poorest-fed slaves in the United States. As in the slave
states of [America], the slaves occupy small buildings near to
their masters' residence, known as the "negro quarters," so
their imitators in Liberia, notwithstanding the masters mostly
live in bamboo huts themselves, many of them not sufficient to
protect the pious patriarchs from the weather, let the colonist
himself be barefoot, and three parts naked, let him feel the
gnawings of want ever so keenly, still he is never too poor to own
slaves. . . . These slaves are generally obtained by purchase from
the native parents, after arriving at such size and age as to be
able to labor, at prices varying from eight to fifteen dollars.

The Americo-Liberians, as they began to designate themselves early on, constituted only 3 percent of the population: they established a government in Cape Mesuardo (renamed Monrovia after the American president and ACS patron) that rivaled and often surpassed the oppression and brutality of the French and British authorities on the native inhabitants in their colonies. Despite the fact that the colony of Liberia was modeled on the democratic rights and privileges of the United States, these basic principles—even some of the most basic civic and humanitarian privileges, including the rights to vote and to education—were denied to the indigenous groups that had been living in Liberia long before the arrival of the Americans. While the country adopted the motto "The Love of Liberty Brought Us Here," there was no misconstruing the intent that the implied rights and privileges of liberty were the unique province of the Americo-Liberians.

When the British contested the Americo-Liberians' claims over territory close to Sierra Leone, a British colony, and claimed the right to tax the people inhabiting the area, the Liberian federation of colonies responded in 1847 by proclaiming Liberia to be a united and independent republic, with full sovereignty over the indigenous peoples. Yet most of the colonies would have preferred to remain private ventures of the colonization societies—the Americo-Liberians were colonizers themselves on a par with Britain and France, and wanted the financial, military, and political backing of their sponsors at home to reinforce and consolidate their holdings more than they wanted independence. Typically, the colonization society provided the new settlers with about six months of support in the form of cash, food, and clothing. With the declaration of independence, however, even this modest subsidy was discontinued, plunging the already precarious new state and its founders further into misery. In this way, Liberia, or at least its settler community, enjoyed the unique distinction of being the only country in Africa, perhaps the only country in the history of the modern world, to have actively sought to be colonized: First in 1893 and again in 1908, Liberia petitioned the United States to make Liberia a political protectorate. On both occasions the United States refused.

The country's constitution was written by a prominent professor at Harvard Law School, Simon Greenleaf, who was also the president of the Massachusetts Colonization Society. Greenleaf's interpretation of the U.S. Constitution was selective, and he incorporated at least one clause into the Liberian constitution that made a mockery of any analogies to the U.S. Constitution, which guaranteed that "all men are created equal." Greenleaf's clause—"The great object of forming these Colonies being to provide a home for the dispersed and oppressed children of Africa, and to regenerate and enlighten this benighted continent, none but persons of Color shall be admitted to citizenship in this Republic"—made Liberia an apartheid state from its inception. Under law, the indigenous people could not vote or marry Americo-Liberians or attend their schools. They were even barred from admission to the best hospitals, the good jobs, and from sitting in the front pews in church. Only in the mid-20th century did this begin to change.

With the cessation of grants from the United States, Liberia had no choice but to increase the revenue generated by its own economy. The government devised numerous schemes to do so, among them laws adopted to squeeze the maximum amount of tax revenue and other payments from the disenfranchised indigenous population. In 1868 the government established the Liberian Frontier Force, a brutal and highly repressive military division that was composed mostly of indigenous people and used by the government to extort what were known as "hut taxes" from other indigenous people throughout the country. The LFF also was deployed to capture natives to work on a variety of government- and privately-owned projects, including road construction, and on plantations producing sugar, coffee, and cotton for export. In addition the natives were expected to grow food for the consumption of government officials and the landed aristocracy. At best, the arrangement was akin to the feudal relationship between master and serf in medieval Europe. At worst, it was the basest form of slavery that can be imagined—as Nesbit called it, "the slave's slave."

But even these cruel and draconian measures did not suffice to ward off economic disaster for the country. World prices for its export commodities were falling, and the Liberian government remained insolvent and faced the likely prospect of bankruptcy. In 1871 Britain made a loan to the government, but this only provided temporary relief and made the country vulnerable to annexation by Britain in the event of a default on the loan. By the 1920s Liberia's economy had deteriorated to such an extent that the government asked the conservative administration of U.S. President Warren G. Harding for a $5 million loan. The legislative bill to which Liberia's loan request was attached failed to pass in the U.S. Senate, and Liberia faced the real prospect of being annexed by Britain or France. By this time, Britain and France controlled all of West

Africa with the exception of Liberia, which had not been appropriated because it enjoyed some limited protection from the United States. But Britain and France, with their then indomitable military superiority and strong presence in the region, were a threat to the heavily outnumbered Americo-Liberian settler community. The Americo-Liberians were well aware that the indigenous population would not defend them. They were extremely vulnerable therefore, and their future was once again uncertain.

For the first time, though certainly not the last, relief for Liberia came in the form of a multinational corporation rather than from a government or charitable fund. The Liberian government's desperate need for new funds led to, among other things, negotiations with the U.S.-based Firestone Corp. In 1926 Firestone was granted a 99-year lease to establish a million-acre rubber plantation near Monrovia. The Firestone rubber plantation was soon the largest of its kind in the world, and for the ensuing 35 years the company was Liberia's largest employer. In return for the concession the government was granted a percentage of the annual revenues, and a large loan was secured through the company, much of which went toward the retirement or reduction of the Liberian national debt.

Infusions of cash from Firestone headed off a near-term political and financial disaster, but scandal soon erupted that again jeopardized Liberia's status as an independent nation. The Liberian government was accused of selling indigenous people into forced labor, both at home and abroad, to the Spanish island of Fernando Po, a charge that soon implicated Firestone as well. The Liberian government denied all involvement, as did Firestone, but the president of Liberia, C. D. B. King (illustrious ancestor of my mother's paternal clan), was forced to resign in 1930 after the League of Nations launched an inquiry in 1929 into the allegations. Unfortunately, the enormity and gravity of the scandal did not have a lasting impact on the various forms of oppression of the indigenous populations, which resumed almost as quickly as the new government came into office. Despite overwhelming international condemnation, the Americo-Liberian settlers were replicating—and even surpassing in degree of degradation and inhumanity—the very conditions that their ancestors had rebelled against in the United States.

A further economic reprieve for the country came in 1943, when Liberia and the United States signed a mutually beneficial defense pact that gave Liberia its most visible role on the world political stage since the infamous Fernando Po slave-labor scandal. Liberia declared war against Germany and Japan in 1944, though it is clear that for Liberia the alliance with the United States was motivated by economic rather than geopolitical considerations. When I was growing up, although we were made to feel proud of our contribution to the Allied war effort, there was a running joke about Adolf Hitler's reaction upon learning of Liberia's declaration. He was said to have placed his hand on a map and asked his generals: "*Wo ist Liberien?*" to which the general responded, "*Es ist unter ihrem kleinen finger, Führer*": "It is under your little finger."

The United States had good reason to seek an alliance with Liberia. The Japanese occupation of Southeast Asia had cut the Allies off from vital sources of rubber, which was urgently needed for the war effort. Aside from Sri Lanka, the only natural source of rubber available to the Allies was the Firestone plantation in Liberia. Under the terms of the 1943 bilateral defense agreement, an international airport, Robertsfield, was constructed with U.S. aid. The airport also became a strategic refueling point for Allied war planes. Shortly thereafter, Pan American Airways, then the world's largest international airline, began providing transatlantic service between New York and Monrovia, finally reuniting the Americo-Liberians with the country that they had never left behind emotionally.

Foreign interests continued to dictate the course of Liberia's economic progress and political orientation throughout the war. Substantial U.S. investments in the development of the country's transportation infrastructure followed: hundreds of miles of road were built, and a deepwater harbor was constructed in Monrovia, all to support the Allied war effort. Meanwhile, the improved infrastructure enabled the Americo-Liberians to further expand their jurisdiction beyond the coast and into the Liberian hinterland, where numerous ethnic groups resided. In this respect they again took a page from the book of the European colonial powers on the continent. The Americo-Liberians simply used their guns and cannons to appropriate the land from local rulers, who were still defending themselves with spears and knives.

The Americo-Liberians took advantage of the long-established tradition among the native people that the land was communal property and therefore could not be sold. They claimed it as their own. An additional instrument of Americo-Liberian hegemony was the concept of "treaties of friendship." These treaties were ostensibly defense pacts signed with local rulers who were for the most part illiterate. But they were ruses used to create fear in the minds of the tribal chiefs, stipulating that the settler government would defend them against potential aggression by other tribes, the French, and the British. Usually these treaties were modified at a later date by the Liberian government, and, presto! The chief would learn that he had signed away his sovereignty.

A third method of inland conquest by the Americo-Liberian government was the subcontracting of expeditionary journeys to outside entities, often private European mercenaries, who invaded territory they regarded as *terra nulles* because no civilized person (meaning whites and Americo-Liberians) had ever been there, which in their opinion made it eligible for appropriation or annexation.

William V. S. Tubman, president from 1943–71, is often referred to as the father of modern Liberia. His administration was responsible for two major policy milestones, one political, the other economic. The first was the enfranchisement of the indigenous tribes (who comprised roughly 97 percent of the total population) and of women. This was a highly controversial, though politically astute and practical, move, as Tubman had rightly reached the conclusion that the economic contribution of all Liberia's citizens was essential to the political survival of the country. His second revolutionary act was the introduction of what he called the Open Door policy, which was designed to encourage foreign corporations to help exploit the valuable natural resources in the Liberian interior, where the majority of the population resided. The Open Door policy was opposed vigorously by many Americo-Liberians, who believed that such a strategy would threaten their economic and political supremacy by opening the economy not only to foreigners, but to the much larger and more threatening indigenous community. Yet it was clear that for the country to remain viable, foreign capital and expertise were needed to extract the resources. They were of no value so long as they remained embedded in the land.

And Tubman also recognized the importance of one of Liberia's most industrious people, the Mandingo. These Mande-speaking traders (who make up the maternal side of my mother's lineage) were not nearly as likely to be conquered by settler force and chicanery as many of the smaller, less organized tribes. The Mandingo were far better disciplined, politically and culturally cohesive, and had centuries-old commercial interests and traditions that they were determined to protect from settler interference. While the Americo-Liberian military might have prevailed, the settlers were never able to fully demobilize the Mandingo trade network because of the Mandingos' extensive geographic footprint, which went well beyond the political boundaries of Liberia, reaching through much of West Africa into the large area south of the Sahara Desert.

The Americo-Liberians detested and disdained the Mandingo for their belief in Islam, and envied their commercial successes, their entrepreneurial drive, and their refusal to labor for others on the assumption that one cannot make good money in that way. But their financial acumen also earned them the grudging respect of the Americo-Liberians. Tubman went so far as to exempt the Mandingo from the compulsory labor that was required of other indigenous groups, and in the 1950s, when the Open Door policy went into effect, he actually encouraged Mandingo emigration from neighboring Guinea to Liberia. Taxes paid by the highly enterprising Mandingo on their trading activities did much to relieve the government's debt burden.

The Open Door policy worked. There was a marked increase in foreign investment in Liberia. The decade between 1958 and 1968 alone saw the establishment of new and expanded operations by many foreign-owned companies, including Firestone, Bong Mines (iron ore), and most important in terms of economic impact and revenue to both the country and my family, LAMCO.

These corporations opened up a range of new economic prospects for Liberia and its most enterprising citizens. Apart from the Americo-Liberian elite, who already had appropriated huge economic sectors for themselves through their land holdings and interests in contracts with foreign investors, those who benefited most from the foreign-driven economic prosperity were the ever-enterprising Mandingo and some hardworking immigrants, among them my father, who had absolutely no government connections but had come to Monrovia in search of what was referred to widely elsewhere in West Africa as the Liberian Dream because of its American connections and the U.S. dollar, which was adopted by the government as the legal tender replacing the British pound in 1940. Other important beneficiaries were the indigenous Liberians who, for the first time in the country's history, found themselves with new educational opportunities and contending for jobs in which their qualifications, and not their contacts or their ethnicity, were the determining factors.

While Tubman's Open Door policy indirectly benefited the indigenous people, it did not go nearly far enough. The majority of the population was still represented and taxed by a tiny minority of wealthy and powerful elites, and the prospects for ending the apartheid system were grim. Tubman himself was ruthless in suppressing political opposition, both within the Americo-Liberian dissident groups (who felt he had gone too far with his reforms) and among the indigenous people, who felt he had not gone nearly far enough. The irony is that in the aftermath of World War II, as countries all over the globe began to anticipate the prospect of decolonization, the plight of the indigenous Liberians was ignored because the colonizers happened to be the same color as the people they had colonized. Because of racial stereotype, the world did not acknowledge that Liberia remained a colony under a minority-settler control, no different from South Africa, Namibia, and Rhodesia, and in many respects worse. In retrospect it is hardly surprising that the end to the Americo-Liberian regime, in the 1980s, came with such ferocity. Beyond the very rudimentary sense of the term as defined by the geographic contours that the Americo-Liberian settlers were able to carve out for themselves in a land that they had seized from the indigenous people, Liberia has never been a nation. This goes a long way to explaining its sad predicament today.

5

What Pappi Built

Given the strange saga of Liberia, my little town of Yekepa seems all the more astonishing; by the mid-1960s, it easily could have been mistaken for any small town in Western Europe or the United States.

With a workforce of only 5,000 to 7,000 (about 25,000 citizens when all dependents were included), Yekepa boasted an internationally accredited school, a modern hospital, large supermarkets, hotels and restaurants, a library, a movie theater, an arts and crafts center, a post office, a police force, a radio station, and access to French-language television broadcasting services from neighboring Côte d'Ivoire. It had a golf course, an Olympic-size swimming pool, and equestrian facilities. It was in Yekepa that I learned to play tennis with my older brother, Claudius.

My family lived in a standard company house, a simple but comfortable one-story bungalow with three bedrooms, one bathroom, a living room and dining room, a kitchen fully equipped with Ericsson appliances, and a veranda in front. The houses were painted white and had flat zinc roofs, but we all individualized them with decorative arts brought over from foreign countries or with local items such as batik curtains, hanging lamps with shades made of straw, African masks, and other beautiful art. Unlike in most of the rest of the country, each house—which we lived in free of charge—came with netting for the windows and doors to protect us against mosquitoes and other unidentifiable flying objects that thrive in the tropics. We had a reliable supply of water, electricity, and even our own telephone exchange; our home telephone number was 276. I could reach Pappi at work by dialing 474 and Mummy at 500, the LAMCO hospital. As the community grew, a prefix of "1" was added to the numbers. Public phones were located throughout the town, and usage was free.

The houses were clustered into six distinct areas, and one's area of residence was determined by one's status within LAMCO. Our home was in Area F, which was the area with the nicest houses, generally reserved for the company's most senior executives and many of the white people. Pappi was not among the most senior managers, but the particular circumstances under which he had been hired, his Presidential Medal of Bravery, and the fact that he had been promoted rapidly to paymaster general afforded him a special status in the LAMCO start-up team, which entitled him to many of the perks usually reserved for expatriates and high-ranking political appointees made by the Liberian government, which was a major shareholder in LAMCO. By the time I came along, my father had been allotted a company car—a Volkswagen Beetle, the standard-issue transportation for senior management. This made us a middle-class, two-car nuclear family in the tropical jungle of Africa, as Pappi held on to the Mercedes that had brought him such good luck.

My memories of those early years in Yekepa are a fantastic

fusion of Western influence and African traditions. I remember the women of Lola, Mandingo traders who lived just about ten miles away in Guinea, who woke before the sun rose, faced Mecca, and said their morning prayers, and then gathered their calabashes for the journey to the communal well to fetch water for the day's domestic chores. The distance between their huts and the water station—which also served several other villages in the vicinity—was short by local standards: only two and a half miles. They lit their charcoal fires in their outdoor kitchens to make *sairi,* an invigorating porridge made of milk, rice, and sugar, for their men and children. The women then prepared for their daily ten-mile trek into Liberia, to the crowded open-air market in the center of Yekepa, large enamel bowls balanced skillfully and effortlessly on their heads and filled with bananas, pineapples, oranges, guavas, papayas, mangoes, and grapefruit. Yekepa, with its few thousand middle-class Liberians and Western expatriates, was a particularly attractive market for the women of Lola. They depended on us. So with their infants attached to their backs by colorful *lappas* cloths— best described as sarongs—they walked for miles and miles on their way to market. Their route took them through our neighborhood, and as a very small girl I joyously anticipated their arrival each morning as they strode single-file along our street. I marveled at their regal bearing, their inherent nobility. To the endless amusement of my parents and my three brothers, I would imitate them, placing, with the help of my nurse, Rebecca, an oversized bowl of fruit atop my own head and a doll on my back, and walking around the garden with my hands placed firmly on my hips, mimicking the melodic chant that they sang, a sort of advertising jingle announcing their arrival: "Fine bananas, fine bananas."

I remember too the fully functional playhouse that Pappi built for me in our neatly mowed backyard in Area F. I remember our family's annual visits to the well-kept Victorian-style house of my paternal grandparents, Mamma Ade and Pappa Larry, in the small mountain village of Gloucester, overlooking the capital city of Free-town, Sierra Leone, and to Fofana Town, Liberia, where Ma Kema, Mummy's mother, lived. Ma Kema was always dressed in tradi-tional African attire, a vibrant *lappa* wrapped around her and her head always covered, as she was a Muslim. She and Mummy resem-bled each other, but you could tell that Ma Kema's life had been much harder by the way she seemed bent over, as if always under some sort of strain. Her English was not the best, so I communi-cated with her mostly with hugs. In my callow youth I had seen her as a kind but illiterate woman, and had even had the arrogance to want to teach her how to read. If I had bothered to learn one iota of what Ma Kema and her people knew about business and entrepre-neurship, I probably would not have had to attend business school—or would have done much better while I was there! Ma Kema could not read or write, but she could definitely crunch num-bers—and she did it all in her head.

I remember particularly the celebrations of the Christmas holi-days, a special time in Liberia, and not only for Christians like us. Many of the Liberians would dress up in raffia costumes, covering their faces with wooden masks that represented various ancestral spirits, and would dance on impossibly high stilts to the shrieking delight of us children. They were incredibly nimble, capable of amazing physical contortions even while they were moving their bodies in time to the music.

The stilt dancers were accompanied by an eclectic mix of instruments: drums; rattles made from a wide variety of materials ranging from gourds to cans and swung in nets laced with seed pods or nuts; horns, flutes, and xylophones; and various stringed instruments, such as acoustic guitars and homemade lutes, which were fashioned from a gourd and fitted with horsehair strings. Typically, there was a master of ceremonies with whom the lead dancer would engage in banter for the entertainment of the audi-ence. We children would hang on his every word. No doubt much of his sly humor and morality tales, intended for our parents, went over our heads.

The dancers traveled around the country throughout the month of December in informal bands that presented a rich blend of minstrels, acrobats, and choreography. Their performances not only called upon numerous traditional chants, legends, and myths about great ancestors and warriors, but also included new verses extemporized to fit the occasion. At Christmastime the performances often focused on the importance of being generous toward others and not to be greedy or selfish. These stories would be told as folktales, similar to Aesop's fables, often with Spider or Monkey as the central character. Spider, or Ananse, as he is known, is portrayed frequently as an arrogant know-it-all, but he always gets his comeuppance at the end of a tale. The following is one of my favorite stories about Ananse:

> *Ananse, who had a ravenous appetite, was invited to two village feasts that were to be held at approximately the same time. He became concerned that if he went to one, he might not make it to the other. To avoid this, he tied two pieces of rope around his waist and told each village chief to pull on the rope when his feast was about to begin. This way, Ananse reasoned, he would be certain to make it to both feasts. Unfortunately for Ananse, the feasts both began at precisely the same time. As a result, each chief pulled his end of the rope simultaneously. One rope pulled poor Ananse in one direction, and the other rope pulled him in the opposite direction with equal force. When Ananse was a no-show at both feasts, the chiefs tugged even harder. Ananse was almost split into two, and the chiefs abandoned their efforts.*
>
> *When the feasts were over, the chiefs and the inhabitants of the two villages went in search of Ananse, each group approaching from the opposite direction. They found poor Ananse lying on the ground, at death's door. They took pity on*

*him and helped untie the ropes. Ananse was so embarrassed
that he ran away. From then on, greed was never again heard
of in either of the two villages.*[1]

I suspect that much of this spectacle was a tribal-lite version,
watered down for Western consumption, of the tradition of the
secret societies that were still common among many of the indigenous groups of Liberia.

In Yekepa, the Christmas season began even before the traditional festivities, with the celebration of Santa Lucia on the 13th of
December each year. This was a tradition imported by the Swedes,
but the children from Norway and Denmark also participated. In
honor of the Lucia, who according to the legend was burned at the
stake because she refused to marry a pagan, the girls would dress in
white robes with red sashes, holding candles in their hands as they
walked in a procession through the crowd. The boys, who also carried candles, dressed in plain white gowns and tall, cone-shaped
white hats. When I first arrived in America many years later, I could
not help but wonder at the parallels between this garb and that of
the Ku Klux Klansmen who terrorized black people on that side of
the world. But in Yekepa, of course, we were unaware of such faraway evils.

One girl, usually a blonde, was Lucia. Lucia was crowned with a
beautiful green wreath, glowing with candles. With her hands
folded as in prayer, she would lead the procession through the
crowded streets. The festivities would end in the Lutheran church
with the serving of wonderful Swedish delicacies, such as *glög*
(mulled wine), lutefisk and herring, Pepparkakor (ginger cookies),
and other goodies. To add local flavor, palm wine, a sweet local
liquor extracted from the palm tree, was served also.

During the weeks following the Lucia celebration our garden
glowed every night with the Christmas lights that Pappi had strung
through the hibiscus hedges and bougainvillea blossoms that he

had lovingly cultivated. He hid loudspeakers in the hedge, which played Christmas carols softly throughout the warm African evening. Pappi always made sure to stock up on snowflakes, available for purchase in cans at the supermarket that LAMCO ran for its employees.

In the months leading up to the holiday I would tell my parents what I wanted for Christmas. Pappi let me know that he was saving up my wishes and forwarding them to the North Pole. If I was good, he assured me, the gifts would come. Finally, on Christmas Eve, the most anticipated evening of the year, we would go to church. Upon our return, my best friend, Ana Peterson, and her mother would come over to our house. The "Ralph-Petersons," as we called them, lived next door. Ana's father, Ralph, a mining engineer, was one of my father's closest friends, and here is a story that illustrates why. One day when I was four years old I was playing with Ana and another Swedish girl, Pia, at Ana's house. Pia, who was a snob, told Ana in Swedish, which I did not understand at the time, that Ana should tell me to go home. Ralph Peterson, passing by in the hallway, overheard her, stopped and said to Pia, in English so that I could understand, "If Monique goes home, you go home." He could have said it in Swedish, and I would have been none the wiser about all that had occurred. I ran home afterward and told my parents the whole story. They understood at that point what a good friend Ralph was.

We spent every Christmas with the Ralph-Petersons. Shortly after Mrs. Peterson and Ana arrived at our house, there would be another knock on the door and in would walk Santa Claus. Both Ana and I, terribly afraid, would run to Pappi with tears streaming down our faces. Claudius, on the other hand, who was two years older than I, would be completely calm, even though I was typically the one who was all bravado. For some reason I just could not overcome my paralyzing fear of this big man in the red suit and the long white beard.

Santa Claus was not having much fun, either. Here he was bringing gifts, and pandemonium was breaking out. Ana was crying and cringing. I was sobbing inconsolably, which caused my beloved dog, Ajax, a Rhodesian ridgeback, to start howling. Santa judiciously kept his distance, handing the gifts over to Pappi, who in turn gave them to Ana and me. Santa gave Claudius his gifts directly, and I was always jealous that my brother had the nerve to make direct contact with the man in the red suit. I always promised myself that next year, I would no longer be afraid of Santa.

After Santa Claus left and Ana, Ajax, and I had regained our composures, we opened our presents as the grown-ups watched. Strains of "O Little Town of Bethlehem," "O Come All Ye Faithful," and "Silent Night" drifted in from the garden. Before long there would be a knock on the door, and in would walk Mr. Peterson to join in the festivities. I loved Ralph like a second father. Ana and I would fly into his arms, show him our presents, and breathlessly describe our latest encounter with Santa.

The year I turned five, there was a terrible accident. Ralph was an avid motorcyclist and he frequently took Ana and me on rides, even though Pappi tried to discourage this. One weekend, on one of his biking excursions not far from Area F, Ralph signaled to make a left turn. As he turned, a car speeding up from behind ran smash into him. Ralph was killed instantly. The week that followed was a sad time. Ana and her mother accompanied Ralph's body back to Sweden for good. I never saw them again.

Christmases after that were never quite the same. I distinctly recall the first such holiday following the departure of my best friend. Pappi had disappeared mysteriously. There was a knock on the door, and in walked Santa Claus. Santa had on the same red suit and sported the same long, white beard, but this time his face was black. Still, I was petrified. I began sobbing hysterically, and Ajax, always on cue, chimed in. Mummy tried to calm me down, but it was no use.

Figuring out the mystery of Santa Claus many years later only heightened my love and admiration for Pappi. Each year he would send to his friends in Sweden and Norway a list of gifts that he wanted for us. He then would arrange to have them transported, usually by a LAMCO employee returning from vacation in Europe the summer before. That person would keep the gifts hidden in his house until shortly before Christmas. Then Pappi and Mummy would have the gifts wrapped and taken to Santa for delivery to our house on the eve of Christmas.

If Pappi put an enormous amount of planning into the effort to make sure that Claudius and I, and eventually my two younger brothers, first Herbert and then Abayomi, had exactly the kind of Christmas that we used to read about in our books, he put even more effort into our education. This was extremely important to Pappi, probably the most important consideration of all, after the health and safety of his family. He was determined to give each of his children the best education possible. But he believed that there was no way that he could accomplish this goal by sending us to school in Liberia, thus committing himself to a life of extraordinarily hard work in order to give us options that he could never have dreamed of for himself under British colonial rule.

My father, Emmanuel Abayomi Maddy, was born on February 13, 1928, in Freetown, Sierra Leone, the British colony that inspired the American Colonization Society to found Liberia in 1821. It is somewhat surprising that what was from the start a dreadful and inhumane social experiment would later be emulated by the Americans in Liberia.

When the American Revolution ended in 1783 the British were no longer able to send their convicts to the New World. They needed to search for another depot for them. One area they considered was a territory located on the west coast of Africa named Sierra

Leone by Portuguese explorers in the 15th century who, viewing the area from afar, thought the peaks of the country evoked the shape of a lion. They called it Sierra Lyoa, which means Lion Mountain in Portuguese. By the time the British learned about it almost 300 years later, the name had been corrupted to its current Sierra Leone. Only a few British subjects had visited the area, including a botanist named Henry Smeathman, known by the sobriquet "Fly-Catcher." Smeathman had entrepreneurial aspirations and, in addition to exotic bugs and beetles, he hoped to discover material wealth in the form of gold and other valuable resources on his expedition to Africa. He was severely disappointed—and barely escaped with his life. Upon his return to Britain he described Sierra Leone as unfit for human habitation, particularly by whites. He predicted that if 200 of the most hardened British convicts were transported to even the healthiest part of Sierra Leone, 100 of them would die within 30 days, and the rest within six months. Nevertheless, looking for a solution to the overpopulated prison system in Britain, the government looked to the west coast of Africa. However, many in the government feared that Sierra Leone was so close to Britain that dispatched convicts would be able to find their way back by boarding the numerous ships that sailed along the West African coast en route to Asia. Botany Bay, on the more remote continent of Australia, was eventually selected instead to be the British offshore penal colony.

But there was another important reason the British were determined to lay claim to Sierra Leone, despite its unsuitability as a penal colony. A number of black American slaves had joined forces with the British during the American Revolution because the British had already outlawed slavery in England, in 1772. In return for their support, the British promised these "Black Loyalists" their freedom after victory against the colonial rebels; having lost the war, however, they were not in any position to grant the Black Loyalists their freedom, and instead sent them to Nova Scotia, the

Caribbean, and England. Despite the outlawing of slavery there, those sent to England did not receive the welcome they had anticipated. They joined the blacks already there who, though free, still faced overt racism and social ostracism and were unable to start their own businesses or even find jobs. Other than those working as domestic servants, they were mostly vagabonds, living principally on the streets of London, Bristol, and Liverpool in poverty, sickness, and despair. The British population in general was vocally hostile to their presence. The following excerpt, taken from an article titled "Candid Reflections by Edward Long," a white supremacist, was representative of the general sentiment of many British after the decision was taken to abolish slavery:

> *The public good of the Kingdom requires that some restraint should be laid on the unnatural increase of blacks imported into it. Negro immigrants are idle, dissolute and a drain on the [welfare system]. Lower classes of women in England are remarkably fond of the blacks, for reasons too brutal to mention; they would connect themselves with horses and asses if the laws permitted them. By these ladies they generally have numerous brood. This will contaminate English blood within a few generations—beyond salvation. From the chance, the ups and downs of life, this alloy may spread so extensively, as even to reach the middle and then higher orders of the people, till the whole nation resembles the Portuguese and Moricos [members of the Muslim people of mixed Berber and Arab descent, inhabiting North West Africa] in complexion and baseness of mind.*

Despite the harshness and hostility of the environment in which they lived, not many blacks in England were eager to trade the certain evils of England for the speculative perils of Africa, a continent with which they had no direct connection. It had been centuries since their ancestors had been shipped to the New World as slaves, and they themselves had been born in England or America. However, a religious group of do-gooders called the Saints determined that they knew better and that it was in the best interests of the blacks that they be sent to Africa, where they would be in their own environment and able to thrive as they never could in Britain. This is how the "Back to Africa Movement," led by one of the leaders and most actve member of the Saints, Granville Sharp, was started.

The Fly-Catcher, ever the opportunist, saw a renewed chance to profit from his otherwise futile voyage to Sierra Leone. In his view, the blacks sent to Sierra Leone could work for him on plantations that he would set up along the West African coast. Thus, a distinctly unholy alliance was formed among the racists, the religious, and the unscrupulous to rid the kingdom of its "black" problem. In 1776, while the convicts were being boarded on ships headed for Australia, a few hundred blacks were rounded up by force and placed on a ship headed for Sierra Leone, with all the promise of malaria, yellow fever, typhoid, and a host of other unknown tropical diseases, not to mention the hostile local people, awaiting them. Joining the 350 blacks on board were some white artisans and officials, whose job it was to set up and manage the new settlement, as well as about 150 prostitutes, whose job it was to procreate. Anna Falconbridge, the wife of a ship's surgeon who encountered some of these women in Sierra Leone, interviewed one of the prostitutes and wrote:

> [S]he said men were employed to collect and conduct them to Wapping, where they were intoxicated with liquour, then inveigled on board of ship and married to Black men, whom they had never seen before; that the morning after she was married, she really did not remember a syllable of what had happened over night, and when informed, was obliged to inquire who was her husband? After this, to the time of their sailing, they were amused and buoyed up by a prodigality of

fair promises, and great expectations which awaited them in
the country they were going to: 'Thus,' in her own words, 'to the
disgrace of my mother country, upwards of one hundred unfor-
tunate women, were seduced from England to practice their
iniquities more brutishly in this horrid country.' (Anna Fal-
conridge, A.M., Two Voyages to Sierra Leone,*) by Anna*
Maria Falconridge.[2]

One-fifth of the passengers died en route, and true to the Fly-
Catcher's prediction, most of them died within the next six months,
either from natural causes or as a result of armed conflicts with the
natives. Perhaps saddest of all, many of the whites and even some of
the most enterprising blacks among the group joined the still
bustling slave trade between West Africa and the Americas.

Eventually the settlement survived, through the force of numbers—in 1808 Sierra Leone became Britain's first colony in West
Africa—the initial group of settlers were joined by blacks who originally had been sent by the British to Nova Scotia and the West
Indies, and by others who came directly from other regions in West
Africa and as far south as what is now Angola. This last group never
made it to the Americas because the ships on which they were being
transported were intercepted by the British Navy as part of their
antislavery blockade, and were freed and released to Sierra Leone.
Some of them found their way back to the countries from which
they had come (modern-day Togo, Benin, Senegal, Gambia, Nigeria, and Ghana), but most, particularly those from farther away,
remained in Sierra Leone and started new lives. These blacks
formed a distinct ethnic group within Sierra Leone, the Creoles, or
Krio, and their tastes, customs, and way of life were far more akin to
Victorian England than to the ways of the indigenous people. The
Maddy klan are Krio, and my ancestors were among those who had
been on a freed slave ship that had set sail from Nigeria.

Like the lives of his parents, Larry Beresford Maddy and Rosalyn Adesemi Maddy, Pappi's early existence was shaped by the economic and social imperatives of British colonialism. His family's beautiful, tranquil village was named after the Duke of Gloucester, nephew to the king of England and president of the African Institution, a British organization of abolitionists and social reformers dedicated to commerce and civilization in Africa, particularly in Sierra Leone. Gloucester was founded in 1816 by Africans liberated by the British from slave ships on their way to the Americas. They settled there because of its rich fertile soil and cool climate. The village quickly became a major supplier of fruit and vegetables to the rest of the country.

We visited Pappa Larry and Mamma Ade in Sierra Leone about once a year, and my memories of those trips are few but powerful: the taste of Mamma Ade's fried shrimp and *kanyan* (a type of peanut paste), and her beautifully tended garden, for which she had won many awards. I remember the gentleness of Pappa Larry, and our trips to the luxury hotel, Cape Sierra, on the nearby beach, where I would show off my swimming and ride the giant waves of the Atlantic Ocean. Pappa Larry and Mamma Ade, who was by then confined to a wheelchair, did not accompany us, because they were unaccustomed to and uncomfortable with such luxuries. Cape Sierra was in fact a white elephant that was built by the country's president, Siaka Stevens. To my young eyes it seemed like the epitome of heaven and gracious living. I wished that we could stay there forever. It did not occur to me then to question the imbalance between staff and guests (probably a five-to-one ratio), or to contrast the hotel's opulence with the relative poverty of my grandparents and the simplicity of their lives. A quarter of a century later these white sandy beaches—so pristine and alluring—would be littered with dead bodies, victims of one of the most horrific civil wars on the African continent. Thankfully, Pappa Larry and Mamma Ade did not live to see the enormous tragedy that would engulf their tiny country and demolish all the hope and promise they had held when they finally won their independence from Britain in 1961.

Pappa Larry was subjected to both the advantages (a decent education) and the disadvantages (second-class citizenship) inherent to British colonial rule. He was inordinately proud and of unyielding rectitude, traits he passed on to my father. Both he and Pappi attended the Grammar School at Regent House in Freetown. Founded in 1845, the school's mission was to find "productive avenues" for the huge numbers of liberated African youth streaming into Sierra Leone after the collapse of the slave trade and vigorous antislavery enforcement by British vessels. An early motto of the school was to "educate the boy properly and all things will be added to him and society." In reality, of course, the school helped to perpetuate British rule in Sierra Leone and everywhere else on the African continent, by educating the black youths to support British values and society and help uphold their authority.

Christian missionaries ran the grammar school, but matriculation was open to students of all faiths. The curriculum, which was based on that of English grammar schools, included mathematics and Latin, biblical and English history, geography, and music. Pappa Larry was a gifted student, proficient in Latin, and he rose to the position of clerk of the court—a prestigious position for an African at that time, but still well below his abilities. Only British civil servants qualified for the senior government positions.

"When I was young," Pappi told me, "Mamma Ade would send me to take my father's lunch to him at the courthouse. Pappa Larry, one of the highest-ranking Sierra Leoneon employees, was not permitted to eat with the British functionaries in the canteen. Instead, he was relegated to his own special lunch area—directly outside the courthouse toilet! Every day I would watch my father eat his lunch there and wonder how he managed to remain so calm and humble in the face of such humiliation. He put up with every insult that was hurled at him by the insensitive and often ignorant colonial administrators. Pappa Larry would tell me that it was the British that were humiliating themselves by their actions and their treatment of the Sierra Leoneans, and so he would only pray for them."

Pappa Larry played an important support role in drafting the constitution for the newly independent Sierra Leone, and was a junior member of the delegation that went to London to negotiate the terms of independence with the British government; he therefore remembered Sierra Leone's Independence Day, April 27, 1961, with immense pride and nostalgia. The entire country was filled with euphoria at the reality of self-rule, a phenomenon that was resonating throughout much of Africa as one country after another gained independence. Like many of his countrymen, he basked in the certainty that the country's future, and that of its children, was bright. Pappa Larry retired shortly thereafter and he and Mamma Ade remained in Gloucester for the rest of their lives. Mamma Ade, my namesake, was a strong and proud woman, and a gifted cook and gardener. She was the entrepreneurial one in the family. In addition to being one of the first women prison guards, she supplemented Pappa Larry's less than generous government salary by selling produce from her garden and baked goods from her kitchen. As a result of their combined efforts, my grandparents were able to build the nicest house in Gloucester, which abutted the village church, an Anglican church to which they belonged, and to which Pappi would continue to contribute long after he had left Sierra Leone.

But my father was not as forgiving as Pappa Larry. Colonialism had marked him, not so much for the impact that it had on himself, but for the humiliation he had to see his father go through in his own country. I think this fueled his determination to teach us never to accept second-class citizenship, and indeed, he was incensed when, later in life, an American college sent me an application to apply for a scholarship reserved for "minorities" only. When he read the forms and understood what "minorities" were, he was repulsed and insulted by the ludicrous notion that anyone would believe I needed special help because of the color of my skin, rather than as a reward for my own accomplishments. "Monique, never let anyone call you a minority," he advised.

Immediately upon completing the grammar school in Freetown at the age of 18, Pappi went in search of broader horizons. He tried to stow away in the hold of a trade ship, the *Oreo*, that was going to Dover, England. He was discovered at the last possible moment, but the ship's captain liked something in this young man and offered him a job as a member of the crew of one of the company's vessels that sailed among various ports along West Africa.

It was at this time that Pappi's own entrepreneurial abilities first began to surface. He purchased records in Freetown to sell when his ship docked in Monrovia. He then purchased Arrow brand shirts, stockings, and beauty products through one of the Firestone distributors in Monrovia—and sold them when he sailed back to Freetown. It was a modest introduction to the world of business, but it provided him with a good grounding in the fundamentals of supply and demand and in how to work market inefficiencies to his advantage.

A year later, Pappi decided to settle permanently in Liberia to pursue a better life. Thanks to LAMCO, he was able to.

Once he was comfortably ensconced in the company hierarchy, we had access to the best health care and education available in Liberia. The LAMCO International School was attended by the children of the local LAMCO executives. But here was where Pappi was again exceptional. For him, the best in Liberia was not good enough. As a child in Sierra Leone, he had experienced the British-run educational system and he felt that the Swedish-run school in Yekepa was neither as academically rigorous nor as discipline oriented. He himself had not had the opportunity to go to college—only the most privileged Africans of his generation had done so—and his ultimate goal was to make sure that we all earned Ph.D.s, which in his mind meant that the foundation of our education had to be solid. "Without a solid foundation," he said, "the rest of the house can not be built."

I in particular benefited from his resolve. He felt that it was critical that I become fully independent. "I don't want you to have to count on a man to support you," he told me time and time again. "You need to be able to count on yourself so that you will never have to put up with anybody mistreating you." A good education, he reasoned, would ensure that.

He wanted to give us the freedom to be what we wanted to be. He would say to my brothers and me, "I will have no money to leave you, but with your education, you can be whatever you want to be." He made it clear that "if you want to be a street sweeper, if that is your passion, be the best street sweeper that you can be and do your work with dedication and humility, and when you get tired of sweeping the street, you will always have your education."

His relatives and friends teased him, challenged him, and even criticized him for his unconventional convictions. But he remained undeterred. The same year that the Ralph-Petersons left, he decided that the time was coming for Claudius and me to be sent away to boarding school. I am not quite sure how Mummy felt about this at first, but she believed in Pappi and supported him fully when it came to decisions regarding our education and upbringing. As she herself had been sent away by Ma Kema to live with her adoptive Americo-Liberian family so that she could have access to a better education within Liberia, the concept was not extreme, though the distance certainly was. Mummy, who had also spent a year studying nursing at Boston University, understood and appreciated the value of a first-class education. She and Pappi therefore obtained a list of British boarding schools from one of the British executives working for LAMCO and began a vigorous campaign of writing letters of inquiry.

By the end of my kindergarten year I had been accepted for admission to Leelands School, in Kent, England. Claudius also was headed for Kent, where he would attend an all-boys school called Glencot House in Somerset. About a month before I was to leave I received a nice long letter in lovely handwriting from someone in England called Goolie Rajabie. In her letter she told me all about life at Leelands, and explained to me that she was going to be my "big sister." I did not know then that all first-formers (first graders) like myself were assigned big sisters, and that big sisters were obligated to write to their new protégées prior to the start of the school term. I read Goolie's letter over and over until I knew it almost by heart and it had practically fallen to pieces. My excitement knew no bounds: Finally, I was going to have my own sister!

On the day of our departure, August 20, 1968, a few days after my sixth birthday, I got dressed in a special green trouser suit that Mummy had purchased for the occasion. Pappi, Mummy, Claudius, and I all piled into Pappi's old Mercedes for the long drive to Monrovia and Roberts Field, Liberia's only international airport. The airport, or more accurately, the airstrip, was the same one that had been built, along with a deepwater harbor, by the United States at the outbreak of World War II to serve as a key logistics base from which to transport natural latex, which was essential to the Allied war effort, especially after Malaysia, another major producer, fell to the Japanese. We said good-bye to my beloved Herbert and Abayomi and to Ajax. At age two and three respectively, they were both too young to understand what was going on. I myself had only a hazy understanding that we were all going on some sort of long vacation focused on my older brother and me. I must have sensed, though, that something bigger was happening. In the weeks, days, and even final minutes before we left, relatives and friends of my parents kept coming to our house, taking Claudius and me aside and urging us to behave ourselves and not embarrass our parents or our country. I recall too that they kept asking Pappi how he could do what he was doing, since we were both so young.

On our way to the airport, we stopped in Fofana Town to see Ma Kema. Our family visited Ma Kema a couple of times a year. She had two homes, one in Fofana, the other in Monrovia, and she divided her time almost equally between them. The drive was always fraught with excitement and anticipation. Most of the cars, vans, and trucks raced along the narrow one-lane, mostly dirt roads at speeds over 100 mph. The vans and taxis were all dangerously overcrowded with people, animals (usually chickens and goats), and commercial merchandise. These public transportation vehicles bore names and slogans painted on their sides and in the rear— SUMMIT TO MOUNT SINAI, GATEWAY TO GALILEE, PASSAGE TO THE PROMISED LAND—as if warding off impending doom or at least preparing the vulnerable passengers for their possible fate. During the dry season, Pappi would hold the steering wheel with one hand and place the back of his other hand on the windshield to counter the force of the avalanche of stones catapulting into us by the force of the vehicle racing in the opposite direction. This usually kept the window from shattering, but not always. The thick cloud of red dust would render visibility to no more than a few yards, and he would have to bring the car almost to a full halt, until it settled. By the time we reached Ma Kema's my hair was a shade of coppery brown that I would today pay good money to achieve.

She gave Pappi bitter kola nuts, which she traded in, so that he would be able to stay awake for the long drive back to Yekepa. I know Ma Kema was opposed to sending me off to England, but she never tried to interfere with the decision. Not having had any formal education herself, she probably felt that the LAMCO school was more than good enough. The fact that she had sent Mummy away at a young age must have certainly been on her mind too. Mummy had been the last of Ma Kema's seven children and the only one to survive infancy. Ma Kema suffered the pain of not knowing her own child so that she could give her a chance at life. Given her devout belief in Islam, I can only imagine how hard doing so must have been for her, knowing that unlike Ma Kema and "her people," as she referred to all Mandingos, my mother would be brought up as a Christian and deprived of her rich cultural heritage. Ma Kema did not see why Mummy and Pappi would want to pay this same high price in the name of some fancy education. But the decision had already been made.

The world that I was about to enter could not have been more different than the one in which my dear Ma Kema lived. Fofana Town was a typical small African village, with lots of mud huts closely clustered together. But it was always bustling with activity—graceful women and tall, handsome men, all dressed in their beautiful native attire conducting all sorts of business: family and religious rituals, domestic chores, and community affairs. In the yard were goats, chickens, and always a few cows. The inhabitants spoke Mandingo, which I did not understand, but they all treated us with immense respect and affection. In our attire, language, and religion we were strangers in their world, and we would not have had such intimate access to Fofana Town if it were not for Mummy. At the age of six I had little inkling of just how rich and complex that world was and what a proud lineage Ma Kema, and by extension I, was a part of. To me they were natives who could not read or write, and I felt sorry for them. Soon it was time to say good-bye. In that world we did not say things like "I love you." It wasn't necessary. I could feel it to the core, and no words that Ma Kema could have used would have conveyed the depth of feeling that I knew she had for me. I was happy when I saw Pappi slip some money into Ma Kema's hand, which he always did when he visited her there.

Then we were on our way. I was thrilled. Within a few short months, I would be seeing real snow. For some reason, I had the impression that unlike the snow that Pappi purchased in the cans at Christmas, real snow was a deep, indigo substance, flecked with white, and I could not wait to see this magical substance blanketing the earth. But I was apprehensive too, because Pappi—who had been to Europe several times—had told me that there would probably be something called "snowball fights." I imagined snowballs to be as hard as tennis balls, and the thought of having them thrown at me was not appealing. Claudius did not do much to allay my fears. He told me that if I did not behave myself he would throw snowballs at me. "Pappi, tell Claudius to stop," I said, as I did every time I felt Claudius was out of line, which usually was twenty-four hours a day. I wondered how I would handle the situation when Pappi was no longer there to run to.

My parents had agreed that Mummy would accompany us to England on this first trip, and that Pappi would remain at home. Pappi knew it would be hard for her to let us go, and he wanted her to have as much time with us as possible. Mummy was also practical, and I looked up to her as a world traveler because I knew she had been to America. Since he was not accompanying us, Pappi used the five-hour journey to the airport to dispense paternal advice. He kept reminding us to write home, to take care of each other, and to work hard. The flow of advice became a torrent, well watered with tears, mine, when it came time to say good-bye. It hadn't fully registered on me until we were actually at the boarding gate that Pappi was not coming. First he pulled Claudius aside and said a few words to him. I am sure he told Claudius that he should take care of me—he always did. Then he lifted me up in his arms. One final time, he impressed upon me my good fortune in being able to attend school abroad: "Monique, remember to always do as you are told, do it willingly, and with a smile, and behave yourself. If you do well in school everyone will look up to you and will respect you. Remember, if you don't know where you are going to, remember where you came from." This was one of his favorite sayings, one that he would often repeat to me over the years. Like our neighbors had done in Yekepa, he told us that it was important that we not do anything to bring shame upon the family. Finally, he reminded me to be proud of my family and my heritage, but to be careful to reach out to others, and to respect them and their cultures.

Pappi felt that any failure or shortcoming in his children was a failure of his own. But the truth was that he did not even have to say it. Even at the age of six, I knew how hard he had worked on our behalf, and that alone was sufficient reason for me to do him proud. Throughout my childhood, almost every time I stumbled upon a problem, I asked myself what Pappi would have done in this situation. Today his words continue to set a powerful example for me.

And so at the age of six, crying and clutching my letter from Goolie Rajabie and a few other possessions, I said good-bye to Pappi for the year and got on a Swissair jet to England.

An African Girl in England

And what was my most thrilling first experience upon landing in England? The train. After landing in London, we went to Charing Cross station and boarded a train for Kent. I had flown in a plane before, when we visited Mamma Ade and Pappa Larry in Freetown, but I had never been on a real train. I marveled at the people getting on and off, and at the blue-suited conductor with a loud voice and a silver machine hanging from his neck that punched our tickets. Up to that point my entire experience with trains was limited to the 165-mile railroad line that LAMCO had built from Yekepa to Buchanan to transport ore to the coast. The once-a-day passenger train that traveled the ore line was called a rail-bus. The railroad had only two tracks, one for each direction, and the rail-bus did not make any special stops like this one did, with people getting on and off constantly. In Liberia, the roadbed was hemmed in on both sides by forests, with only a few villages scattered here and there. When the villagers along the roadbed saw the rail-bus going by they would take a break from whatever they were doing, usually simply walking, or washing their clothes in a lake, and smile, wave, and in the case of the children, jump up and down. The travelers would wave back. Here it seemed nobody waved; Mummy, Claudius, and I were the only ones who were excited. I kept looking at the people on the train, and wondering what their lives were like and what kind of houses they lived in. I imagined myself following one of them home.

Eventually we arrived at our stop, where Claudius's tall headmaster was waiting for us. He greeted us warmly. I remember that he called Claudius "Master Maddy." That worried me, because I knew that from then on, Claudius would think that he was the boss.

We dropped Claudius off at his school, Glencot, in Somerset. The headmaster told us how charmed and pleased he was to finally meet us. He then gave us a tour of the campus. The staff members who greeted us during our tour were all friendly and were determined to make Claudius feel welcome. But at day's end, as Mummy and I prepared to leave him and head on to my school, Master Maddy started screaming, kicking, and carrying on. He said that he was not staying, that he wanted to go back to Liberia, and that he would run away that night. I was mortified. I remember wishing that he would run away before he brought more shame on the family, and that we would never find him again in this big country. Mummy was putty in Claudius's hands, and he knew it. Pappi, on the other hand, would not have tolerated any of this nonsense.

Who was being the baby now, I thought. Eventually, after Claudius had cried himself into exhaustion, Mummy and I took off for Leelands. I did not see him again until the end of the school year, when he and I traveled back to Liberia for the summer holidays.

Now it was my turn. Miss Mary Barkley, the head of my new boarding school, picked Mummy and me up at Glencot for the drive to Leelands. Miss Barkley was impressive looking. The first thing I noticed about her was the deep frown that seemed permanently etched in her forehead. What was she so worried about, I wondered? Could she be worried about me? She had salt-and-pepper hair and was dressed primly in a long skirt, a sweater, and a tweed blazer. She must be old, I thought, maybe 30 or more. I clung to Mummy. I believed that the minute I was left alone with this woman I would be in big trouble.

She had done nothing to deserve this harsh assessment. On the contrary, she mostly smiled at me and asked me a series of innocuous questions: Are you happy to be here? How was your flight? Are you looking forward to Leelands? I responded mostly in monosyllables, with my head buried in Mummy's skirt. Meanwhile, I kept a wary eye on Miss Barkley's peculiar little dachshund, Ramsey, who was decked out in a little coat that was quite similar to Miss Barkley's blazer. I had never seen an animal wearing clothes, and I concluded that this woman and her dog were strange creatures, indeed. They would have been laughed out of Yekepa.

During the drive to Leelands, Ramsey and I were in the backseat of Miss Barkley's Mini. He kept jumping into my lap and licking my face. I did not like it one bit, but I was far too fearful to say anything. I thought of Ajax, and how much I missed him already, which only made me despise this intrusive little creature all the more. Ramsey was not a real dog. He looked like a sausage.

As the car swayed along the winding English country roads, I began to feel sick. My face must have given me away, because Miss Barkley turned and asked me if I wanted a sweet. "If you're feeling sick, dear," she said in a firm but pleasant voice, "just let me know, will you, and I'll stop the car." But I was far too embarrassed to speak, much less confess that I needed to vomit. I wanted to whisper in Mummy's ear, so that she could tell Miss Barkley. But she was out of reach in the front seat, unless I wanted to be rude. I had learned already not to whisper in front of others. So I decided to hold my breath, though my strategy did not work, and with one great surge I vomited all over the back seat, all over Ramsey and his coat. Miss Barkley managed a tight smile, and told Mummy, "Not to worry, Mrs. Maddy; it is not a problem." After she and Mummy had cleaned me up, she once again reassured us that this wasn't at all unusual. I was relieved to learn that it was customary to vomit in Miss Barkley's car and on Ramsey. She must have lodged the memory of that incident in part of her brain, because for the entire period that I was in her care she took special precautions any time we had to drive a distance together. She stocked up her car with hard candy, and before we set forth on our journey extracted a promise from me that I would warn her if I started to feel sick.

We spent the remainder of the first day visiting the school, meeting the teachers and administrative staff, and touring the facilities. I was shown to my dormitory room, which had six white wrought-iron beds, all neatly made. I was introduced to "Nurse." I never did learn Nurse's real name. Whatever it was, though, it could not have been more apt than Nurse. She was the person primarily responsible for enforcing discipline and strict adherence to all of Leelands's rules, and she comported herself like an army drill sergeant. I decided on the spot that I would make certain never to cross her path again. That, as I soon learned, was impossible, for Nurse was involved in almost every aspect of our daily lives. The only time we were free of her watchful gaze was when we were in class.

Toward the end of the day came an experience that was certainly novel for Nurse: Mummy had to teach her how to deal with my hair, the likes of which Nurse confessed that she had never come across before. She therefore wanted to learn how to "manage" it. As the novelist Graham Greene, who spent several years in West Africa, aptly observed: "The African hair which looks as though it will never grow enough to demand any effort in fact needs constant attention." Even though I had grown up with lots of Europeans, I had not paid much attention to just how different our hair textures were. At home my hair had been "managed" by my own nurse, Rebecca, who braided it on a daily basis. Since there was no

Rebecca here, an alternative solution was necessary. Mummy was well prepared. She pulled a heavy black comb out of her pocketbook, a weapon that was to be left with Nurse, and proceeded to rake and tug it through my hair. It was sheer torture, as Mummy yanked on what felt like every individual strand. I wondered if my scalp was going to separate from my skull like an orange peel from an orange. I was in excruciating pain. At home Rebecca combed my hair patiently in small sections at a time. However, Mummy must have figured that she did not have the luxury of time to stand on ceremony. Nurse and Miss Barkley, who were looking on intently, kept marveling aloud at how brave I was to tolerate what was obviously pure torture. Mummy continued at her work, undaunted. Given my hair's natural texture, it did not fall to my shoulders when Mummy released it, but instead stuck straight out and up into the air.

When Mummy was finally finished, she produced a barrette that pulled my large mop neatly back together into one big bunch on top of my head. (My fate was sealed in that instant: I gained the unwelcome nickname "Topknot.") I later realized that being brave during Mummy's unintentional assault was a serious blunder, because in doing so I forever relinquished my right to cry when it came to my daily grooming by Nurse. My salvation came several weeks later, when Nurse decided that emulating Mummy's grooming was too time-consuming, and I was left to comb and brush my own hair just like all the other pupils. The first thing I did when left to my own devices, of course, was to stop inflicting pain on myself. The topknot went away. I merely brushed my hair back and placed a headband over it, which sufficed to keep it all down and in place. From that point on I stopped being Topknot and once again became Monique. For the rest of the year I allowed my hair to pursue its natural tendencies, which certainly did not bode well for Rebecca when I returned home nine months later for the summer break.

Now the time had come for Mummy to leave me among these strangers in this strange land. I was frightened and did not want to be left behind. Like Claudius before me, I began to weep piteously, clinging to her skirt, begging her not to abandon me. I like to think that I maintained a little more dignity than my brother, in that I did not kick anyone, or threaten to run away. I just cried and cried, inconsolably. But soon she was gone, and I found myself entrusted to the care and custodianship of Nurse and Miss Barkley. Despite my trepidation, I steeled myself to act courageously.

So began my education at Leelands, for which I credit a strong academic foundation that would serve me throughout my career. In those days there were only a few children from Africa at English schools, and I was the first at my school. For that reason Miss Barkley had thought long and hard before offering me a place at the school. She later confessed that she had been seduced by the picture of me that had accompanied the application form. In it she saw a "cheerful, happy, and somewhat mischievous little girl."

I was the only black person at Leelands, though it took me a long time to realize that. I also was one of few students from overseas. Sheila Ma hailed from Hong Kong, and Goolie Rajabi, my "big sister," came from Persia. Goolie was in the senior form and was extremely popular, and I was lucky indeed to have her as my school sister.

Daily life at Leelands was strictly regimented. Nurse woke us up ringing a loud bell at about seven-thirty in the morning. Winter uniforms consisted of a heavy brown tunic worn over long-sleeved yellow shirts, and brown blazers. In the spring we wore yellow-and-white-striped pinafores. Before every meal, Miss Barkley would say grace: "For what we are about to receive may the Lord make us truly thankful." To which we would all respond in unison, "Amen," before taking our seats, about ten girls to a table that was always headed by one of the seniors. Breakfast always began with cereal and milk. The next dish, for reasons known only to the cook at Leelands, was invariably something on toast: baked beans on toast (my favorite), scrambled eggs on toast (tolerable), or fried tomatoes on toast (revolting). This was accompanied by either tea or cocoa. It was not until I came to America many years later that I discovered that orange juice was a breakfast drink. At Miss Barkley's seat, which shifted from day to day because she took turns to eat with all of us, there was always toast served on a nice silver toast rack with a pretty jar of bitter orange marmalade on the side. I was so envious of that little setup; it looked so nice and elegant.

After breakfast, we had to go and see Nurse again, this time to get our vitamins and any special medications that were required. These were stored in the medicine cupboard, which was kept locked at all times, and Nurse had a special list of all the pupils and which medicines each was supposed to take. To our young minds, anything that was kept locked or off-limits, just like the marmalade, must be valuable—something that we might want to possess. I remember that Claire Miller had a special medicine that looked just like candy, clear and transparent and oval-shaped. I knew it must be delicious. We were each allowed only two sweets a day, given to us by Nurse after the lunch period. This was not enough for my palate. I was therefore dying to get one of Claire's sweets. One day, when Nurse had her back turned, and with encouragement from some equally daring classmates, I snatched one of Claire's tantalizing ovals. Already anticipating the sweet, syrupy taste, I received poetic retribution when I sank my teeth into a deceptively packaged reservoir of fish oil.

After morning dispensary, and before classes, we assembled in the gym for prayers and to attend to other matters of the day. Miss Barkley led these sessions, which were extremely disciplined. Everyone was terrified of Miss Barkley. We sang hymns ("Onward Christian Soldiers," "Oh God Our Help in Ages Past," and the like), and listened to a prayer by the Reverend Hammond, who lived in the vicarage nearby. Then came general announcements and information on any other special topics that were not part of the normal course of events. At these morning convocations we sat in columns by classes. At the beginning of the term the teachers arranged the pupils alphabetically. Once midterm exams were given, however, we were reseated according to our academic performance, with the girl with the highest grades sitting at the head of the column, and she with the worst at the back. It was at times like these that I felt that I was playing by a different set of rules than most of my classmates. I felt that if I did poorly and wound up at the tail end of the column, everybody would think that all Africans were stupid. I could not let that happen.

The idea that I was different was not only in my head. Shortly after I arrived I began to be teased and taunted mercilessly by a classmate named Paula Greenly. I felt that she did this mainly because I did not invite her to my special birthday party: I had asked Mummy and Pappi to have Leelands celebrate my birthday when I was with all of my friends during the term, rather than in August when I was back in Liberia. Paula began calling me a monkey, and telling me that I had a flat nose, and saying that I should go back to Africa. I suffered and cried for several weeks, not knowing how else to react, and because I did not want to risk being called a "sneak" by everybody for telling Miss Barkley. A sneak was the worst thing to be.

But it became intolerable. Finally, I decided to go to Miss Barkley. I was convinced that the teasing was only going to get worse if I did not do something about it. I also knew that Miss Barkley had developed a special fondness for me. Unbeknownst to Paula Greenly and the other students at Leelands, Miss Barkley often would call me into her office to ask if everything was all right. I knew I would get a fair hearing in the dragon's den.

Miss Barkley admitted me to her office, and I tearfully related my tale of Paula Greenly. The headmistress promised me that everything was going to be fine. Sure enough, word quickly spread that Paula had been summoned to see Miss Barkley. The next morning at assembly, after the hymn and the prayers, she delivered a stern lecture. She declared that we were all the same and that those who did not understand that simple fact ought to be ashamed and did not belong to the Leelands family. In fact, she continued, such ignorance was a disgrace to the school, and would not be tolerated at Leelands.

Everyone in the room knew exactly why this intimidating sermon was being delivered at this particular time. And everyone knew that when Miss Barkley expressed an opinion about how to behave, you would be wise to behave that way. I had been popular enough before this episode. Now, though, Miss Barkley's oration in my defense catapulted me to an infinitely higher social plane. From then on I was a special quantity. Everyone wanted to be my friend. Had I been a publicly traded company, my shares would have soared. Conversely, Paula's stock was plummeting, and few people wanted to hold on to it.

Since then I've thought frequently about what Miss Barkley did that day. She made my difference inconsequential, even an advantage. And because of her strong moral authority, her message carried incomparable weight. At the same time, I knew that she had placed a burden on my young shoulders. Now I had to prove that I warranted the great confidence that she had shown in me. I had to excel.

The subjects that we were taught were all basic, including math, nature, history, dictation, geography, science, Latin, English, French, Scripture, gym, and music. I was consistently in the top third of my class, and at times I was number one or two. I will confess that I was pleased that Paula Greenly always seemed to be stuck in the bottom third. Over time, though, I actually felt sorry for her, because she had become quite isolated, mainly due to the episode involving me.

In the middle of that year two new students, Sofie and Nicole Lameux, came to Leelands from France. Neither spoke any English. By virtue of that fact, the Lameux sisters were perceived to be even more alien than I was. Some of the meaner girls started to call them "frogs." Unlike me, Sofie and Nicole never found the courage to complain to Miss Barkley, so their troubles continued until they learned to speak proper English.

Because I did not want to cause Mummy and Pappi pain or worry, I never informed them about these ugly undercurrents in my letters home. Not that I didn't have ample opportunity to do so. Each Sunday, we were all required to write home to our parents. In fact, there was a specific time set aside for this purpose, before church on Sundays. Not only was this exercise supposed to keep our parents informed about our activities, it was also designed to help us improve our writing and communication skills. From my point of view, though, this was a horrendous amount of letter writing. Unlike the other girls who could confine their letters to one standard page, I was writing to my parents on aerograms, which were extremely lightweight but seemed to have acres of empty space. I did not have much news to report from one week to the next, and my letters became rather predictable:

> *Dear Mummy and Daddy:*
>
> *I hope you are well. I am. How are Herbert and Abayomi and how is Ajax? I went swimming on Tuesday. We did breaststroke and the crawl. I had ballet on Monday. I want to take horseback lessons because all of the other girls take horseback lessons and Claudius is also taking horseback lessons. I don't like ballet because it is too cold in the gym. This week we played port, starboard, deck in gym class again.[1] For Christmas I would like to have some new felt pens, a five-year diary with a lock and a Slinky. Could you please tell Miss Barkley that I can have all these? I went to Rachel's birthday party and we had chocolate cake. It was fun. Etc. etc.*
>
> *Lots of Love (XXXXX) from Monique [X (love) X (like) X (hate) X (adore) X (love)]*

Even with a substantial amount of padding, I just could not keep coming up with enough new things to fill up all the acreage on those light blue sheets. I therefore decided to enter an alliance with one of the seniors, Penelope Williams. Penelope had good penmanship, and I thought she would be a good communicator too; besides, the seniors always seemed to have a lot more going on than us first formers. I asked her if she would write my letters to my parents on Sundays, in return for which I would do favors for her, such as working on her garden (all the girls had little garden plots that we had to maintain and for which prizes were awarded). Penelope agreed to write my letters, but politely declined my horticultural services—she must have noticed my sorry little plot. It was evident that I had not inherited Mamma Ade's or Pappi's green thumbs. On the first Sunday that we implemented this new arrangement, I took my seat at the table in the hall as usual, and Penelope was at hers with the rest of the seniors. I pretended to be writing my letter. Miss Barkley, walking up and down the hall, failed to notice anything amiss. At the end of the period Penelope managed to get my letter over to me, and I was absolutely delighted. The handwriting was beautiful, both sides of the page were full, and the letter provided Mummy and Pappi with breathless descriptions of all the interesting things we were doing at Leelands. I knew that Mummy and Pappi would be thrilled with this wealth of information and with the remarkably quick improvement in my penmanship. All I had to do was sign it and address the front in block capital letters, which I did. This way Miss Barkley would never know.

The following Monday morning I was summoned to Miss Barkley's office. Putting on her sternest face, she demanded to know who had written the letter to my parents. Briefly, I tried a counteroffensive, asking how she knew so much about my letter, in light of the fact that school administrators weren't supposed to read our letters before they posted them. But I wasn't arguing from a position of strength, and I knew it. I received a good dressing-down, as did poor Penelope, who had merely been trying to help me. For the next month of Sundays, I had to sit in Miss Barkley's office while I wrote my letter home. Obviously, I never again used a ghostwriter.

At Christmastime at Leelands we celebrated by producing a nativity pageant in the local church. The major roles, including those of the Angel Gabriel, Joseph, Mary, King Herod, and the Three Wise Men, almost always went to the upper-class students. The younger students were assigned bit parts or took their place in the choir.

The principal responsibility of the Three Wise Men was to parade majestically down the aisle of the church bearing their gifts of gold, frankincense, and myrrh for the newborn king. This was a plum assignment in the Leelands social hierarchy, definitely the province of the upper-class students. But because it is written in the Bible that the three kings came from the East, it was acknowledged they must have been dark-skinned (or at least darker than the average British schoolgirl). This presented the Leelands play director with a small dilemma.

Goolie Rajabie's skin was darker than most of the girls', and as a result she was always chosen as a Wise Man. For the second king, another upper-class student would have her skin made dark by the application of a dark foundation cream that gave her the appearance of being black. Years later in America I learned that this procedure was referred to by Americans as "blackface" and was a social taboo, but there was no such stigma or nefarious motive at Leelands. The director was merely trying to make up for a bona fide deficiency. I had the only authentic Wise Man complexion in the school, and so each year I was plucked out from underclass student obscurity and elevated temporarily to the big leagues. True, I was far shorter than the other two Wise Men. But Leelands was not about to let the genuine article go to waste. To the chorus of "We Three Kings of Orient Are" I paraded proudly up the aisle, head held high, bearing my frankincense for my savior, the baby Jesus. I was convinced that everyone in that little church envied me because they knew that I was the real thing—or at least one of his direct descendants.

These kinds of racial subplots played themselves out, for better or for worse, in many of my experiences at Leelands. As a result of the British colonial experience in Africa, many in England automatically assumed that all Africans were excellent athletes. I was African, thus I must be a good runner. Being basically a well-mannered little girl, I did not want to disappoint.

As it turned out, others' high expectations of me gave me a tremendous psychological edge and desire in this area, which ultimately were reflected in my performances. I was convinced that I could not be defeated; my rivals believed that they could not beat me; and therefore I never was. I even became addicted to the adrenaline rush I got each time I heard the stern words: "Runners, take your marks." I raked in bushels of medals, shields, and trophies. Sports Day was more like Maddy Day, or the Maddy Invitational. It was held twice a year, and all the parents came to campus, except mine, of course, as they were too far away. On those days I felt like I was Georgie Best, a popular British soccer player at the time who played for Manchester United and on whom we all had a crush. Many of the parents would seek me out to wish me luck and tell me how much they were looking forward to seeing me run my races. Even as I took my marks I could hear the buzz that anticipated my performance. Under these conditions, losing was not an option. Curiously, this was the inverse of the same type of racially-biased psychology that the British had used for centuries to conquer and rule the "colored" races. Through their numerous decisive military conquests of distant lands, they had successfully created and propagated the perception among the "natives" that the white race was superior to all others. It was a myth that prevailed for centuries without serious challenge from the conquered subjects, cowed as they were by the sheer bravado of the British. At least until a young man called Gandhi came along and redefined the rules of the game.

In my own case, what was happening was that I was actually training a lot harder than everyone else because of the additional pressure that I had imposed upon myself. But I also was perpetuating a myth that I was not at all interested in debunking—just as the British had been spurred by their early victories to continue their conquests, made possible by their seemingly invincible naval and military superiority. Although none of us knew it at the time, the natural superiority that was attributed to me by the people at Leelands was nothing but racial stereotyping. I discovered this for a fact in America many years later, when as a runner I frequently was outperformed by people of all races. Yet I would not be telling the truth if I did not admit that these racial delusions shared by me and my schoolmates (and our elders), no matter how dubious, had given me a good head start in the arenas that count: those of mettle and confidence. Indirectly, I learned to appreciate the value of mental discipline and to apply the astounding power of the mind to achieve my goals. These lessons have served me well whenever I've encountered an obstacle. I have undertaken the conditioning necessary to overcome that barrier and attain my goal.

On balance, Leelands did a lot for me in numerous apparent and inconspicuous ways. My guardians taught me to use my differences to my advantage and to take pride in them, and even to use them to excel. They provided me with large doses of positive reinforcement. They gave me the necessary academic tools and the strength of character to distinguish myself, and freed me to reach for seemingly impossible dreams. I owe an enormous debt to the formidable Miss Barkley.

7

Back to Africa

After almost five years of schooling in England, Claudius and I learned that we were going back to Liberia. "Master Maddy" was ecstatic. By now Claudius was at his second school, having been expelled from Glencot, after running away to find his way back to Liberia. At age 8, with no money, he had not made it far. Pappi likely lectured him with the old Krio proverb: *"Bush noh de foh trowe bad pikin."* "Bad children may not be thrown into the bush," meaning, no matter how naughty a child may turn out to be, he cannot be disowned by his family. Then he found him a new school, Holmewood House, in Tunbridge Wells, Kent. Claudius was wildly popular there. If the trophies that I had won at Leelands were impressive, they were nothing compared to the war chest that Claudius accumulated. He was a star and excelled in every sport that he tried: fencing, soccer, cricket, and horseback riding. The nurses loved him; the teachers loved him; his fellow students loved him. It all seemed to come naturally, as if he felt it was his due. But unlike me, who wanted to remain in England with Miss Barkley, Nurse, the other staff, and my schoolmates, Claudius missed Liberia and was perfectly happy to leave all of his adoring fans behind.

Because of the prohibitive cost of travel, we only went home to Liberia once a year, during the summer break. This meant that I had nowhere to go during the short school-year holidays. I spent the Christmas and Easter recesses in Norway with close friends of my family, former LAMCO employees who had moved back home. But during the shorter holidays, of which there were quite a few, I had to be placed in homes that the school found for me. These were strictly business transactions; my parents would pay for my room and board at an agreed-upon daily rate. I was a foster child, and these stays always made me miserable. I never once went back to a home where I had already spent some time—I did not want to. There were usually other children, the natural children of my foster parents. Once one of these children told me that I looked like a scarecrow. Another time I was told that I had to use a separate bath because the children did not want to turn black by bathing with me. At Leelands we bathed two to a tub, and nobody had turned black because of me. While all the other girls at Leelands lived for the vacation days, I dreaded and hated them. I never complained to anyone about it, but Miss Barkley must have sensed that something was amiss. Many years later I learned that the school had experienced great difficulty in finding these temporary homes for me. Miss Barkley and my parents decided that this was not a good or healthy situation for me.

They did not, however, share their decision with me until the summer of my eleventh year, 1973, after I was already back home in Liberia. In other words I left Leelands thinking I would be back in the fall—I had been told that I was going home on vacation—but in fact I was going back home for good. This was devastating to me. Not only would I not continue on to the Benenden School, where most of my Leelands friends were going, not only had I not had a chance to say good-bye to my friends there, but I now found myself an outsider in my homeland.

It was 1973 and the first time in years that I had lived at home with my entire family. Claudius, who seemed ecstatic to be home in Yekepa again, was 13, Herbert was 7, and Abayomi was 6, and I hardly knew any of them. Not only was I a stranger to my own family, but five years at a proper English boarding school had taught me to speak English differently from everyone else. Suddenly I had to make new friends, and find a way to fit into a life that, aside from good old Ajax (he still remembered me!) was now as foreign to me as Ma Kema's had been on the eve of my departure.

She, for one, was thrilled that I was back, and was among the first to come and visit, bringing huge sacks of the oranges that grew on her land; she knew I could not get enough of them. She had been on a pilgrimage to Mecca for a second time during my absence, and had brought me back a ViewMaster that showed the beautiful sights of Mecca and Medina and other holy places in Saudi Arabia.

Much had changed in my family since I had been away. Mummy was now the head nurse at the modern hospital that LAMCO had built and staffed with doctors and nurses from Liberia and all over the world. Herbert and Abayomi were now enrolled in the LAMCO International School. And Pappi, after working for LAMCO for 20 straight years, had concluded that he would not be able to send his children to the best schools on a LAMCO salary alone, no matter how hard he worked. While Claudius and I were away he had opened a small snack bar at Sandy Clarke Square, the central square of Yekepa, where most of the major stores and recreational facilities were located. He had begun with a small operation. He had set up a bar where LAMCO workers could stop by on their way from work to have a cold beer before going home. This proved to be quite a success, so he decided to rent some additional space in the commercial area from LAMCO to open a restaurant. He called his new sidewalk and indoor restaurant Monique's and put a small picture of me skiing in Norway on the front counter, but almost immediately everybody referred to it as Maddy's. He hired a manager to operate the establishment, though he discovered that when he tended to it on the weekends and his days off, the profits almost quadrupled. So he fired the manager, resigned his position at LAMCO, and took over the operation of the establishment that he soon converted into a full-service restaurant.

On the menu were Pappi's pepper chicken, prepared according to his own secret recipe, as well as pork chops, steaks, fish, and on Wednesdays, Liberian food was served. Palm-butter, made from the kernels of the palm tree and served with rice, was the most popular dish, especially among the Europeans, who loved Liberian food. Even though the restaurant was small, about 15 tables in all, they were always full and booked for parties and dinners; luckily for Yekepa, Pappi offered take-out.

Maddy's was famous throughout the area for excellent food and service, and indeed, Pappi was always always gracious to his customers, because he viewed the restaurant almost as his home, and the patrons his friends. The community was so small that this was an accurate perception.

One thing I must say is that Pappi never overcharged, even in a market where the competition was vastly inferior and people would have been willing to pay double the prices on the menu. Pappi wanted to keep his patrons loyal. It was as if an unknown power was guiding him. As one of his customers remarked, "Maddy, everything you touch turns to gold." He imported a machine from Italy to make ice cream—possibly the best ice cream in the country. "My ice cream is democratic and delicious," Pappi was proud of saying. At only 10 cents a cone almost anyone in Yekepa could afford the occasional, and even frequent, indulgence. This was a concept that I would call upon many years later when I founded my telecommunications business—to provide a service that was available and affordable to most.

Pappi also purchased a Volkswagen van, which he had engineered to be an ice cream truck. It was painted beautifully in red and blue to match the cups that the ice cream was served in, with MONIQUE'S scripted on both sides. Ma Kema provided a hardworking and honest driver-cum-salesman named Moussa to drive the van all over Yekepa, ringing a bell that signaled his arrival. This was important, because Pappi rightly feared that given the local economics it would be easy for a driver to run off with the entire van. Getting a driver from Ma Kema's large extended family was like having a bonded worker. The insurance could not get any better than that.

For thousands of LAMCO employees Maddy's was a popular spot to relax in at the end of a grueling day, especially for those who worked in LAMCO's iron-ore mine. Dinner was the main meal and reservations were sometimes made months in advance. The setting was simple but idyllic. Patrons ate al fresco, shielded from the elements by a large canvas covering the dining area. At night the moon and millions of stars gently accented the dimly lit terrace, and soft music played in the background. Whenever there was a torrential downpour, the waiters would fold up the chairs and tables quickly and the customers would squeeze into the much smaller interior dining area. But these occasions were rare. Usually the weather cooperated, and good food, drink, and lively conversation in multiple languages flowed freely. At 11:30 every night Pappi would play "O Danny Boy," a favorite of his, and the only song that he had ever learned to play on the guitar. This was the cue for the customers to leave, and in each dining party there was always someone who knew the routine and would turn to his fellow diners and say, "Maddy wants us to go home."

The obstacles to launching a small business in Yekepa, even in the relatively insulated LAMCO environment, were formidable. Pappi soon found that running a restaurant in Africa almost always entailed backward-integrating into your entire supply chain, as locally available inputs needed were either of inferior quality, not available, or available only intermittently. For the restaurant business that meant one also had to be in the farming, food processing, and shipping and handling businesses. The day-to-day running of the restaurant was challenging enough, but it was these ancillary yet critical activities, which in a more advanced country would have been outsourced, that were the real drain on his energy. Take the ice cream machine. In the United States, even in the 1970s, one could merely pick up the phone or a catalog, research a product, place an order, send a money order and have the product in a matter of weeks, if not days. But when Pappi contacted Capigiani, the Italian manufacturer of the ice cream machine, they had not even heard of Liberia, let alone of Yekepa. Several letters of inquiry went unanswered. It was only through logistical support by LAMCO that Pappi was able to complete the purchase. He always bought machines in duplicate, in case one of them broke down. Often the second machine would serve as an emergency source of parts, because spare parts would take weeks, if not months, to arrive.

To serve the ice cream, cones were needed. At first Pappi was able to procure them from the local supermarket, but the quantities were never sufficient and the unit cost was too high. So he found a Lebanese supplier in Monrovia who had an ice cream vending business. But the shipments would be delayed, often stale, or too often, in crumbles. It was not long before he realized that he had to get into the cone-manufacturing business; yet another machine and spare were ordered. This meant that once a week, a day we all dreaded, the entire family got up at 4:00 A.M. to make the cones from scratch. The machine was stowed in the garage, which is where we made the fresh cones that were, I must say, perfect when eaten warm.

Even basic food supplies were difficult to obtain. The local meat was not tender enough, so Pappi ordered the meat through the LAMCO supermarket. He also ordered frozen chickens this way, from Denmark. This was expensive, however, with the extremely high markup that the supermarket charged—there were no allowances for wholesale pricing. So he found the supermarket's supplier and arranged to import the chicks from Denmark and raised them in a section that we cleared on our land and transformed into a small poultry farm.

Securing the newborn chicks from Copenhagen proved even more complicated than securing the ice cream machines. Upon receipt of payment, which was arranged through LAMCO, the supplier in Denmark would arrange for a third-party shipper to send the chicks by airfreight to Liberia. A telex would be sent to Pappi conveying the details of the airway bill so that he would know when to go down to Robert's Field, near Monrovia. Each of these journeys meant negotiating those treacherous roads, most of which were barely passable in both the rainy and the dry seasons, and every time that Pappi drove off in the Mercedes, I was petrified that it would be the last time that I would see him. Like the railway bed, the route from Yekepa to the airport was bordered by tropical rain forest with tiny villages thinly scattered along the way. The only gas stations for miles at a time were crude contraptions with gas of questionable quality. These stations, usually located under the shade of a tree by the side of the road, tended to be communally run by a small village of up to 30 people. The gas was dispensed from a glass bottle that was hanging upside down from a pump and had a rubber-hose attachment through which the gas was pumped into the car's tank. At the more prosperous of these establishments, an old dilapidated generator might be heard, churning noisily away, providing a modest and uneven stream of electricity to a single flickering lightbulb suspended above the fuel pump. Even this was a luxury, as most of the villages along these roads had no public utilities whatsoever. The gas might have arrived at these stations already contaminated with impurities. Then it might be diluted with water by the enterprising villagers desperate to stretch their limited resources. Pappi always left Yekepa with a full tank of petrol and filled up in Monrovia for the return journey.

It was not unusual for him to arrive at Roberts Field only to learn that the expected cargo had not arrived from Denmark as promised. The problem was that there were no direct flights from Denmark to Liberia, and the shipment had to transit through European countries such as Switzerland or Germany. As I sit at my computer and write this, I realize that I can log on and get a tracking number for a Federal Express shipment that I have made and identify exactly where it is at any moment of the day en route to its final destination. But a low-volume, faraway customer such as Pappi did not receive the best customer care. The next flight he could get his cargo on would arrive in Monrovia a week later at the earliest. So he would have to make the long and arduous journey back to Yekepa empty-handed and dispirited, then drive back down the following week in hopes that this time the chicks had made it.

But that was not the only problem that we contended with. One morning, shortly after Pappi had transported the two hundred newly arrived chicks from the airport in Monrovia and put them into the chicken coop, we woke up to discover that about five of them had been killed. We figured out that it was a snake that was to blame. We put a mongoose in the coop with the chickens, as they were known to kill snakes. It seemed like a good idea. The next morning we discovered that we had made a tremendous mistake. One by one the mongoose had killed each of the little chicks, whose tiny carcasses lay scattered across the ground. I fully understood the loss—the chicks, the time, the money. We could not just call up the local supermarket and order replacements, as one would be able to do in any Western country. Instead, the entire routine, beginning with placing the order to Denmark, would have to be repeated. I wanted to cry for Pappi, because I looked in his face and all I could see was defeat. And there was nothing I could do to fix it.

These excursions and the mongoose incident eventually took their toll on Pappi, and before long we were knee-deep in the poultry business. He ordered an incubator from Europe, put the roosters and hens in there, and soon the chickens were hatching right on our property. The days of ordering chickens from Denmark were over. Furthermore, many of the inhabitants of Yekepa began to rely on our poultry farm for both fresh eggs and chickens. The former were in high demand year round, and the latter were in particularly high demand at Christmastime and at New Year's, when chicken in various dishes was often served, and the local equivalents, malnourished and poorly bred, were poor quality compared to ours.

Pappi did everything grandly, so it was no surprise when some jealous tongues in Yekepa began wagging about Claudius's and my return from England. Maddy has run out of money and can no longer keep his children abroad—he isn't any better than the rest of us, some people said. Pappi believed fervently that all was possible for both him and his family. But the logistics of having two young children out in the world on their own had proved overly complex. Moreover, with our long absences, he was missing us and felt he did not really know us and that it was impossible for him and Mummy to develop the kind of natural bonds they had established with Herbert and Abayomi. He had therefore decided that it was best to bite the bullet, bring us back home, and settle for the LAMCO International School, where all of the company's senior managers sent their children.

Pappi was not prepared for the reception, or lack thereof, that we encountered. The Swedish principal, Torbjörn Ranefelt, wrote a letter to Pappi informing him that there was no room for Claudius and me, and that we would have to enroll in one of the schools that had been established for the children of the most junior staff of LAMCO—the natives.

Pappi was livid. To him, this was a blatant case of racism, which conjured up memories of injustices from his own childhood days under the British colonial rule in Sierra Leone. I am not so sure; after all, Pappi was no longer an employee of LAMCO, which was the criterion for getting into the school. Yet, one could argue that Mummy still worked for LAMCO at its hospital and, as head nurse, she was quite senior. One thing that was sure was that the international school would make room for any European student who arrived midyear, as it was part of the contract between LAMCO and all its international employees, even the most junior ones. Pappi knew full well that Mr. Ranefelt would never have dared suggest that white children go to what were known as the indigenous schools.

The principal had crossed the wrong person. I had never seen Pappi so angry, and I do not think I ever did again. Practically dragging Claudius and me behind him, Pappi took us to the campus of the international school. We sat outside Mr. Ranefelt's office with the secretary and the head teacher while Pappi raged inside at the principal. I learned later that he flatly accused Mr. Ranefelt of racism, and made it clear that he would not sit idly by while his children were discriminated against.

We then left his office and drove directly to the office of Pappi's longtime friend, Olle Wijkström, the managing director of LAMCO. A series of urgent phone calls and meetings followed, including a visit by Mr. Ranefelt to Olle Wijkström's office. Within a few days Claudius and I were enrolled in the LAMCO International School.

Mr. Ranefelt not only lost this battle, but also left for good at the end of the year. It was rumored (and of course we fervently believed) that Pappi's defiance had played a major role in his departure. Around the village, the "Ranefelt incident" was celebrated for a long time. Pappi had become a hero to many of our friends and neighbors, who were in awe of his determination. But anyone who knew him well knew that he would fight tenaciously to give us access to the best education possible. In fact, he would risk almost everything for his children. Displeasing the local power structure could have been bad for his new restaurant venture, but when Pappi was fighting for his children, he took no prisoners.

The school, while the best that Yekepa had to offer, was rarely as challenging or as interesting as Leelands had been. This was a period of tremendous adjustment for me. I missed my old Leelands schoolmates. Try as I might to imitate the local manner of speaking—for instance a Yekepa local would say *"ha di go di go?"* meaning, "how are you?" To which one was expected to respond: *"I fine ya."* I could not manage it. And soon I became shy, spending most of my time with my family, on my studies, and helping Pappi at the restaurant for a couple of hours each day.

There were bright spots, of course, and slowly I began to assimilate into the life and culture of Yekepa. There was the time I met the princess. One way to meet royalty and other famous people is to live in offbeat places like Yekepa. There fame carries much less currency, so there is tremendous ease of access when fame comes to town. My earliest recollection of such an encounter was when Princess Christina of Sweden visited our school. She was in Liberia on behalf of the Red Cross, which was running a program to transport food from Roberts Field to Mali, a country that had been hit with a severe drought. The school authorities whipped us into frenzied anticipation of her arrival. They pleaded with us to be on our best behavior to impress her royal highness and the entire population of Sweden, which would witness the event on television.

I was fascinated by the prospect of her visit. Hans Christian Andersen fairy tales had been my constant companions during my days in England, and still were in Liberia. I therefore considered myself an authority on royalty. I knew how a true princess should look, act, and carry herself. I mentally pictured a young, beautiful woman with long flowing hair like flax; dainty feet; a diamond tiara; and a silk or gossamer gown, flanked by a coterie of aides. How surprised and disappointed I was when into our classroom walked Princess Christina, bespectacled, crownless, and definitely not young, her short, limp hair plastered to her face on account of the tropical heat, flanked only by a few Red Cross personnel and the soon to be departed Mr. Ranefelt.

During those years, Pappi's restaurant did well, but it was not easy. His days began at 4:00 A.M. and did not end until midnight. I often felt guilty knowing that he was working himself into the ground just so that my brothers and I could have a good education. I tried to help wherever I could. After school I would go down to the restaurant to help serve the ice cream to the customers. I think Pappi enjoyed the company more than the help. After a few hours I would go home to play and do my homework and try to stay awake until Pappi came home. As I heard his Mercedes pull up to the house, I would run out to see him, even if I was in bed, and join him and Mummy at the table, as he ate a late dinner. Afterward, he would reconcile his books. He brought home the daily receipts from the restaurant in a small white sack. A good day's take was $400; on a bad day, for instance, when much of the expatriate community was on vacation in Europe during the months of June through August, it could be as little as $30. The cash was then placed in the rusty old Jacobs Crackers tin that he kept locked away in his and Mummy's bedroom.

When I was not helping Pappi at the restaurant or doing homework, I was usually getting into mischief. Hunting, as we called it, was one of my favorite pastimes. I was eleven years old, and with Herbert, Abayomi, and a few of our friends, we assembled what we assumed were the tools of the trade. In our arsenal were our walkie-talkies (which never worked), air guns, cutlasses, a Swiss Army knife, and several slingshots. We would drive our Mini Hondas (which we had begged and pleaded Pappi to get for us) to the edge of the bushes. Fortunately, LAMCO had not cleared away all of the bush from Yekepa, so we were still able to go to the outlying areas that remained virgin rain forest and pretend we were in "savage" and dangerous territory. We would then trek into the forest for two to three hours in search of dangerous animals. Although we never encountered the lions, cheetahs, or leopards we were looking for, these expeditions gave us the chance to escape the comfort and civility of the LAMCO sphere of influence and enter raw and untamed Africa. In our minds we were the explorers Livingston and Stanley, whom we had read about in school. Occasionally we shot rice birds, and every now and then we would kill a rabbit or a mongoose.

On one of these excursions Parviz Bazargani, whose father was from Iran and mother from Germany, and from whom I got my first ever kiss, was running away from a ten-foot-long, fast-moving black mamba snake and mistook my leg for a branch. As he hacked his way through the bushes to safety, his knife landed in my knee. Everyone froze in fear and amazement as they watched me fall, blood gushing out of my wound, knowing that a black mamba was on the loose. The knife was stuck at a neat forty-five degree angle, but I was too afraid of the additional pain I would suffer if we attempted to remove it. I refused to cry, however; I was the only girl in the group and I felt that I had to show that I could be as tough as everyone else. The boys carried me safely out of the bushes and an ambulance took me to the hospital, where Mummy was on duty, as was Parviz's father, who also happened to be LAMCO's chief physician. Parviz and I had a lot of explaining to do.

After I was all stitched up, I pleaded with Mummy not to tell Pappi how the accident had happened. She did not oblige, and that evening my warrior days came to an abrupt end.

From then on I had to cure my jungle fever by scouting gigantic bug-a-bug (termite) colonies where I could marvel at the highly sophisticated caste system in which the queen ruled over millions of soldiers, workers, and other peons. They all seemed to exist solely for her pleasure and protection; even the demure king appeared to bow to her every whim. Meanwhile, she remained hidden, buried in the basement of this impressive structure, as hundreds of thousands of workers carried individual pieces of dirt into the dwelling, sometimes reaching upward of ten feet. I am ashamed to admit that on several occasions I selfishly demolished the fruits of their hard labor in my quest to ferret out and pay homage to their noble queen. Luckily for me, no black mambas ever appeared, as they are known to find refuge in these structures when they have been abandoned.

The most important memory to me during this period was the year in which Pappi built his dream house. Pappi always had wanted a house of his own, one that did not belong to LAMCO. But Pappi was also cautious. The decision as to where to build the house required much thought, foresight, and speculation. He wondered what would happen to Yekepa when the iron ore in the Nimba Mountains had been exhausted. Moving to Monrovia, the capital, was an alternative, as Pappi was quite certain that the capital would always be there and thriving economically. But that would be almost like moving to a developing country from a developed one. Monrovia's water supply was intermittent, electricity was rationed, and telephones were a luxury to which only a few had access. Pappi also considered moving the family to Las Palmas, on the Canary Islands of Spain. The primary reason for such a move would have been stability, because he often feared that the deep chasm that existed between the Americo-Liberians and the indigenous peoples of Liberia would one day erupt into some kind of conflict or rebellion, especially as more and more of the indigenous people were becoming educated and were traveling abroad, thanks to companies like LAMCO. Over the years there had been growing signs of tension between the ruling elite and the indigenous populations, as more and more of the latter demanded a greater say in their own government. In addition, Pappi had received numerous proposals from Europeans to franchise his restaurant, and had so far declined. In the end his passion and love for Africa won out, as did his faith in the long-term prospects of Yekepa.

As he did with all projects he undertook, he became intimately involved with all the details of building the house from start to finish. First he secured the best site in the Yekepa area, overseeing the entire land-surveying process. The property he selected was high atop a hill and afforded a spectacular view of the entire town that

LAMCO had built. He worked closely with a Swedish architect to design the house. He personally selected beautiful ornate rocks from Mount Nimba to use on certain portions of the house, and the best mahogany from the forest. I helped with the rock selection. While on a trip to Rome in connection with the ice cream machine purchases, he chose marble for the living room floors. Like the house his parents had built in Gloucester, his was the most beautiful in town. The house, the first and the only that he would ever own, was the culmination of Pappi's pursuit of a better life. It was here that he dreamed of spending his retirement, and of creating a permanent refuge for his children and grandchildren. Which is not to say that Pappi turned his back on the community: He was the prime sponsor of one of Liberia's lead soccer teams, and he gave mostly to the church and an organization for the disabled. But he imagined a place to which his family would always be able to return, even after the bounty of the mines had been exhausted.

We lived well, especially compared to most other Africans. Each year, Pappi took at least one member of the family to Europe for the summer holidays—Norway, Sweden, Germany, Spain, and Italy. Some in Yekepa found these annual jaunts by the Maddys surprising. Their expectation was that only Europeans would go on European vacations (which were paid for by LAMCO as part of their contracts).

But this was just another way in which Pappi was exceptional. Whenever he could afford it, he would provide us with wonderful, stimulating, eye-opening opportunities. Our vacations were primarily meant as fun, of course, and as a way for our family to enjoy spending time with one another. But I think they were also intended to show us that we were just as good as anyone else, and that we did not have to conform to a stereotype; that we could enjoy these kinds of opportunities. If that was his goal, he certainly succeeded.

8

Building a Metropolis in the Jungle

Many Westerners who have come across me over the years have assumed that I must be a member of some tiny, superrich elite class—perhaps the daughter of a dictator or a diamond potentate. Or I am asked, "Was your father a diplomat?" The truth is that thanks to one private company, LAMCO, a substantial middle class emerged in Yekepa. In fact, all of us who lived there were better off and much safer than the vast majority of Liberians, because LAMCO in effect was our government, and was a much more efficient and enlightened version than the government that ruled over the rest of the country.

The 1950s had marked what appeared to be the beginning of a brand-new era of economic promise for Liberia. The economic possibilities and prospects looked bright, and it seemed that the years of the country constantly living on the brink of bankruptcy had passed. Spurred by the government's Open Door policy and its generous tax and investment incentives, numerous foreign companies were exploring new business opportunities in Liberia. Once dependent on one major commodity—rubber—and on one multinational corporation—Firestone—Liberia began to diversify its economy through the investments of up to fifty multinational corporations and countless other medium and small enterprises. The principal lure to interested foreign investors was the promise of rich mineral deposits such as gold, diamonds, and iron ore believed to be buried in Liberia's soil. Foremost among these prospectors was a group of American business concerns that entered negotiations with the Liberian government regarding the possibility of prospecting for iron ore. The leader of this group was Lee Detwiler, an American business promoter, a smooth-talking wheeler-dealer with limited access to capital but sufficient international contacts to put a consortium together of the scale and scope required to launch a major venture like LAMCO, who for years had been scouting the African continent for investment opportunities.

Desperate for cash, the Liberian government needed little convincing. In 1953 it awarded the Americans a 70-year concession, granting rights to explore, mine, process, manufacture, and engage in any other business activities that would enable them to exploit the iron ore and any other potential natural resources they might discover in the 500-square-mile area covered by the concession.

The American companies then incorporated as Liberian American Minerals Company (LAMCO J. V. Inc.) to exploit the concession. But as they had no industry expertise and lacked financial resources they approached potential partners, one of them being Sweden's Enskilda Bank, owned and controlled by the vibrant, financially astute, and entrepreneurial Swedish tycoon Marcus Wallenberg. Wallenberg contacted Gränges Corp., Sweden's leading private iron-ore exporter at the time. Gränges, anticipating the sale of half of its assets in Lapland mines to the Swedish government, was flush with cash, and they took an interest in the proposed venture in order to maintain its dominant position in the ore business. In the fall of 1954 the iron-ore exporter was able to put together a syndicate of six Swedish operating companies, called the Swedish LAMCO Syndicate, to acquire an interest in the American concession agreement. Gränges bought a 50 percent stake in the company.

By May 1958, the Americans and the Swedish syndicate had formed a joint holding company, Liberian Iron Ore Ltd., and two years later Bethlehem Steel, the world's second largest iron and steel company, agreed to acquire 25 percent of LAMCO's shares. More important, Bethlehem agreed to purchase at least a quarter of the future iron ore production of LAMCO. Thus emerged LAMCO, the company that would do more than any other single corporation before or since to radically alter and improve the physical, economic, and even the political landscape of Liberia.

Mining is a highly capital-intensive undertaking. It is clear that such an ambitious project as LAMCO, capable of injecting life into the entire Liberian economy, could not have been undertaken by a small- or even by a medium-size company. Early investment estimates called for a quarter of a billion dollars. Deep pockets were a sine qua non, and were provided principally by Bethlehem Steel and Enskilda Bank, the latter with access to a diversified and extensive financial network. A strategic investor was also critical to the project's success, and was provided principally by Bethlehem Steel and Gränges Corp. The Liberian government provided the concession, for the most part stayed out of management's way, and at least temporarily, sustained political stability and predictability. It was not a genuinely stable environment, but one that the government imposed and maintained by force and intimidation, rather than by popular will.

The complementary strengths of the Swedish syndicate, Bethlehem Steel Corporation, and the Liberian government facilitated

LAMCO's successful launch. Bethlehem's contacts guaranteed loans from the American market. The Swedish connections, under the leadership of Marcus Wallenberg, who visited the country on several occasions and met with Liberian president William V. S. Tubman, paved the way to financial arrangements with European lenders and secured purchasing agreements with a number of German ore importers. In other words, the financing and the marketing of LAMCO were enhanced by the multinational and concerted approach adopted by the various shareholders. The Liberian government, which had a lot to gain from the success of the venture and even more to lose from its failure, adopted a laissez-faire policy and went out of its way to cooperate with its multinational partners, including allowing for investments into the development of both physical and social infrastructure in Liberia to be made directly by LAMCO rather than through royalties paid to the government for use at its discretion, in which case it is highly unlikely that the infrastructure would have been built. Years later I would wish that my own company, Adesemi (which was the successor name to ACG), could have enjoyed any of these advantages. Unfortunately, other than a priori political stability, we had none of them.

Even in its infancy LAMCO was regarded as a paradigm of foreign investment in the developing world. At the time it was one of the largest private investments in Africa. By 1960, building and construction had begun in Yekepa. Three years later the railroad and Buchanan port facilities were complete, and in that same year, 1963, the first loads of ore mined in Yekepa were sent by rail to the port of Buchanan and shipped out to the world. Many foreign dignitaries, including presidents of newly independent African countries, came to Yekepa to view its operations. The expected returns to the investors had to be sufficiently high for them to be induced to build what for all intents and purposes amounted to a developed enclave within a developing country—economic development subcontracted to the real experts. The infrastructure was complete with physical plant, human resource development, social services, and an administration capable of managing a highly diverse and complex community of people from all over the world. It even included a private police force, referred to as the Plant Protection Force. The only major missing component was a defense force that would have permitted LAMCO to protect its borders from the ravages of external conflicts. Not surprisingly, LAMCO's Liberian employees had far more loyalty and patriotism to the company than to the country.

That said, I do not mean to convey the impression that LAMCO's track record in Liberia was totally without blemish, or that Yekepa was some sort of utopia. Initially the company was not unionized, as that was illegal in Liberia, and they suffered their share of labor unrest. During one strike in 1965—the workers were demanding better pay, more equitable housing distribution, and improved relations between management and labor—about 300 strikers ran around the mining site for two days, laughing, shouting, and brandishing heavy rocks and cutlasses. At one point a group of them stormed the office of the general manager, an overweight American by the name of Richard Lowe, leaped onto his desk, and menaced him with their cutlasses. After a moment of stunned surprise Lowe leaned back in his chair and burst into laughter. This response apparently satisfied the mob, which roared and departed Lowe's office to continue their cavorting elsewhere.

In retrospect, this should have prepared the LAMCO officials for more serious disputes to come—disputes that involved Tubman himself ordering machine-gun-toting troops into Yekepa to quell subsequent strikers' unrest. In the end it was because of LAMCO's foreign shareholders that the Liberian government was forced to allow the formation of trade unions and was required to establish guidelines outlining legal processes to be followed in settling management-and-labor disputes. Thus, the strike led to the formation of the National Mine Workers' Association of Liberia.

LAMCO's early projects included a 165-mile railroad, paved

roads, ore-handling installations (for blasting, crushing, and transport), a deepwater harbor in the port of Buchanan, and complete physical and administrative infrastructure to accommodate residential communities at its two major centers of operations, notably Yekepa and Buchanan.

Although the risks and ownership of LAMCO were shared among LAMCO's major shareholders, Gränges Corp. managed the day-to-day operations of the company. As a consequence it was the Swedish business philosophy of "social investment" rather than the Liberian one that permeated and defined the nature and scope of the company's investment and management style. This philosophy included not only physical improvements, but investments in social infrastructure, such as schools, community centers, hospitals, and housing. These investments were made not out of charity but because of the bottom-line need for increased worker productivity and loyalty. In all but name, LAMCO assumed the responsibilities that normally fall under the scope and province of government. Had LAMCO not made these investments in Yekepa, including providing education for thousands of indigenous Liberians, significant improvements in health care, and stimulated entrepreneurship, it is doubtful that the mining project would have been a success.

Erland Waldenström, president of Gränges from the late 1950s through the company's sale to the Electrolux Corp. in the late 1970s, published a small pamphlet in 1963 that outlines the movement of capital between industrialized countries and the developing world. Waldenström's view reflected the reigning Swedish multinational management philosophy at the time: The "ultimate aim" of any interaction with an underdeveloped country "must obviously be to see that diversified, vigorous and economically viable enterprise and investment is established in the developing countries, and that this, rather than gifts, is made the permanent foundation for their economic growth" (*The LAMCO Project—A Commercial Contribution to African Economic Development,* by Erland Waldenström, 1963).

Waldenström also provides some guidelines for foreign interests investing in less developed nations, citing LAMCO as a successful example of cooperation between the developed and developing countries: "It is undoubtedly a great advantage in such cases if the government or private investors in the developing countries can be brought in as participants, thus shouldering some part of the financial risks of such enterprise. Our experience in LAMCO has been that such ownership tends to reconcile divergent interests and to promote the kind of mutually confident collaboration that inclines more to partnership than to the relationship between giver and receiver." (ibid.)

Acting on its investment philosophy, LAMCO made investments in Liberia that changed the social and economic prospects of tens of thousands of Liberians. The Liberian government was fully aware of the improvements brought about by the company. In a 1973 statement in the company's monthly news publication, Liberia's president, William R. Tolbert, said: "As the largest economic enterprise in Liberia, LAMCO employs a sizeable sector of the national work force. Hence, its contribution to the Liberian economy is substantial, both in terms of wages and social services, and in terms of infrastructural amenities, which include housing, roads, schools and hospitals. Thus LAMCO has become not only an example of enlightened industrial influence, goodwill and cooperation, but also a most welcome and beneficial entity within our country" (*LAMCO News,* November 1973, p. 2).

So what was this contribution, exactly? LAMCO allocated a full 50 percent of its $275 million initial capital outlay to investment in physical infrastructure that was not operations specific and could be used by other industries in Liberia, and to social investments. Of this amount, approximately $137.5 million went toward economic infrastructure, including roads, port facilities, and railways. About

$27.5 million went toward social infrastructure deemed essential to the long-term viability of LAMCO. These investments included health facilities, housing, and schools. By any measure this was a staggering investment, and it generated long-term benefits for LAMCO's employees, for residents in the surrounding towns and villages, and for businesses throughout the country that emerged to meet the additional demand stimulated by LAMCO's activities. The changes arising from LAMCO's investment were nothing short of revolutionary.

Among the most striking improvements made by LAMCO was in health services. Prior to LAMCO, the people in Yekepa had relied exclusively on witchcraft and the traditional medicine man for health care. With the arrival of the company, however, a hospital was built, in 1963, beginning with 54 beds and four doctors. As the population of Yekepa grew the hospital grew as well, adding a pediatric ward and a maternity and child-care clinic. Foreign and local physicians staffed the hospital, along with foreign and local nurses, among them Mummy. The hospital initially was viewed with a high degree of skepticism on the part of some of the locals, who believed that they would either be cured automatically upon their first visit to the hospital or that modern medical science was a fraud. But after much education, and more important, concrete results, they came to trust the system and understand the importance of ongoing and even preventive care. By 1970, LAMCO was treating approximately 130,000 outpatients, most of them local to the Yekepa area, but many from the outlying areas as well. In an average year, 4,700 patients were admitted. The hospital assisted in some 1,200 births each year. Resources at the hospital—including a laboratory, an operating room, an X-ray department, and a pharmacy—were as sophisticated as those of many European hospitals of comparable size. Employees and their children were routinely inoculated against harmful diseases. Infant mortality fell well below the national average, and life expectancy increased.

In cases where local treatment was not possible, patients often were sent overseas, especially to Sweden, for more complex diagnosis and treatment. While LAMCO did not entirely eliminate the influence of native superstition and the belief in the local medicine man, it certainly convinced local residents of the power and effectiveness of modern medicine, proper nutrition, and hygiene in improving their health.

LAMCO also built a water purification plant in the village, which treated approximately 1.1 million gallons of industrial and residential water daily and reduced the incidence of water-borne diseases that previously had been pandemic in the tiny community. The company paid particular attention to sanitation, preventive medicine, periodic checkups for students in all the schools, regulation of agricultural products, especially locally-slaughtered livestock and other locally produced crops. Only the privileged elite in the country had health care comparable to that which even the most junior member of LAMCO received in Yekepa.

LAMCO's educational mission in Liberia was twofold. First, the company considered education to be a critical component of its overall business strategy. Advanced vocational training was given to workers. Primary and secondary education was given free of charge to their children. Within twenty years the number of students in the system each year was up to 5,000. Initially all the schools in Yekepa were run by LAMCO. As the number of students and schools grew, however, LAMCO subcontracted out the management and operations of some of them to other organizations. For example, in 1967 the Catholic Mission was engaged to operate the Area N school, soon to be called St. Joseph's School. And in 1973, as part of the ongoing attempt to promote Liberian management in the affairs of the community, some of the schools were fully integrated into the Liberian educational system.

The schools transferred to the government followed the curriculum established by the Liberian Ministry of Education and were run according to the national academic calendar, which was from March to December. The international school, with students from 14 countries, remained fully under LAMCO management and offered a much more diverse and complicated curriculum and ran on the European and U.S. academic calendar, from September to June.

Employees of LAMCO also were offered numerous supplemental training opportunities, allowing local hires to master skills to eventually replace higher-cost expatriate workers in more advanced jobs. The company's training program was complemented by contributions made by the Swedish International Development Authority (SIDA), the Swedish government's foreign aid organization. This was an example of a working public and private partnership, and its success was due mostly to the fact that the private company was in charge and the development agency was given a specific area of expertise in which to operate. Exceptionally talented Liberian employees were sent to Sweden, America, and other foreign countries for short and long-term advanced training courses in civil engineering, electrical engineering, administration, and general management. Pappi attended one of these courses in Stockholm while he still worked for the company. For those who merely wanted to improve their basic level of education, an adult night school offered classes from grades three through twelve, enabling employees to obtain a high school certificate. Some of these night classes were also open to privately employed household servants of LAMCO staff for a fee, usually paid by their employers, and many of them took advantage of the opportunity for a chance to improve their own earning and professional prospects.

Thanks to LAMCO, the residents of Yekepa were insulated from most of the infrastructure, management, and administrative deficiencies of the rest of the country. The weak link was schooling: Even the best school only went up to the 9th grade, at which point all the expatriate children would return to their countries of origin to continue their educations. Most of the Liberian students at the LAMCO International School moved to the capital city or elsewhere in the country where there were more advanced levels of schooling, including universities. As Claudius and I approached the ages of 16 and 14 respectively, Pappi again began to look at the bigger picture. Where could we go to obtain the best education possible? Claudius, having completed the 9th grade at the international school two years earlier, already was attending an all boys Catholic boarding school, Carroll High, not far from Yekepa. But Pappi viewed this as a short-term arrangement. Once Claudius graduated from there, Pappi's goal was to send him abroad to college. He wanted to prepare me for college as well, and figured that the best way to do so was by sending me to a rigorous high school, possibly in England. He had in mind that I would eventually go to Oxford. We began discussing the options that were open to us. For Claudius, the solution was relatively simple. Claudius had become a star tennis player in Yekepa—so much so that many of the senior LAMCO executives wanted to play against him. One of LAMCO's top managers was impressed enough that he arranged for LAMCO to give Claudius a scholarship to attend college in the United States. Because he knew of someone already attending the school, Claudius applied to Bridgeport University in Connecticut and was accepted in 1977. The search for a school for me was more difficult. One idea was to send me to the Annie Walsh Memorial School in Freetown, Sierra Leone. Like Pappi's alma mater, Annie Walsh was founded by the Christian Missionary Society of the Anglican Church in 1816. The actual Annie Walsh was a young English girl whose dream was to do missionary work in Africa. Unfortunately, she was killed in a tragic accident before she could fulfill her dream. Her parents established the Annie Walsh Memorial Fund in her honor, which was subsequently pooled with the funds already collected by the Christian Missionary Society and used to build a campus in Sierra Leone to educate young women up to the high school level.

I did not relish the idea of moving to Sierra Leone, and I told

Pappi so. While I had loved our periodic visits to Mamma Ade and Pappa Larry over the years, apart from the luxurious Cape Sierra Hotel, I remember Sierra Leone as being a relatively backward country—even when compared to Liberia. After all, hadn't Pappi himself left there to come to Liberia in search of a better opportunity?

Perhaps my attitude hurt him; his education in Sierra Leone had served him well enough. Was I any better? But when I balked, I was still young and insensitive in the way children can be. Besides, I had ideas of my own.

For reasons I could not articulate at the time, I had reached the conclusion that America, not England, was the land of opportunity for me. Claudius was already in America, I had watched lots of movies about America, and many of the Americo-Liberians who visited the States raved about it, considered themselves American more than Liberian, and treated us "bush people" as inferior. I felt that by going to America I could get rid of this stigma.

Pappi, on the other hand, had never had good feelings about America, having grown up in the British educational system. Another contributing factor was the behavior he had witnessed on the part of the Americo-Liberians toward the indigenous people in the country, including him, as a native of Sierra Leone, which they regarded as only marginally better than the Liberian natives. These descendants of repatriated American slaves were frequently insufferably arrogant toward their "native" countrymen and all other Africans that were not descendants of American slaves. They referred to the former derogatively as "country people." But Pappi's primary concern about sending me to school in America was not the Americo-Liberians' ugly bigotry but the torrent of bad news about the United States that had made its way across the ocean to Liberia, stories of crime, drugs, and delinquency unheard of in Old Man Yeke's cocoon. The media reinforced Pappi's perception that the United States was a vast wasteland where an innocent African could easily get lost or lose himself.

No matter. I was almost always able to get my way with Pappi. He and I had a special bond, and generally I could wear him down with argument, charm, and dogged persistence. I knew that it was only a matter of time before I would convince him that America was the place for me.

I had as my coconspirator Mummy, who with her previous educational experience in Boston began looking at different possibilities on the East Coast, especially in the Boston area. After our first choice, a school called Cushing Academy, about an hour west of Boston, turned out to be too expensive, we fell back on our second choice, St. John the Baptist, an Episcopal school in Mendham, New Jersey, which had been advertised in a *Good Housekeeping* magazine that Mummy had purchased in Liberia. So I got my wish: In January 1978, at the age of 15, I would be heading to school in America.

Ma Kema

Mummy and I once again traveled the familiar route to Monrovia, where she was putting me on the plane, this time alone, to New York's John F. Kennedy Airport. Naturally, on our way there, we stopped to say good-bye to Ma Kema at her residence in the capital.

After all these years I still could not understand why Ma Kema had not just moved in with us in Yekepa. Situated in the heart of the capital, not far from many luxurious homes owned mostly by elite Americo-Liberians, her Monrovia residence was a major transit point for Mandingo traders operating between the coast and the Sahel, the southern boundary of the Sahara. But to a westerner's eye, Ma Kema's home in the city would have appeared as nothing more than a slum.

It always seemed to me that going there was like descending into a grotto of centuries past. First we had to navigate the steep, rocky decline that led to the densely populated compound, consisting of rickety dwellings made mostly of corrugated iron sheets and subdivided into numerous little sections that served as temporary lodgings for thousands of traveling Mandingo traders who were all Ma Kema's people. Conceptually, it was like a satellite office of a large corporation.

The roots of this commercial system were centuries old. The Mandingo people (also known as the Mandinka) are part of the Mande speakers of the Sahel region, different groups of which built the ancient West African Kingdoms of Ghana (c. 800–1240, ruled by the Soninke) and Mali (1240–1550, founded and ruled by the Malinke after their defeat of the Soninke). These groups controlled and thrived as a result of the lucrative trans-Saharan trade, which consisted principally of exchanging gold from Wangara and Bambuk for such items as salt, clothing, and manufactured goods, transported along the caravan routes from Africa north of the Sahara by Arab and Berber traders. The kingdoms were well armed and they built thriving cities, such as the Ghanaian capital of Kumbi-Saleh, that were as complex and sophisticated as many European cities of the time. The majority of their people were farmers and herdsmen who were required to pay taxes for the upkeep of the kingdom.

The increasing contact between the Soninke and northern Africans resulted in the conversion of many of the Soninke to Islam, which by then had spread throughout North Africa and southern Spain. By the beginning of the 13th century the kingdom of Ghana began to decline due to a number of factors, including increasing desertification, which made farming in the area much more difficult, and growing competition from other major groups in the region. Among these were the Muslim Malinke, who now controlled a new source of gold, at Bure, in the upper Niger River region. The Malinke were led by the great epic warrior Sundjata of the Keita clan, who united a number of lesser Malinke chiefdoms to form the empire of Mali, the capital of which was Niani, close to Bure. A number of trading and cultural towns emerged in Mali, including Jenne, Gao, Walata, and Timbuktu. Mali was a formidable kingdom that became famous for its religious scholars and rich cultural traditions. It was during this period that Mali was made even more famous by the pilgrimage of one of its most prominent kings, Mansa Musa, the direct descendant of Sundjata, to Mecca in 1324. It is said that he had up to 15,000 people in his entourage and took so much gold with him that the value of the metal in Egypt decreased by 12 percent as a result of his shopping spree there, and that it took a number of years for the price to recover.

In the town of Jenne a group of Muslim traders emerged; they were known as the Dyula. The principal commodities that they traded were gold and the kola nut. Kola nuts were an important and profitable commodity because they were one of the few stimulants that the Muslims were allowed to consume. The kola nuts grew in the tropical forest region that now belongs to Côte d'Ivoire and Liberia, and were shipped across great distances by Dyula porters traveling through thick rain forests, barren savanna, and the unforgiving heat of endless deserts. The kola nut was therefore considered a luxury that was popular in the Sahel region, where there were large populations of Muslims. The Dyula were Ma Kema's direct ancestors.

After Mali's fall and subsequent absorption into the Songhay Empire, an act that was completed by the 15th century, the Dyula continued to play a prominent role in the long-distance trans-Saharan trade, particularly in the principal city of Jenne. According to accounts provided by Portuguese traders along the West African coast:

> *The most lucrative aspect of the trade seems to have been the time-honored exchange of Saharan salt for West African gold. The salt was carried by camel from the Sahara to Timbuctu in large blocks of up to 200 pounds each (a camel would carry two such), and then shipped in, presumably Songhai canoes (each of which might carry some 20 tons or so) to Jenne, where it was*

worth something like 8 ounces of gold (£32 or $160, when these currencies were on a gold standard) per hundred pounds. This was roughly twice its value at Timbuctu, so the trade was pretty lucrative. . . .

A Malinke merchant trading in these products in the 16th century could therefore make up to £30,000 gold ($150,000) a year. Other items imported to Jenne in this way were brass, copper, blue and red cloths, silk, and spices. At Jenne the salt and other commodities were packed and shipped further south by caravans of up to two hundred porters. The merchants would return with slaves and gold dust. A portion of the commodities were invested locally, while the surplus was used to make further acquisitions from the North. (P. 91, Valentim Fernandes, 1507; A History of Africa, by J. D. Fage. Routledge of London, 1995.)

The Dyula were devout Muslims, and everywhere they went they took elements of their faith and heavily Arab-influenced culture with them. As they migrated they settled mostly in large market towns, where the best trading opportunities were found. These frequent displacements often required them to settle among other ethnic groups and to accept second-class or "alien" status among the populations into which they settled. In this way they became adaptable and resilient in periods of rapid and at times violent disruptions in society, traits that would prove invaluable and critical to their survival as a group, all the way up to the 21st century. Their attitude toward work was akin to what was much later referred to in Europe as the "Protestant" work ethic. Major European proponents of this theory, such as the French and German theologians John Calvin and Martin Luther and the German economist Max Weber, merely articulated (and got the credit for) what the Mande peoples had been practicing for centuries. Hard work was viewed as a natural complement to their religion. In later years they were referred to as "Black Jews" by those who envied them and felt threatened by their economic success.

Over time the discrimination they suffered from other ethnic groups, as well as their strong Islamic faith, provided them with a distinct and powerful sense of shared identity that governed their politics, their social lives, and their commerce, even when the national governments of the countries they inhabited tumbled into utter chaos. They settled in present-day Ghana, Côte d'Ivoire, Liberia, Sierra Leone, Guinea, and Mali, and maintained close commercial links that still transcend geographic and political borders. This unity was and is the secret to their success and prosperity, and the key to their survival against the ostracism and open hostility they frequently face from other ethnic groups. While they may not have physical boundaries to define them, the Mande-speaking peoples are in almost every other sense a nation—and a powerful one at that, because of the tremendous economic clout that they wield in many parts of West Africa and their intense loyalty to one another.

One of the leaders who emerged among the Dyula was Samori Touré, the scion of an animistic Dyula trading dynasty from Futa Djallon, the highland region of west-central Guinea. As a young adult he converted to Islam, a decision that would later prove instrumental to his ascent to power. For many centuries, Samori's family had been engaged in the trade in gold dust from Bure and cattle from Futa Djallon. Under the command of Samori, the Dyula used their extensive trade network to secure arms, especially from neighboring Sierra Leone, which, because of the British settlement there, had some of the most advanced weapons in the region. Between 1865 and 1875 Samori conquered and consolidated the neighboring Dyula city-states to form the powerful and prosperous Mandinka empire. By uniting the formerly competing states he significantly enhanced trade, creating a tremendous amount of wealth for the enterprising Dyula merchants, of which there were many.

He extended his empire to incorporate the all-important Bure alluvial gold fields in the North. By the end of his period of conquest, the Mandinka empire came closest to reunifying all the Mende-speaking peoples under one leadership, similar to the role played earlier by the Mali empire.

In addition to revitalizing and expanding the trade links, Samori restored much of the scholastic and artistic glory of the ancient Mali empire. Rather than selling his conquests into slavery he ordered them to build his empire and recruited them into his military. He also promoted Koranic studies and built new mosques. He promoted self-reliance in various areas by commissioning local ironsmiths to replicate firearms previously imported from Europe. Impressive as the empire of Mandinka was, however, it could not overcome the military might of the French, to whom it succumbed in the late nineteenth century.

The mystique of Samori Touré lived on through his grandson, Sékou Touré, the first president of the the independent Republic of Guinea, who would later avenge his ancestor against the French, only to have them retaliate by practically ransacking the country. Sékou Touré diverged from most of the other African leaders of former colonies of France, who chose limited independence by electing to remain within the "French Community," as it was called, and remained bound by the constitution of the Fifth French Republic. Abandoned by the French, who adopted an all or nothing approach to Guinea's defiant stance, President Touré turned to the Cold War embrace of Premier Nikita Khrushchev and the Soviet Union.

The French and British colonization of West Africa, for all of the ethnic fissures that it exploited and exacerbated, was unable to disturb the solidarity and fierce entrepreneurial drive of the Mandinka, who by the end of the nineteenth century were active across West Africa and always in the avant-garde of commerce. They rightly believed that they could develop new economic opportunities from the ground up in any country in the region because of their extensive and highly effective trade and financial networks, assets that were unparalleled by any other group in West Africa, foreign or indigenous.

As Yves Person Samori, a noted chronicler of the Mandingo, observed,

> *The Mandingo developed a strategy of establishing themselves in villages or towns through trade. They would send a sort of advanced team of traders to live among the local people and establish themselves within the community. The first such diplomat became the jatigi, or landlord, and welcomed fellow Mandingo who arrived late and became their sponsors, assisting them in their transition and integration into local life and commerce. These traders adjusted and adapted to the local population, learned their languages, contributed to local economic development, and thus became respectable and highly valued members of the community. When other itinerant Mandingo traders came down to trade, they served as hosts and facilitated their entry into the market.* (From Konneh, *Religion, Commerce and the Integration of the Mandingo in Liberia*, p. 13 as quoted from Y. Person's *Samori: Une Révolution Dyula*. Dakar: Ifan, 1968, pp. 109–205.)

When the Americo-Liberians encountered the Mandingo in the 19th century they found that the Mandingo were not so easily dismissed or repressed as many of the smaller, less-well-organized tribes that the settlers had relatively easily defeated, forced, or tricked into submission. The Mandingo were far better organized, stronger economically, and had well-entrenched positions that they were determined to protect from settler interference.

But with superior military power the Americo-Liberian settlers were able to retain their dominance, at least in the coastal areas. Beyond that, their success was limited because even when they penetrated the interior, especially with their Liberian Frontier Force, for the purposes of taxing and exploiting the labor of the indigenous people, they were never able to dismantle the Mandingo operations. Their sophisticated commercial network enabled the Mandingo to dominate trade within the hinterland, and they were first to capitalize on the foreign investments made in Liberia by companies such as Firestone and LAMCO by quickly establishing transportation, construction, and other services that catered to the demand stimulated by these investments. The Mandingo are first and foremost entrepreneurs and traders. They therefore do not like to labor on behalf of others—for instance, you would never see a Mandingo working as a "houseboy" for an Americo-Liberian family or for any other ethnic group, for that matter.

The Mandingo lead a dual life. They are devoted to Islam, an essential bond that unites them and creates a sort of regnum in regno. Yet they are extremely secular and pragmatic when it comes to their business dealings, which President Tubman well understood when he invited them to immigrate from Guinea to participate in Liberia's growth. To the Liberian government, Mandingo commercial activities constituted foreign investment every bit as much as Firestone and LAMCO's activities did. The Mandingo are exceptional traders, artisans, scholars, and are driven to excel in everything that they do. They treat their work or profession as a manifest destiny passed on from one generation to the next. While their economic drive appears to some to be relentless and evokes envy in other groups, their diligence serves a much deeper purpose than a mere desire to accumulate wealth. The Mandingo do not live ostentatiously. On the contrary, even the wealthiest of them are frugal and prefer to live a Spartan life. What they earn they tend to reinvest in their businesses, rather than acquire personal luxuries.

Also important is their ability to create businesses that have ripple effects, in that they create shared opportunities for growth. This makes them far more resistant than the general African population to the political and economic upheavals of the governments around them. Their strong bonds create informal banking and insurance mechanisms that are self-regulating in poorly regulated and inefficient markets. As one scholar notes:

> *A Mandingo trader receives protection and hospitality from a blood brother in his trading adventures. There are certain families that entered into such pacts and always watch out for each other. For example, if a Konneh Mandingo trader entered a territory for trade purposes, he would look for a Tarawallie or Kante for support. The reason is that historically these families established blood pacts that required them to help each other at all times. Blood brotherhood is an agreement by two people or families to protect and support each other. It is a give-and-take relationship and has no limitation in terms of its requirements. Thus, the Mandingo trader traveled widely knowing that there would be a blood brother to help him or that he would be able to establish one.* (Paulime 1968, 12–27; Jabateh, 1991). Taken from *Religion, Commerce, and the Integration of the Mandingo in Liberia,* by Konneh, p. 17.)

Ma Kema's family members were admirable trustees of this rich and empowering legacy. It was mostly from her and others in Fofana Town that I learned of the rich traditions of the Mandingo peoples. At the time these stories seemed more like images out of the pages of *Arabian Nights*—I pictured ancient caravans and weary porters as they proceeded in their dusty treks across the ocean of sand, into the Sahel and down into the steamy tropics—than anything to do with me and my relatively cosmopolitan and contemporary existence. I did not yet appreciate or understand their struggle and their triumphs or their relevance to my own life in the twentieth and twenty-first centuries.

One thing I did understand was that Ma Kema ruled her seemingly unruly world. In this compound, as well as at Fofana Town, she was the *jatigi*. A tremendous amount of business was carried on in her grungy Monrovia lair. The travelers traded in kola nuts, cloth, cattle, and gold, just as their ancestors had for centuries. The cooking area was outside, as were the bathing areas. Like the rest of the structures in the compound, the bathrooms were made of corrugated iron, but they were not covered. The bather got a bucket of warm water from the communal tap, and then proceeded to the washing stall. The water was never clear like the water we enjoyed in Yekepa. Here in Monrovia, the tap water was often a light brown, a by-product of the rust that had accumulated in the pipes through which the water flowed. In the morning a visitor was likely to see this water being used to do the washing. Clothes would be soaked in large tubs and spread out to dry on rocks under the strong glare of the sun. After a few such cycles, even black clothes tended to fade to white.

Large groups of young children would scamper around the compound half naked, perhaps playing in the puddles of stagnant water along the narrow dirt trails that separated the structures, seemingly without a care in the world. I remember their large, protruding bellies and thinking that this signaled malnutrition, and in fact it was a symptom of a lack of diversity in their diets—a problem of vitamin deficiencies rather than a lack of food. Coming as I did from a middle-class background I would wonder, Who are all these wild-looking children? The answer was complicated and foreign to my own experience. The entire compound was "family." The children were considered children of the entire clan, so all were "brothers" and "sisters." Little attention was paid to which child came from which parents. Through Ma Kema I was related to each of them, although I knew none of their names and would probably never see them again. The journey upon which I was about to embark and the tragedy of what lay in store for Liberia and the Mandingo people would make that impossible.

In contrast to the external surroundings the interiors of these structures were absolutely spotless, not even a spec of dust. As our eyes grew accustomed to the dim interior light, Ma Kema would signal to the people around us to bring in chairs. The requisite number of three-footed wooden stools would miraculously appear, seemingly out of nowhere. For her part, Ma Kema sat in the corner on the dirt floor, which was covered only by a straw mat, an area that at night was converted into a bed by the addition of a long wooden bench and a straw mattress. Conspicuously next to her on another wooden stool were a folding travel alarm clock, which we had given her many years ago on the occasion of her first pilgrimage to Mecca, and a simple flashlight—her "tor-shee light," as she called it.

Not a typical family portrait by Western standards, to be sure, but typical in Ma Kema's world and in many ways quite happy, because the entire family was protected and secure. No one was ever abandoned. When the children became old enough, they would help with little chores around the compound, and a few would attend the Koranic schools, where they learned to read and write. All of them were taught the traditional values of family, religion, and commerce, and as they grew older increasingly were assigned more adult responsibilities. When they reached their twilight years they were cared for lovingly, often in the same compound into which they had been born. It was a setting that comprised the complete cycle of life.

As a young teenager, of course, I understood almost none of this. To me, it was all dilapidation and chaos. I could not understand why anyone would choose to live this way, especially when they had well-to-do relatives like us to whom they could turn. Every time we visited I was acutely embarrassed. I thought of Paula Greenly. I would imagine how my schoolmates at Leelands would react if they were dropped into the middle of all this. I thought of their grandmothers with their salt-and-pepper hair neatly coifed, aprons secured around their rounded figures as they prepared afternoon tea of scones and jams in their quaint little cottages by the sea. I thanked God that they would never see me here amidst this misery and despair and all of these weird people.

Yet as I sit and reflect today, I have to wonder if Ma Kema, though never a judgmental person, did not have as much or even more cause to be embarrassed about the oddness of our appearance and mannerisms among her people—our Western clothes; our inability to communicate in any of our native languages; our obsession with comfort and our books, as opposed to the life she lived and the lasting relationships she built, which in her mind constituted the truer education. I now realize that Ma Kema's world was the most authentic form of sophistication—it could not be feigned, and there were no artificial trappings. It could only be attained and understood when experienced through the Spartan existence that they chose to lead, where values and loyalty ruled over all else. They worked hard, not for the comforts that money could buy, but as a means of protecting the entire community. But at the time that thought never even crossed my presumptuous mind.

Ma Kema first came to Liberia from Guinea with her parents in 1920. My great-grandparents, Sékou and Mama Bilite, were born in Guinea toward the end of Samori Touré's rule. Their daughter, Kema Bilite, was born around 1905. The Bilites were devout Muslims and professional merchants, like most Mandingo, specializing initially in gold, cattle, and kola nuts. They first settled in the northern Liberian town of Sanniquellie, the capital of Nimba County, not far from what would eventually become Grassfield.

At the age of 15, Ma Kema was "given" to the district commissioner of the county, an Americo-Liberian. The position of district commissioner was typically a political appointment that went to the less politically connected Americo-Liberians. Because they were posted in the hinterland, away from the relative sophistication of Monrovia, it was difficult to induce the best or the better connected of the Americo-Liberian elite to accept these posts. The job of the district commissioner was essentially to protect the Americo-Liberian interests in the region he governed and to extract as much money and goods as possible from local chiefs and their constituents and from foreign corporations operating within his jurisdiction on behalf of the government. The incumbent had immense powers and few official constraints over the exercise of his authority. He was a minor despot and could get virtually anything he wanted. One day he had decided that he wanted Ma Kema.

Although a Christian, the commissioner had no objection to polygamy. Ma Kema was the third of his wives, and by the time she was in her early twenties she had given birth to seven children. But my mother, Julia, was the only one to survive. Soon after Mummy's birth, Ma Kema and the other indigenous wives were sent away at the request of the commissioner's Americo-Liberian wife. Ma Kema's parents were only too happy to have her back. They arranged a second marriage for her to Mamadou Fofana, like her a Mandingo and a Muslim. Mamadou was a prosperous cattle breeder, and together he and Ma Kema purchased 400 acres of land near the town of Tapeta. They settled there in what they called Fofana Town, with numerous family members, including Mamadou's other wives and their children, all of whom I grew to know and became fond of. The village was not far from the extensive rubber plantation established by Firestone in the 1920s. There were rubber trees on their property, and Mamadou and Ma Kema became a supplier of latex to Firestone. She also continued to trade kola nuts and other goods, including various fruits, vegetables, and cattle. These products were sold along a well-developed Mandingo distribution channel.

Shortly before the outbreak of World War II the British author
Graham Greene visited Fofana Town and other villages around it.
Ma Kema told us that hers had been among those of the villages that
received him. To them, he was not a famous writer or the British
agent that he would become, but a crazy white man in search of
adventure—a welcome novelty in the communities and to the peoples
that he and his cousin, Barbara Greene, visited, led by a caravan of
porters that literally carried them through the dense tropical rain forest. In his travelogue *Journey without Maps,* he provides the following description of the typical village that he visited in the hinterland:

> But though all the villages at which I stayed had these com-
> mon properties—a hill, a stream, palaver-house and forge, the
> burning ember carried round at dark, the cows and goats
> standing between the huts, the little grove of banana-trees like
> clusters of tall green feathers gathering dust—not one was quite
> the same. However tired I became of the seven-hour trek
> through the untidy and unbeautiful forest, I never wearied of
> the villages in which I spent the night: the sense of a small
> courageous community barely existing above the desert of trees,
> hemmed in by a sun too fierce to work under a darkness filled
> with evil spirits—love was an arm round the neck, a cramped
> embrace in the smoke, wealth a little pile of palm nuts, old age
> sores and leprosy, religion a few stones in the center of the vil-
> lage where the dead chiefs lay, a grove of trees where the rice-
> birds, like yellow and green canaries, built their nests, a man
> in a mask with raffia skirts dancing at burials. This never
> varied, only their kindness to strangers, the extent of their
> poverty and the immediacy of their terrors. Their laughter and
> their happiness seemed the most courageous things in nature.
> Love, it has been said, was invented in Europe by the trouba-
> dours, but it existed here without the trappings of civilization.
> They were tender towards the children (I seldom saw a crying

child, unless at the sight of a white face, and never saw one beaten), they were tender towards each other in a gentle muffled way; they did not scream or "rag," they never revealed the rasped nerves of the European poor in shrill speech or sudden blows. One was aware the whole time of a standard of courtesy to which it was one's responsibility to conform. (Graham Greene, *Journey Without Maps,* New York, Penguin Books, 1978, pp. 79–80.)

After World War II and the economic changes resulting from increased investments in the country, Fofana Town too began to change. A paved road built by Firestone and the U.S. government, linking part of the hinterland to the Atlantic coast to the south, passed along Fofana Town, transforming it into one of the important points of contact and exchange for many Mandingo traders. The road was paved up to Gbanga, and north of there, all the way up to the LAMCO area, most of the road was nothing more than a long dirt track. Like most roads in Liberia, this one was full of perilous twists and turns. At night there were no streetlights for illumination—just the moon, stars, and headlights of oncoming vehicles, when they actually had them. During the rainy season the road was a river of thick, red, viscous mud; during the dry season, an opaque haze of dust. Potholes wide and deep enough to swallow Mack trucks were part of this strip of land that passed for a road. It was an unavoidable death trap, a highly incompatible fusion of the modern (the vehicles) with the primitive (the almost virgin tracks of land).

Even if a driver avoided being involved in one of the numerous, mostly fatal accidents he encountered along the way, his vehicle was still likely to break down, and its occupants usually were forced to wait a day for mechanical support or the right spare parts to arrive. Here again the Mandingo network and business savvy shined. Villages such as Fofana Town became full-service rest stops open 24 hours a day, with mechanics, gasoline, lodging, and food. I am not sure why, but many of these breakdowns occurred in the dead of night; often Ma Kema herself would get up, grab her torshee light and her kerosene lamp, and walk down the road to attend to marooned travelers. Their cargo, consisting of such items as sheep, goats, chicken, fresh fruit, and vegetables for sale in one or more of the major markets, would have to be unloaded and stored as best as possible, and the travelers themselves would be given mats to sleep upon. In the morning they would be given water from the nearby stream to bathe in and a hearty breakfast. There were no phones or other modern forms of communication in Fofana Town, but word already would have been sent, via another passing vehicle, of the need for spare parts or additional vehicles to rapidly transport the passengers and their wares to their ultimate destinations. Usually all of these services would be provided by people within the Mandingo network.

At Fofana Town the residents also grew numerous fruits and vegetables. When harvested they would find their way to the major points of sale, usually towns and cities throughout the country, including Yekepa and the capital city of Monrovia, using the tightly controlled and efficiently run Mandingo transportation system to get the products to market. Among my favorite memories of Ma Kema's farm were the orange trees. The oranges were nothing like the oranges that I later discovered in Europe and America. They were not even orange—they were green, even when ripe, and absolutely delicious. There was one particular two-week period of my childhood during which I became very ill with malaria and pneumonia. All I could stomach were dry Jacobs Crackers and fresh oranges. Word was sent to Fofana Town of my illness and of my craving, and soon several sacks of oranges were dispatched by taxi along those tortuous roads to our house in Yekepa.

Peter, our houseboy, would peel each orange in the traditional African way, first cutting away the thin layer of skin with a knife, as African oranges are infinitely juicier than Western oranges and it was too difficult and messy to peel it by hand. Peter did so expertly, in a circular motion, beginning at the top, so that when all the skin had been removed it was still in one long curly strand. A thin layer of white rind would be left and the orange would then be placed in the refrigerator, like a cup, to cool. As soon as I was ready for an orange, Peter would cut a hole in the middle, from which I could suck the sweetest juice that ever was. I felt special knowing that each orange had been picked especially for me and delivered by Ma Kema's Mandingo network. I have no doubt that her oranges did every bit as much to cure me as the huge doses of antimalarials that I had to take.

In addition to rubber trees, fruits, and vegetables, Ma Kema also sold kola nuts wholesale, a major part of her business. There is still a tremendous market for kola domestically and in the Sahel region. I always found it amusing that the Mandingo were frequently criticized for consuming too much kola—which, their critics argued, gave them an unfair advantage over their business competitors. It was like accusing the winning team of practicing too much.

The Mandingo are financially astute people. Long before I learned about the fundamentals of investing—of arbitrage trading and such fancy-sounding formulas as $PV = 1/1+r_1$, $IRR = (FV/PV)^{\wedge}(1/n)-1$, or the Black-Scholes formula, at Harvard Business School—it turns out the supposedly illiterate Mandingo had been practicing these concepts for years. The absence of an official futures market did not deter them from creating an informal one that worked just as effectively, and more to their advantage. For example, rice is the staple food in Liberia. The Dyula trader might purchase a contract for rice in Nimba County, where the price is high, and sell another contract for rice in Bong County, where the price is low, locking in a profit because of the price differential between the two markets. He is aware of such opportunities for arbitrage because of the strong Mandingo network in the communication and transportation industries. They also would purchase rice when prices were low and they anticipated shortages due to various meteorological factors, and sell them at elevated prices when supply was low. I always wondered how it was that when there was a shortage of rice at home and in the entire country, we would send word to Ma Kema, and within days a taxi would appear with several sacks of rice.

After her husband Mamadou died, Ma Kema split her time between Fofana Town and her compound in Monrovia. She visited us in Yekepa about twice a year, usually staying only a week or two at a time, often during the summer holidays when I was home from boarding school in England. She always brought us little toys that even in my youth I thought she could ill afford, given the simple and rustic life she lived. During her visits with us she would stick as much as possible to her habitual lifestyle, which, I am embarrassed to admit today, I was ashamed of. I found it odd and primitive. Instead of using a toothbrush to clean her teeth, Ma Kema used a small twig picked from the flowery mannagézé tree. She refused to shower in the bathroom and would instead shower outside early in the morning, when it was still dark, using her own oversized kettle that she filled with water. She paid special attention to the washing of her feet. She was beautiful, even in her old age, and serene.

Because of the tremendous cultural chasm there was a certain distance between her and us, which I regret today. While we ate in the dining room Ma Kema would sit in the kitchen, apart, eating alone. No matter how much I insisted that she join us she would not consent to eat with us. She would just shake her head and smile, as if there was something that I did not understand. I often wondered why my parents let her eat alone. Then I thought that perhaps it was because she ate with her hands that she preferred to eat alone.

It was only later that I learned that it was not unusual for the Mandingo, when in the midst of "infidels," which we were, to eat apart for fear of encountering something that was forbidden, such as pork. I loved to watch her eat. She would shape the grains of rice into exquisite bite-sized ovals, which she would then dip into a sauce and ever so elegantly put into her mouth, without creating a single spill. Imagining the horror that this would elicit from Nurse at Leelands, I would say, "Ma Kema, why don't you eat with a knife and fork?" To which she would respond that when God had created her he had not equipped her with a knife and a fork.

Ma Kema was a deeply spiritual woman. She adhered strictly to the teachings of Muhammad, praying fives time a day no matter where she was at the appointed time. She wore a veil when she prayed, but even when she wasn't praying her head was covered with a scarf. She fasted from dawn till dusk during Ramadan, despite oppressive heat and humidity. When she was sitting down she always had her *tasbih,* the praying beads, in her hand, as she conversed with God. Ma Kema made the pilgrimage to Mecca and Medina twice, on both occasions leading a group from Fofana Town. I remember the glow in her eyes when she returned from the first trip, during which she had brought me the ViewMaster. I came to understand that for even the poorest Muslim in Liberia, failure to go to Mecca is almost akin to failure in life. Likewise, when Ma Kema returned, it was as if she had fulfilled her mission on earth and that she was ready for death at any time; it was no longer something that she feared.

I once asked my mother why Ma Kema did not want to come and live with us, why she preferred her Spartan life in Fofana Town over ours of comfort and convenience. It was many years before I fully understood her reply. "Ma Kema wants to be with her people," Mummy said.

The implication was that we were not her people. Mummy had after all been raised by the Christian and aristocratic King family. By the time I appreciated how much Ma Kema had sacrificed in her life, especially for her daughter, it was too late to talk to her about it. Imagine giving birth to seven children and losing all but one before they had emerged from infancy. Wanting to give her year-old daughter a better chance of survival, Ma Kema sent her to live with her sister, who was married to an Americo-Liberian. The first time Ma Kema saw her daughter again was when Mummy was six and under the impression that her adopted Americo-Liberian family was her real family. She therefore was surprised to meet her real mother, Ma Kema, for the first time, and they were together for only a few days. Until my mother was fully grown she was rarely able to see Ma Kema. I can hardly imagine the pain Ma Kema must have felt, but she never talked to us about it, or complained, and I was far too young to ask. I sometimes wonder if she regretted her decision. But she had no choice. It was life or death, and for Mummy, she naturally chose life.

On the day of my departure for the United States Ma Kema came over to the house in which we were staying, just a few blocks away from her Monrovia lair, a former stately mansion that was now in visible decay. The house belonged to Mummy's *paternal* family, the Kings, with whom she had been sent to live after completing her high school studies. Graham Greene had visited this house as well, during its prime, shortly after it was built by former president C. D. B. King, the father of Mummy's second adopted mother, Ellen, whom we called Big Teetee, who now lived in the house on Front Street. Big Teetee lived in it with one young "country boy" to help her get around, two of her grown-up daughters, and more rats than people—big, huge rats. The family had indeed fallen from grace. In 1929, King and his government had been investigated by the League of Nations for being involved in the sale and trafficking of slave and child labor to help boost Liberia's foreign exchange earnings. As the Spanish delegate to the League of Nations, Salvador de Madriaga, attested at the time, in response to the inquiry into the slavery charges:

> *Liberia . . . has a treaty with Spain whereby she provides Spain with black labor for Spanish cocoa plantations in Fer-*

nando Po at the rate of twenty-five dollars a head. Slavery? Oh
dear no! All these laborers are free citizens of a free republic.
(I. K. Sundiata, *Black Scandal,* Philadelphia, Institute for the
Study of Human Issues, p. 11).

The situation was so dire that Britain and France wanted to see
Liberia dissolved and apportioned between them, as they already
controlled all the surrounding regions. Liberia survived, and while
the government was cleared of all of the major charges, King was
forced to resign, although he flirted with the possibility of a rerun.
Shortly before his departure from Liberia, Greene met with him
and had this to say:

I visited Mr. King a few days later at his farmhouse outside
Monrovia. With an old blue bargee's cap on the back of his
head and a cigar in his mouth, he put up an excellent imita-
tion of the old simple statesman in retirement. There was no
doubt that he was a sick man. We both drank a good deal of gin
while he went over and over the events of his downfall. From
his obscure corner of West Africa he managed to attract quite a
lot of notice with the shipping of labour to Fernando Po and
the pawning of children. He had feathered his nest nicely: he
had his own little plantation of rubber trees he was waiting for
Firestone to buy; he had his two and a half houses. But he hadn't
really any hope of a return; he was quite ready, he said, if he
was elected, to accept the League of Nations plan of Assistance,
tie his finances to European advisers, put white Commission-
ers in charge of the interior, give away Liberian sovereignty
altogether, but he knew quite well that he wasn't going to be
[re] elected.[1] All the rumours of the Firestone money, all the
speeches meant nothing at all. He was complying with a cus-
tom; one could see that he would be glad to go back to bed. He

*had had a finer fling than most Liberian Presidents: banquets
in Sierra Leone, royal salutes from the gunboat in the har-
bour, a reception at Buckingham Palace, a turn at the tables at
Monte Carlo. He stood with his arm around his pretty wife's
shoulders on his step while I photographed him, a black
Cincinnatus back on his farm" (Journey Without Maps, Gra-*
ham Greene, p. 242).

It was unusually cold that morning, with a thick layer of fog hanging in the air, as Mummy and I stood outside Big Teetee's house waiting for Ma Kema to arrive. As she struggled up the hill in her
rhythmic, slightly bent-over gait, Ma Kema emerged from the dew like
an apparition, swathed in her richly textured traditional attire. In retrospect I remember the fatigue, so visible in her face. Suddenly I had
an urge to change my mind, to give up my American dream.

Ma Kema had a surprise for me. She took my hand, and into it
she quietly slipped a $20 bill. The bill was like most of the U.S.
paper currency then in circulation in Liberia—old, crinkled, looking as if it had been dug out of a swamp. At some point it had been
torn in half and then carefully taped back together. Even then I
knew that, for her, giving me 20 dollars represented a tremendous
sacrifice. I felt awful taking it. But I also knew that not taking it
would have been worse.

I burst into tears. As I clutched that ratty old bill I knew that this
was almost certainly the last time I would be seeing my kind and
gentle grandmother. To her, America might as well have been
Mars. She surely had no idea what one could buy on Mars with
twenty dollars. But she was determined to keep me from harm. She
did not know, not that it would have mattered to her, that I had two
$100 bills in my pocket that Pappi had given me for emergencies.
She did not understand that a year's tuition in the States was going
to cost my parents several thousand dollars, and that the airfare

would be at least another thousand. She would do her best by me, according to her own standards.

Much later that same day I arrived in the United States for the first time. Once again, I had said good-bye to my family amid rivers of tears and oceans of well-intentioned advice. This time, though, it was different. This time I had gotten exactly what I wanted. But what if Pappi was right? I had heard stories about people who left Africa for America, never to be heard from again. What had happened to them? Would it happen to me? I had seen the movies to which Pappi had referred—full of drugs, murders, and mayhem. Most prominent in my mind was a scene, probably a kaleidoscope of images, in which one big black car pulled up to another big car, a gun emerged, someone was shot, and the big black car containing the shooter sped off with a squeal of tires. Would that happen to me?

During the flight I had tried to calm down. I had tried to persuade myself that my fears must be groundless. After all, hadn't Mummy and Pappi learned about St. John the Baptist by carefully scrutinizing its handsome brochure? Hadn't that brochure depicted a beautiful lake for skating, nuns strolling across the lawn in their black-and-white habits, girls in uniforms, tennis courts, and lots of other amenities? Had we not written a series of nice, long letters back and forth, confirming how wonderful it would be?

Once the Pan Am 747 had landed it was too late to turn back. Terror mixed with excitement: I was actually in America. I had butterflies in my stomach. It was as if I had won the lottery. Even if I never made it beyond the airport, for the rest of my life I could say that I had been to America. In the eyes of the Americo-Liberians, until you had been to America you were a native savage. Even some of the Americo-Liberians, who so loved to condescend to their "native" compatriots in Liberia, could not make this claim: "I've been to America." This had to be the equivalent of the epiphany that Ma Kema had experienced the day she first arrived in Mecca, Saudi Arabia, so many years before, the journey without which her life would not otherwise have been complete. As my turn to be interrogated by the immigration authorities approached I prayed that they would not turn me back. I nervously handed all my official documents over to the officer, including my F-1 visa, signifying that I was a student and that I had been accepted by a U.S. school. Yet, just based on my experience in England and traveling in Europe with my family, I had been through enough of these barriers to know that even if all of my documents were in order, I was still at the mercy and caprice of the individual officer. After I fielded a few perfunctory questions, the loud thump and quick release of the instrument used to stamp my oversized green Liberian passport signaled to me that I had made it. Now, officially, I was welcome to enter.

Unfortunately, the warm greeting I had pictured was not forthcoming. When I emerged from Customs I expected to be met by someone holding a sign with my name on it. (St. John's had assured my parents that this would be the case.) There were many uniformed drivers standing around and holding placards, but my name was not among them. It was already evening, winter in New York, and I was alone and miserable. I longed for Mummy and Pappi.

Eventually, I became convinced that no one was coming for me, and that I had to call the school. My challenge was to get some change for the pay phone. My heart pounding, I went to a nearby concession stand, and, handing over one of my $100 bills, asked the man behind the counter for change. He snorted, handed the bill back to me, and told me he could not change a hundred. The only other money I had was the $20 bill that Ma Kema had given me. There was no way I was going to surrender that precious keepsake. I had resolved to hold on to that link to her forever.

After waiting for almost half an hour, though, I was getting scared. I started to think that people were staring at me. Maybe I would get mugged, or even shot, like so many of those poor people in the American movies about life in New York. My resolve was ebbing; I had overestimated my own courage. It was January, and all I had to keep me warm was a lightweight, white wool cardigan.

I had only two choices: to beg for 10 cents from passing strangers or to surrender Ma Kema's twenty. It suddenly struck me that Ma Kema had intended with her gift to protect me from unknown dangers. I walked back to the concession stand and reluctantly handed over the bill.

The clerk held the bill between his thumb and forefinger, barely disguising his disgust. "What is this piece of shit?" he sneered. "Where the hell has it been?"

I had no words to answer him. Twenty-five years later I can still recall the deep piercing pain his words caused me. I had handed over my irreplaceable memento to this man in order to get a dime to make a phone call.

Ma Kema died less than a year later. Stranded in the States by the cost of a transatlantic plane ticket, I could not attend her funeral. I was told that people from all over Liberia attended it. Many were complete strangers to our immediate family, and yet all were part of Ma Kema's greater family. Even the poorest among them came bearing gifts of sheep, goats, cows, chicken, money, firewood. They came to show their respect and affection for a remarkable woman, a shrewd businesswoman, a natural entrepreneur who had worked hard and given back to her community—who throughout her life had welcomed and assisted every stranger she encountered with warmth and empathy.

At that time I did not fully grasp the scope of my own loss. Today, I would give almost anything to be able to speak with Ma Kema. And I would give almost anything to gain one-hundredth of the wisdom she possessed, or to accomplish even a fraction of the good she effected during her lifetime.

The saddest part of this story is that as it turned out, I need not have surrendered Ma Kema's gift. As I was digging through my bag in search of the St. John's phone number I saw somebody running in my direction. It was the school's representative, apologizing profusely for being late.

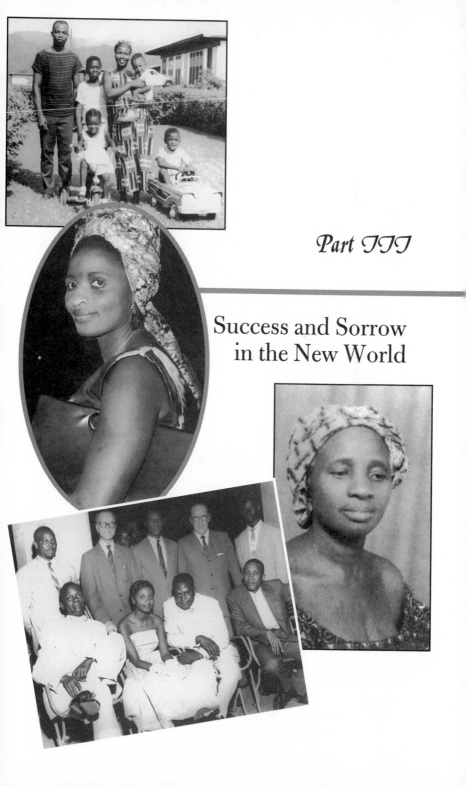

Part III

Success and Sorrow
in the New World

10

Coming to America

She had red hair, freckles, a beautiful smile. She was not particularly tall, and she weighed something over 250 pounds. I thought gleefully that I would soon be that big, too, because in America I could eat all the fast-food I wanted, at any time that I wanted. I had heard Americo-Liberians talk about McDonald's, and it seemed as though if you hadn't been to a McDonald's, or if there was not a McDonald's in your country, you were not yet a part of the civilized world.

Kathy and I wound our way through the outdoor parking lot, and she headed toward a beige station wagon. I peered around each car that we passed, trying to avoid getting mugged. Kathy must have noticed this strange behavior, even though I did my best to conceal my fear. When we finally got to the car she told me that I was skinny. I thought she was insulting or criticizing me, just as people had done at home when they thought I was too thin and would then ask my parents if I was sick or if they weren't feeding me. It wasn't until much later that I discovered that Kathy was paying me a compliment. She then asked if I wanted to make a stop at the nearby HoneyBee Chicken. I politely declined. I certainly did not want to be involved in a shoot-out in a fast-food restaurant on my first day in America. Anyway, the combination of chicken and honey sounded strange and unappetizing. The memory of Pappi's famous pepper chicken came to mind, filling me with nostalgia and making me homesick.

I slumped deep into the passenger seat. My plan was to keep my head well below the window in the event that one of those big black sedans pulled up alongside us and began blasting away. But I just could not resist the urge to gaze out of the window at the sights: the mile-high buildings of New York City in the distance; the lights; the gigantic billboards; the multiple-lane highways; and the ramps and bridges that wove in and out of each other like an industrial tapestry of concrete and steel. At the tollbooths, the collectors did not tote guns. Kathy did not have to bargain her way through the barrier; she simply handed over the posted fare, and we were free to proceed. When we arrived at St. John's a few hours later, it was quite late at night. Kathy helped me with my suitcases and led me to the dormitory and my room. My roommate was already fast asleep; and did not wake up when we turned the lights on. I quietly changed, climbed into bed, and cried myself to sleep. I would have given anything to be back in Yekepa at that moment.

When I woke up it was to the sound of loud disco music coming out of a clock radio on the nearby bed stand. My roommate, whose name was Kathryn, used the radio to wake herself up in the morning. I had never seen one before, and was really impressed at the concept of a clock that could wake you up to music. Thinking of Ma Kema's simple folding alarm clock that she treasured so much, I wondered what she would have thought of this one. Probably not much, but nevertheless I thought it would be a nifty thing to have and decided to procure one for myself as soon as possible. When Kathryn saw that I was awake she gave me a big smile and a "Hi!"

Kathryn was black, although not nearly as dark as me, and huge. I was amazed. I had now met two Americans. Kathy was big; Kathryn was bigger. She must have weighed 300 pounds. How big did these Americans get? In a rush of words she told me she was from New York, her boyfriend was Puerto Rican, and that he was 35 years old. I was scandalized. I had never ever even had a boyfriend. If she was trying to shock me, she was definitely succeeding. Also, I had never experienced such instant and intimate personal disclosure. It seemed that she was revealing to me in five minutes the type of information that it would have taken me five years to share with a close friend. I wanted her to stop, because somehow I felt that she was contaminating me, but I did not know how to communicate that, so I remained silent.

She asked me why I was so black. She asked me if I lived in a hut in Africa. She could never, ever imagine herself marrying an African, she said matter-of-factly. She then asked me if I had ever tried something called "reefer." She had smoked "a joint" just that past weekend, she told me conspiratorially. I had never heard of reefers, or of joints, but I figured it would be smart to just keep nodding in response to everything she said.

I had only been at St. John's a few hours, but already I could sense that this was nothing like boarding school in England. At Leelands a major part of the fun was being able to be naughty, with its risk of being caught. Of course, there naughty meant sneaking food into the dormitories, getting out of bed after lights-out to have pillow fights, and reading banned adventure books by Enid Blyton. Poor Pappi. He thought the Scandinavians had loose morals; what would he say about this? He would have put me on the plane back to Liberia the following day. If Kathryn was representative of the school, then the brochure that they had sent to us, which we had pored over so painstakingly, was terribly misleading.

None of us in Yekepa had had any reason to know about the highly effective and particularly American art of hype: Put the absolute best face on something and then claim that this ideal face is in fact the rule rather than the exception. I soon learned that form is often more important than substance, and that the meanings in what are otherwise the simplest and most universal of concepts is not necessarily objective. For example, the word "lake," which was used in the St. John's promotional material, can be used to depict anything from a mere pond, which was more reflective of the tiny pool of water that the school had on its property, to the Atlantic Ocean, with no qualification required.

When Kathryn and I made our way downstairs to breakfast my new schoolmates stared at me and whispered. Because I was arriving in the middle of the school year and did not yet have the school uniform—a Scottish kilt with a white top and a blue blazer or sweater—I stood out even more than I otherwise would have. The headmaster of the school, Reverend Jim Cromley, welcomed me and invited me to come to his office after breakfast. As soon as I showed up there he asked if there was anything that I wanted. "Yes," I murmured, "I want to call home." What I did not tell him was that I was planning to ask Pappi to have the school send me back to Liberia. I already had my return ticket; it could not be that complicated. The reverend must have suspected something, because he told me that I would feel very much at home at St. John's after a little while.

I spent hours and hours that first day trying to get through to Mummy and Pappi. This meant not only getting through to Monrovia, but also lucking into a subsequent connection all the way up to Yekepa. When I finally reached them I began to cry. I told them that I was cold, and that I wanted to come home. What could they say? They both advised me to be strong, and to give it a try.

But the whole environment and experience was foreign to me, and I really felt that I did not belong. In Liberia, I had been teased and traumatized for being skinny. Here, everyone kept telling me how beautiful I was because I was skinny. In Liberia, one did not boast about one's modest origins. Here, coming from the "projects," like my roommate claimed she did, seemed to be a point of immense pride.

The racial divide at St. John's was actually a yawning chasm. Among the Americans, the white and black students hardly mixed at all, except in gym classes, when intramural teams were selected by the instructor. My classmates, and even many of the faculty, naturally assumed that the color of one's skin determined the kind of music one liked (whites, rock music; blacks, soul music), the way one spoke, and a host of other things that I had never before associated with race. But I was soon to learn from certain comments made that Jews were assigned to yet another category, or perhaps a subcategory, and that if someone had a name that sounded Jewish but was not, that person would go to great lengths to clarify this point. Foreigners were in a separate category altogether: We were outside the matrix, and thus less susceptible to easy typecasting. Indeed, foreignness was one of the few factors that seemed to outweigh race at St. John's. The few international students there tended to hang out with each other, united as we were by the fact that we came from such faraway places as Ethiopia, Liberia, Iran, Thailand, Germany—and even Canada, which by the parochial standards at St. John's also was considered foreign.

From my perspective, our classes were far too easy. For example, in English we studied grammar fundamentals that I had mastered years before in England. Soon I noticed that many of the black students were far behind the others in terms of academic performance. They tended to say things like "you is" and "he be" and confused verb tenses. At the time I assumed that these were honest mistakes rather than affectations or political statements, but the teachers did not bother to correct them. They would never have gotten away with that at Leelands or even at the LAMCO International School. I could not believe that Pappi was paying so much money for this.

A few weeks into the semester Ms. Price, the English teacher, informed us that the class was being split into two. She did not say why. She listed the names of those who would be in the first (advanced) group, and then the names of those who would be in the second group. All the whites were in one group, and the blacks were in the other. One white girl, Ruth, who was slow, wound up in the black group.

I knew that they had made a mistake in putting me with the black-plus-Ruth group. But I had arrived only recently in America and hadn't yet learned the highly effective art of assertiveness and confrontation, particularly when it came to my relations with people in authority. I also thought about Pappi and remembered how he had told me that if I demonstrated my academic capabilities and worked hard, I would win the respect and recognition of both my peers and my superiors. Sure enough, within a week I was moved into the advanced English class. Not long after this shift, the school had to recruit a French woman to teach me French because I was too advanced for the first teacher and kept correcting her. The same soon proved true in math (I ran through two teachers), and I began taking science courses at a neighboring Catholic boys' school, Delbarton's, where they offered more advanced courses, with two other girls, one of them an Ethiopian named Nitirwork, who became one of my best friends.

I excelled in sports, especially those that I had played in England and in Liberia and those that depended a lot on being swift of feet: lacrosse, tennis, soccer, and track and field. Slowly, in and out of the classroom, I tested myself, and I became convinced that I could succeed in America.

As in England, the biggest problem for me in America was where I would stay during the school holidays. While all the other students, including the foreign ones, had family in the United States, I did not. Shortly after I arrived at St. John's, I had tried to make contact with Claudius, who was enrolled in college in Bridgeport, Connecticut, not more than a few hours' drive from where I was in New Jersey. I wanted us to meet, but he was vague with me on the phone and kept putting me off. He appeared to be interested in other pursuits—and tennis was no longer among them. He told me he was actually thinking of leaving school altogether. I just could not understand this. When he had left Liberia a year earlier, tennis had been his entire life—he lived to play every day. What could have accounted for the change? Both Mummy and Pappi knew that something was amiss, but for the better part of a year Claudius had managed to convince them otherwise. In Pappi's eyes it must have seemed as though the disparity between Claudius and me was growing. I was the good girl, working hard to succeed and please; Claudius, on the other hand, while he seemed to excel at anything he applied himself to, often applied himself to the wrong things or chose not to apply himself at all. He was almost unbelievably charming. As a result, he usually was able to get whatever he wanted with a minimum amount of effort. It had been like that for as long as I could remember, and I just could not understand why he did not put his gifts to better use.

Pappi's words—"it is important that you not do anything to bring shame upon the family"—were always in my mind. Perhaps to make up for Claudius's increasingly erratic behavior, I studied all the harder. I spent my short holidays alone at the nearby Convent of St. John's. Okay, I thought, here I can spend my otherwise empty days studying without distraction. There certainly weren't any boys around my all-girls' school to distract me from my schoolwork. I soon learned how to teach myself most of what I needed to know in the coming term, and was also able to start preparing for college in the United States, as that had been the ultimate objective of my coming to America. I had already decided that I wanted to study international affairs, and my teachers told me that the Georgetown University School of Foreign Service in Washington, D.C. was the best place for me to go. I also was told that it was hard to get into, and therefore I knew I needed to work hard.

Flights to Europe were relatively cheap. So that first summer I went to stay with family friends in Norway. However, things had changed, especially the fact that I had aged by five years since my periodic visits to Norway when I was a student in England. I was now almost sixteen, and the father of the family, a man whom I had loved and trusted like a father from the age of six and who had taught me, along with his own daughter, how to ski, fish, and sail, decided that his feelings for me were no longer paternal. That was it for summer vacation in Europe: back to the convent I went.

There were other disturbing changes in my life. Pappi and Mummy told me little at first, but Liberia was at a boiling point. I had taken up Pappi's habit of listening to the BBC every morning, and I was often able to glean enough information from the international news reports to understand that the country I had left behind was undergoing a political makeover, and that even in our little town of Yekepa stability was threatened. Opposition to the government was becoming increasingly vocal and threatening. As I have indicated earlier, many of these changes were fueled primarily by foreign investments in the country, which had led to new roads being constructed farther and farther up into the hinterland, and more indigenous Liberians being educated, often at missionary schools, but also abroad, in America and Europe. These citizens were becoming increasingly preoccupied with the idea of democracy and its potential power, which they felt had been denied to them for over 150 years of Americo-Liberian rule.

Earlier in his presidency, President William R. Tolbert, Jr., had actively discouraged the return of these overseas-educated Liberians to the country, fearing that they would seed political subversion. But in 1978, in an attempt to create some form of national consensus and prevent further challenge to the one-party system, he issued an invitation to all self-exiled dissidents and Liberians studying abroad to return home to help build the country. Tolbert's policy reversal was no doubt also inspired by the visit of U.S. president Jimmy Carter to Liberia that same year. As part of a regional crowd-pleasing tour, more like a press junket cum photo op than a serious political mission, a pattern that would become common with subsequent U.S. presidents touring the region to demonstrate, unconvincingly, Africa's politically correct but ultimately spurious strategic importance to the United States, Carter, his wife, Rosalynn, and their daughter, Amy, made a six-hour whistle-stop visit to Liberia. Carter's contact with the Liberian "natives" on this jaunt was limited to a group of chiefs assembled at the executive mansion, Liberia's White House. They were there to offer him bowls of kola nuts and rice while he discussed "serious" matters of state with the more enlightened Americo-Liberian president. Nevertheless, political reform must have been discussed sometime between the main course and dessert, because it was shortly after this visit that Tolbert reached out in earnest to the Liberian expatriate community.

Many responded to the call, though not necessarily those Tolbert had had in mind. Most who returned were not returning for a slice of the political pie; nor even to bake a new pie. They were determined to take over the kitchen. Added to this political landscape were a number of economic factors that were well beyond the government's ability to control. In particular, world prices for Liberia's principal export commodities, rubber, timber, and iron ore, were declining precipitously, and there was no reason to expect a reversal of the trend. Meanwhile, the price of petroleum, one of the country's major imports, was soaring. To make matters worse, Liberia's principal foreign investors—all major sources of government revenue and employment in the economy— also were being heavily affected. Firestone, which had helped fuel the Liberian economy for decades, had also run out of steam (or, shall we say, was tapped out)[1] due to the increasing supply of natural rubber elsewhere around the globe and the growing use of synthetic alternatives to rubber, both of which pushed down prices.

More and more Liberians were falling below the poverty line. As if this were not bad enough, the government decided that it would raise the price of both imported and locally produced rice, Liberia's staple food, by up to 50 percent. Presumably the goal of the price adjustment was to discourage the import of rice and encourage its domestic production. A major landowner and rice producer himself, Tolbert and others in his government were accused of putting their personal interests ahead of those of the people, as they stood to profit immensely from the price hikes and import curbs. Tolbert had painted a bull's-eye right in the middle of his forehead.

On April 14, 1979, in what became infamously known as the "rice riots," hundreds of ordinary Liberian citizens descended into the streets of Monrovia in protest. They were spurred by one of the new opposition groups, which included among their leaders some of those Liberians who had returned recently to Liberia at the president's invitation. The government responded in its customary manner, by sending the army to control the crowds. The army troops, mostly made up of indigenous Liberians from numerous ethnic groups, refused to fire on their own people.

Tolbert invoked a mutual defense pact that Liberia had signed with neighboring Guinea, which resulted in the dispatch of troops from Guinea to help the police force reestablish law and order in Monrovia. In the end, between 50 and 100 rioters were killed, many others were jailed, and all over the city looters rampaged. The resulting damage to private property was estimated to be in the millions of dollars. The writ of habeas corpus was suspended, but facing tremendous international pressure, and the fact that the government was about to host the annual meeting of the African heads of states and that human rights in Africa was the key agenda item for that meeting, the government could not escape the irony and potential embarrassment, even by African standards. Eventually, therefore, it released the prisoners and abandoned the proposed price hikes. The opposition had tasted victory and the government had shown its vulnerability.

Amid all this domestic turbulence, including an economy spiraling out of control, Tolbert was trying to carve out a grander role for himself, one that would ensure that his name was etched in world history. At the shockingly insensitive "let them eat cake" cost of close to a $100 million, he built a huge, insanely luxurious complex to host the annual meeting of the Organization of African Unity in his bid to become the organization's leader. Sure enough, he was elected chairman of the moribund organization during its four-day star-studded convention in Monrovia.

My family was still in Yekepa, seemingly far away from the events unfolding in Monrovia, but the news traveled quickly, even in that infrastructure-challenged country. This was the first time in my parents' lifetime that Liberia, which traditionally had been one of Africa's most stable nations (by dint of force rather than by democracy), had experienced such a bold challenge to the government's authority.

Initially it was the fall in the global price of iron ore that had the most direct impact on LAMCO and its residents. Here LAMCO had a quantity and a quality problem. The LAMCO engineers had discovered that the original prospectors or geologists had vastly overestimated the iron ore content in the mines in Yekepa. Moreover, after almost 20 years of exploration, the quality of the ore on the Liberia side of the Nimba Mountains was eroding. To reach the higher grade ore would mean higher excavation costs. There was one alternative that LAMCO could and did explore. Part of the Nimba mountain range was located across the border, in Guinea. For a long time this had been an issue of contention between Liberia and Guinea, the border of which was less than 10 miles from

Yekepa. This dispute was why Pappi had been decorated by Liberia's then-president Tubman for securing the maps that proved that at least part of the mountain range was in Liberia.

LAMCO management believed that the company could continue for about another 20 years if LAMCO could negotiate with the government of Guinea to continue its mining operations on the other side of the border, where there was still a lot of untapped high-grade iron ore.

A developing country itself, with an even lower per capita GNP than Liberia, Guinea decided that it wanted its own Yekepa—it too wanted railroads, shipping harbors, loading docks, swimming pools, tennis courts, houses. Instead of using the existing infrastructure it had built in Liberia, LAMCO would have to replicate in Guinea the investments it already had made in Liberia in exchange for the right to extend its operations to Guinea. But with growing competition from iron ore deposits in Brazil, Australia, India, and elsewhere, the proposed deal was a nonstarter.

It must have been about then that Pappi really began to wonder if he had made the right decision in building his dream house in Yekepa. Perhaps Las Palmas would have been the better spot after all. With the passing of the generalissimo, Spain already had discarded much of its political baggage. Liberia, on the other hand, was on the precipice of the kind of political upheaval that had hitherto seemed impossible in our tranquil little hamlet. Factoring in the political situation and the reality of the global market for iron ore, LAMCO's long-term business prospects were not bright; management believed that they probably could operate in Yekepa for about five to seven more years at the most, and at that with a much reduced workforce. To a realist, the future looked dim. But Pappi was ever the optimist.

I was spared many of these details. Perhaps Mummy and Pappi, who wrote to me regularly, did not want me to worry or be distracted from my studies and college applications. By contrast, they, along with Herbert and Abayomi, who were now 14 and 13 respectively, were living with these uncertainties from day to day. Little could have prepared them, or me, an ocean away, for what was to follow almost a year to the day after the "rice riots."

In the early hours of April 12, 1980, the government of President Tolbert was overthrown in a violent military coup. A renegade band of soldiers, led by an illiterate 27-year-old army sergeant named Samuel Doe, who belonged to the indigenous Krahn tribe, stormed the executive mansion and shot and killed President Tolbert as he lay in bed with his wife, Victoria, beside him. The First Lady's life was spared, though she was taken prisoner by the rebels. The rebels then disemboweled the president before descending into the courtyard of the mansion, where they killed every military officer in sight.

When I went to bed in my dorm at St. John's on Friday April 11, the only thing on my mind was Georgetown: I had been told that the letter accepting me or turning me down would arrive any day now. I was convinced that the answer to my future lay in that letter. So when I got up Saturday morning and turned on the BBC world news, I listened in shock to what was happening in Monrovia.

I immediately tried to call home, to no avail; all the circuits to the country were blocked or busy. Probably every Liberian outside of the country, and anyone who knew anyone in Liberia, was trying to call into the country. I kept on trying, day after day, in a state of utter panic. I knew that it was just as difficult for them to reach me by phone, as their international calls had to pass through the international exchange in Monrovia. In the intervening days, my most reliable source of news on Liberia was the BBC, but they only came on a couple of hours each day, and Liberia was just one of the many topics covered. These were the precable, pre-Internet days, and even the scraps thrown my way by the BBC were better than the mere seconds of footage—days after the coup—that the major U.S. television networks deigned to show. Of course all the international news only covered Monrovia, certainly not the far-off town of Yekepa. So without speaking to my parents I had no way of knowing whether or not Yekepa had been directly affected by the horrific events in the capital. Each day the situation became even more menacing, as top government officials were rounded up.

My family finally got through to me on April 15, the same day that I received my letter from Georgetown. I remember noting that it was a thick envelope—I already knew what that meant—but there was no room in my heart for celebration.

The first thing that Pappi told me was that they were all well, but that Mummy had been arrested and jailed for a few hours.

It turned out that in the immediate aftermath of the government overthrow, some young men with bloodshot eyes in military fatigues had gone swaggering to the LAMCO hospital, brandishing their AK-47s. They accused Mummy, who was at her job as head nurse, of not showing them enough respect. Poor Pappi had to drive around Yekepa all day, trying to reason with a bunch of illiterate thugs to let Mummy out of jail. Eventually, with the personal intervention of the chief executive of LAMCO, she was released.

After I heard this story there was not much that Pappi could say to convince me that all was fine. He had no way of knowing what the future held. None of us did.

About a week after my conversation with my parents the world learned just how brutal Doe's new government was. Amid much drunken revelry, and a kangaroo court presided over by a hastily convened military tribunal, most of the top government officials, among them thirteen cabinet ministers, including the father of a friend, Charles Cecil Dennis, who was foreign minister in the Tolbert government and a graduate of Georgetown, were killed in a gruesome public display that was videotaped and subsequently broadcast across the globe. Prior to his arraignment Dennis had gone to the U.S. embassy begging to be granted protection. In his official capacity he had played host to President Jimmy Carter and Secretary of State Cyrus Vance when they had visited Liberia in 1978. He had also received red carpet treatment on his numerous visits to America. He had every reason to believe that he would be protected. But he was not.[2] In what the jubilant masses garishly called the "Monrovia Beach Party," Dennis and the other former dignitaries were stripped to their undergarments, tied to telephone poles lined up along the Atlantic Ocean, and shot execution-style as they pleaded for their lives. Mobs of citizens filled the streets in celebration of the ouster of the Tolbert government, dancing and singing as they went around looting and seizing the property of the murdered officials, and terrifying Americo-Liberians, who were running for their lives.

Doe immediately suspended the U.S.-inspired constitution and established a People's Redemption Council (PRC)[3] to rule the country under his leadership. The PRC was dominated by members of his own ethnic clan. Any Americo-Liberians who could quickly fled to the United States. The irony was that many of them were as poor as the indigenous people themselves. The group of Americo-Liberians who had held on to power was itself an elite subset, with the same few families ruling the country for decades. But the rebels were not going to split hairs over that distinction—any Americo-Liberian was a target.

Once the initial euphoria was over, those who sang and danced at the "beach party" realized that their celebrations had been premature. There were not enough spoils to go around, and the PRC was not interested in sharing the spoils that did exist. It was not long before the mob was turning on itself, with ethnic rifts being encouraged and exacerbated by Doe in his merciless policy to divide and conquer. He attempted to affiliate the normally apolitical Mandingo with his new government. As the Mandingo were a powerful economic constituency, and widely perceived as foreigners in Liberia, he hoped that he could ingratiate himself to them and use them to stave off moves by other ethnic groups, in particular the Gio and Mano, who were from Nimba. The Mandingo accepted his overtures, but Doe's Machiavellian strategy ultimately proved disastrous and costly to the Mandingo, who were merely practicing their long-standing tradition of adaptation to survive.

I waited a couple of weeks before telling Mummy and Pappi about my acceptance at Georgetown. Although Liberia seemed to have stabilized somewhat, I was still not sure what lay in store for me. Could Pappi still even afford to send me to Georgetown University? Who could predict what would happen in Yekepa, given the new political and economic realities? Perhaps the entire family would have to be uprooted; Pappi had already decided that if things continued to deteriorate, he would look into the Las Palmas option, meaning that he would abandon all that he had spent his life building and start over again from scratch in a country where he did not even speak the language. Mummy and my brother Herbert had been planning to come to my graduation. I realized that that trip was no longer certain. I felt guilty for being spared the uncertainty they were living with day to day.

I wondered what Claudius was thinking. I had not been in touch with him for months. From what I had been told of what was going on in his life at the time, I doubt that he was giving Liberia much thought. Even in the midst of the crisis in Liberia, Pappi's letters to me were becoming increasingly despondent over Claudius, who was keeping Mummy and Pappi completely in the dark about his activities. This was especially nerve-wracking for Pappi, who had still not relinquished his preconceptions of life in America as dangerous, especially for a young man.

Claudius did not even call me after the coup, and I did not know where to reach him—I suspected by now that he had dropped out of college—so I called friends of our family in New York City whom I knew kept in touch with him. All they were able to tell me was that Claudius was spending most of his time gambling. He had given up tennis, lost his scholarship, and abandoned his studies entirely. I soon learned that he had taken off to Norway to visit other family friends, where he had fallen in love with a beautiful Norwegian girl who wanted him to marry her and stay in Norway for good. Apparently, this had the effect of sending him running back to the States. He did not bother to reenroll at Bridgeport—or, for that matter, at any university. I soon learned through the New York friends of the family that Claudius was involved romantically, to the point of obsession, with a much older Liberian woman in New York.

In addition to the anxiety he was causing our parents, I also was worried about the impact his behavior was having on Herbert and Abayomi, who looked up to him. It hurt me all the more knowing full well that both Pappi and Mummy were now waking up at the crack of dawn each day to work in the restaurant and laboring until well past midnight, with Mummy continuing to hold her job as head nurse at the LAMCO hospital, to make ends meet. The economy had taken a nosedive with the installment of the Doe government in Monrovia; ore prices were plummeting; government corruption was rife. Few legitimate foreign investors would come into Liberia now.

I graduated from St. John's as covaledictorian, and Mummy and Herbert were there to watch me, but the ceremony was bittersweet. I knew how much Pappi had wanted to attend, but either he or Mummy needed to remain in Yekepa to keep the restaurant open; every dime made was vital to their survival and our education. It had been almost three years since I had seen him, and it would be another full year before I would get the chance to see him again. His unselfishness never ceased to amaze me.

At the graduation, just before I was to give my speech, the president of the school's alumni association told a story to the assembled crowd of students, teachers, and parents. "One thing you can all count on," she told them, "is that Monique will always tell you the truth and say exactly what is on her mind.

"Each year, the association awards an academic scholarship," she continued. "Monique was one of the two finalists, and the choice between the other finalist and Monique finally came down to their personal interviews with the committee. During Monique's interview, she was asked whether, if given the opportunity to do it all over, she would again choose to come to St. John's. In response to this question, she instinctively said 'No.' "

Until then I had often pondered why I hadn't been awarded the fellowship, but not wanting to be a bad sport about it all, I had decided not to pursue it. Finally, as I sat there in the front row, my question was answered. My answer—more along the lines of the court jester stating the unpleasant truth than a cash-strapped pupil eager to prostrate herself for a couple of thousand dollars—had cost me the fellowship. To think that I had assumed that I would be rewarded for my candor!

I wondered how Mummy, sitting in the audience with Herbert, was taking this, especially when $2,000 meant so much to our family. I had answered the way I did because of all the special measures that the school had been obliged to take to accommodate my academic needs. My response had been equally influenced by the high degree of social dysfunction that I perceived within the student body. Even today I am not sure what lesson we students were supposed to draw from this impromptu exposé. I did get some vindication, however. Not long after my graduation in 1980, St. John's was closed down and turned into a shelter for troubled young adults; as far as I was concerned, that is what it had always been. Not that I should hold a grudge, really. St. John's ultimately did right by me, and ensured, by occasionally extraordinary means, that I got the education that I needed to get into Georgetown.

And I was no longer the terrified and lonely little girl who had arrived on that bitterly cold January night two and a half years earlier with a head full of distorted ideas about America. Now I was much tougher, far wiser, and a person of whom Pappi could be even more proud.

Georgetown, Johns Hopkins, and Sorrow

When the much anticipated day for registration and orientation finally arrived I took a train from New Jersey to Georgetown. By this time I was quite accustomed to handling these major life changes on my own. However, I was still melancholy—and envious—when I saw my fellow freshmen being moved in by their parents, who helped them set up their dorm rooms in a way that made them look as if they had lived there for years. My roommate was French, but she was not arriving until the second semester, so I had the room all to myself. That gave me plenty of room, but also left me a little lonely.

During orientation week I set out to make friends. As had been the case at St. John's I soon found that I had the most in common with the international students, of whom there were many, from all corners of the Earth. These associations also evolved because the school tended to treat the foreign students as though we were from another planet and did not know right from left. But of course we were still in America, and some of the odd social patterns that I had noticed at St. John's also manifested themselves at Georgetown. On my first day at Georgetown, I met three people who would turn out to be my closest friends during the next four years: Alfredo was from Hong Kong; Ulrike (Ri) was from Sweden; and Juanita was from Brazil.

The school threw a big orientation party, which Alfredo, Ri, Juanita, and I went to together. The place was mobbed, but we plunged into the crowd. A couple of hours later a young man tapped me on the shoulder and invited me to a party that he said was being sponsored by the "BSA." I had no idea what the BSA was, but I was happy for an excuse to bolt the orientation party melee. I told him that I would bring my friends along.

We met up with the guy on the sidewalk as planned, but when he saw the four of us, he quickly took me aside, pointed at his arm, and whispered that only people of "our" complexion could go to the party. "BSA," he explained, stood for "Black Student Association."

I was speechless. I could not believe that I would be invited to a party based solely on the color of my skin—and that my friends would be turned away for that same reason. Did this young man and his fellow BSA members really think that my skin color might make me a more compatible, congenial, interesting, or likable person? Did they think the opposite of my white friends? Ulrike was the fairest. Juanita (whose father was British) and Alfredo (half Chinese, half Portuguese) both had roughly the same, slightly darker, complexion. Did that mean that Juanita and Alfredo would fit in slightly better than Ri (although still not well enough) at the BSA party? I told the young man, coldly, that I did not want to go to any party that excluded my friends.

That strange racial undercurrent continued throughout my years at Georgetown. I did not feel that I belonged to any particular group. Nor did I want to, because it was clear that such belonging would have limited my opportunities. The upshot was that while I made friends across a wide range of interests and nationalities, I did not make many friends among the black Americans at Georgetown. Those that I did make, I made because I liked them as individuals, not because of the hue of their skin. For the rest, I could not relate to the antagonism they often felt toward people of other colors. I could not explain to them why I did not have a "natural" affinity for soul music over other music genres. I could not explain why their decision to sit together in isolated sections of the cafeteria struck me as a kind of self-imposed exile—or even worse, a nascent apartheid. To the extent that I thought about racial issues at all, I believed instinctively that we were all alike. Many of the black Americans despised me for that belief, or at best thought I was odd. I heard that I was referred to as an Oreo cookie—dark on the outside, white on the inside.

It was at Georgetown that I first realized that education was a process, rather than a goal. I was enrolled in the School of Foreign Affairs, which had an ongoing rivalry with the College of Arts and Sciences as to which one was the toughest to get into. Of course, I believed my school was harder. At Georgetown I had my first in-depth encounters with Plato, Socrates, Descartes, Teilhard de Chardin, Locke, de Toqueville, St. Augustine, Karl Marx, St. Ignatius of Loyola, Adam Smith. It was also the first time that I seriously began to contemplate the meaning of life and to realize that things did not always have to be as they were or as I was told they were. I actually could effect change. The Jesuits were opening me up to a whole new world. One in particular, Father Thomas King, had a tremendous impact on me. Even though I was not a Catholic and had never voluntarily attended mass before, I made sure that every Sunday night at ten o'clock I was at his service. Father King must have been in his mid-fifties at the time, an ascetic and a most profound thinker. His sermons were not like lectures.

They were lessons on how to live a good life, and I hung on his every word as I watched his hands move in the air. He sought to impart the unity of knowledge; that is, that science and theology are not mutually exclusive, a concept that I found appealing.

I had always thought of priests as stern and pious people, at least until I came to America. At Georgetown, I discovered that the Jesuits were of another breed. Some of them certainly knew how to let their hair down. They would drink and party with the students and more than one of them propositioned me. One of the most influential priests, Father Otto Hentz, ran a tight clique of students in which I found myself a hanger-on, by way of Ri, who had fallen in love with one of Otto's followers. Out of each incoming crop of freshmen Otto anointed a small group of clean-cut, all-American young men whom he chose to mentor through their four years at Georgetown and for the rest of their lives. It operated like a medieval cult, with all the requisite plots and intrigues, and met once a week; nobody outside the club ever knew what they talked about or did during those meetings. "Otto's boys," as the students called them, enjoyed various perks, including periodic meetings with the president of the university and even, it was rumored, special access to highly competitive scholarships. Otto tolerated the girlfriends of his chosen only grudgingly and treated them as second-class citizens, and it struck me one day, after observing the whole scene for a while, that this priest's behavior was no different from what I had experienced my first night at college with the guy from the BSA.

Georgetown was the first time I encountered running as a business, with serious competition, contenders, and sponsors. The Georgetown athletics department operated as if it were an independent subsidiary of the larger corporation of the university. I hadn't even known that one could come to the school on a sports scholarship—Juanita (six-foot-three) and Ri (five-foot-ten) were both on full basketball scholarships. They encouraged me to try out for the track team, which I did. When I met with the coach I was absolutely amazed at the degree of professionalism that was applied to sports. For the first time I discovered an institution where athletics were as important, if not more important, than academics. At least that was the case within the world of the full and partial scholarship athletes that I unwittingly threw myself into. I was one of only two walk-ons that year; that is, we were not scouted out of high school by the coach for the specific purpose of running for Georgetown. On the day of my trials I arrived with my tennis sneakers on. I had absolutely no idea that there were shoes designed specifically for running. That was soon to change. By the end of the first week I, like the rest of my team, was a walking billboard for Nike Corp. The shoes, the sweat suits, the shorts, the T-shirts were all provided by Nike. Being on the team gave me access to extraordinary training facilities and world-class coaches. I had never felt so pampered, as far as sports were concerned. And although we were obliged to train hard, we were given excellent physical care.

Until then running for me had been all fun and something that I assumed I almost naturally excelled at, thanks to the stereotyping at Leelands. But here, natural talent was just the beginning—maybe 10 percent. The rest was hard work, as I was about to discover. For the first couple of weeks I left practices hyperventilating and in serious doubt as to the wisdom of pursuing this. After all, 99 percent of the women and men on the track were being paid (via scholarships, that is) to do this; they did not have a choice. I did. Eventually, my passion for running won out, and I stuck with it, although I did not make track the sole purpose of my existence, as so many others on the team did.

During my second year, one of the girls on the team, one of the best runners in the entire country, Mary Wazeter, used to do some self-training at the same early hour I did. She was on a full athletic scholarship, a full ride, as we called it. I watched her, absolutely amazed at how much she put into her workout and how tiny she was. She would tell me how she felt fat, at all of 90 pounds, and how she wanted to do so much better. She felt that she was not measuring up. I could not understand where this woman was coming from. If she thinks she is big, I thought to myself, she must think I am an elephant.

It was shortly after I met Mary that I heard about anorexia nervosa and bulimia for the first time. I hadn't even heard about it at St. John's, much less in Liberia. In Liberia, food was never fetishized; you ate because you could and were grateful for the opportunity. In Liberia, there was so much else to worry about and so few resources that physical health took precedence over mental well-being. There was crazy and there was sane, and nothing in-between. I did not meet a psychologist in Africa until I was well into my thirties—and she was from South Africa. I have yet to meet an African psychiatrist.

It was not long after these independent track sessions that Mary, at home in Wilkes-Barre, Pennsylvania, on school break, found a railroad bridge and jumped right over it, into the ice-covered waters of the Susquehanna River. Her suicide attempt failed, but she became a paraplegic, confined to a wheelchair, probably for life, an experience she later wrote about in a memoir called *Dark Marathon*. In a way, it was because of Mary that I took up long-distance running. There was a 10K race in her hometown to raise money for her medical costs. Until then I was a pure track runner—long distance for me meant 400 meters. But I wanted to show support for Mary and her family, so I trained for the 10K. From the moment I crossed the finish line I was hooked.

During my four years at Georgetown I visited Liberia only once, in 1981 at the end of my freshman year. By then the 28-year-old Samuel Doe and his Peoples' Redemption Council had been in power for a little over a year. It was my first trip back since leaving for St. John's in 1978, and I could already sense that things were changing for the worse. As Mark Huband, the former West African correspondent for the *Financial Times,* put it in the introduction to his book, *The Liberian Civil War*, "Quickly, the PRC came to rule over a country which attracted bounty-hunters, both foreign and Liberian, keen to exploit the inexperience of the new government, bribe their way into contracts, use lax banking laws to launder earnings from the international narcotics trade and siphon off funds granted the new regime in foreign aid." (Mark Huband, *The Liberian Civil War*, London, F. Cass, p. xix)

Rather than creating the national unity that he had promised, Doe pursued a policy of divisiveness, courting especially the loyalty of those of his own tribe, the Krahn, from which group he formed the core of his government. He viewed the members of the Mano and Gio tribes, the groups that constituted most of the population in Nimba, as the enemy, and sought to silence them at all cost. On one occasion a group of randomly selected Mano and Gio were arrested near Yekepa by government troops, taken up to an isolated area in the iron ore mines, and shot to death. Most of LAMCO's local employees belonged to these two groups. My nurse, Rebecca, our houseboy, Peter, and almost all our domestic help and those who worked in the restaurant were Mano or Gio, and they had never had problems with each other or with other tribes before.

The political uncertainty generated by the coup took an economic toll on Liberia that trickled all the way down to businesses like Pappi's restaurant. I was finally old enough to realize just how much it took for this little operation to fund my expensive education now and Herbert and Abayomi's in the future: Mummy and Pappi had decided that they would send the boys to America for college. The trips that Pappi still had to occasionally take to Monrovia were fraught with even more danger than before, as government soldiers manning impromptu checkpoints and looking for money to buy their next bottle of beer, their next cigarette, or their next stash of hashish could emerge anywhere along the 200-mile stretch of road from Yekepa to Monrovia. The wrong look or the wrong answer could have put a bullet in Pappi's head. More and more frequently he was asked for his naturalization papers, as he was still considered a foreigner in Liberia, even though he had been a citizen for over 20 years. Yet if this bothered or scared Pappi he never let on about it.

Doe was an anticommunist, which made him of some value to America during the still frigid Cold War years in which he was in office. The U.S. government, led by Ronald Reagan and under the guidance of his assistant secretary of state for African affairs, Chester Crocker (who coincidentally was my faculty supervisor during my first year at Georgetown), provided Doe with substantial military and financial backing, close to $500 million, between 1980 and 1985. Much of the money was wasted by Liberian officials on luxury cars and lavish personal spending sprees; other than shutting down the Libyan embassy and ordering the USSR to reduce its diplomatic staff in Liberia, little of it went to warding off communists or improving the economic lot of Liberian citizens. In exchange for the funding and for their turning a blind eye to his corruption and brutality, Doe granted the U.S. government staging rights on 24-hour notice at Liberia's sea and airport facilities. These bases were used by the U.S. Rapid Deployment Force and the CIA to launch covert operations in support of U.S. strategic and security interests in the region, especially those threatened by Libya's colonel Muammar el-Qaddafi and by the presence of Cuban forces in Angola supporting the Marxist MPLA government.

This trip to Liberia, coupled with what I was learning at Georgetown, furthered my resolve to make my profession in international development. I decided to apply for a junior year in Paris at the prestigious Institut d'Études Politiques, better known as Sciences Po. I arrived in France in September 1982. If Mendham, New Jersey, had seemed like Sodom when I first arrived in America, Paris was Gomorrah on steroids. We students from America were placed in the homes of French families who wanted to earn a little extra money by renting out spare rooms to students. Unbeknownst to me (and, I can only assume, the program that sent me there), my host family was operating a modest but busy brothel.

The apartment was tiny. In fact, it had only three rooms: one for the madame/landlord, a beautiful psychologist named Marie; one for her 10-year-old twins, a boy and a girl, Piérre and Nicole; and one for me. Marie had the most liberal attitudes about sex I had ever encountered—not that I had encountered much beyond Pappi's Victorian outlook at that point. Even at Georgetown, I had not really dated. I had fallen madly in love only once, with Karl, a Swede I had met through Ri. Karl was a great athlete, sensitive and kind, and he looked like Gregory Peck! I spent a summer with him at his summer cottage in a beautiful village in Sweden, but his parents were there, so we had a relatively chaste summer. I still look back on it as one of the best times of my life, because for once, nothing else was on my mind.

At Marie's, there was always something else on my mind. She entertained men in her bedroom, often more than one at a time. The apartment literally would shake, with screams and growls of pleasure, accompanied by the music of Rossini or Verdi, played at top volume, while the air reeked permanently of the nauseating stench of hand-rolled Gaulois cigarettes, to which Marie was heavily addicted. Men of all sizes, shapes, and appearances would wander naked about the apartment, and I found myself obliged to keep my door locked at all times, as these were frequently men whom she picked up after one encounter at a bar. After several months of biting my tongue, I finally complained to Marie that the situation was intolerable. I could not sleep at night because of all the commotion. Moreover, I told her, I did not feel comfortable sharing my café au lait in the morning with naked male strangers. Marie sighed sweetly and then suggested that the real problem was that I was too much of a prude. If I would join in the fun from time to time, I would not only shed my unhealthy inhibitions but would also bring a dose of genuine exoticism to her soirees.

One winter night, in the middle of one of those soirees, I got a phone call from my parents in Liberia. I knew it must be something important, because normally they wrote, rather than phoned. My mother, in tears on the other end of the line, told me that Claudius, now 22 years old, had been arrested in New York City and accused of murder. The police said that he had shot to death the older Liberian woman he had been seeing. I was in shock. It seemed that all of Pappi's apprehensions about America—where he had still never set foot—were being realized in the most horrible fashion.

Then Pappi got on the line. It was the first time that I had ever heard him cry. The sound, compressed though it was by thousands of miles of phone lines, broke my heart. He kept asking me if I thought it was true. He was asking me for hope, but I could not give him any.

Somehow, I always felt that deep down Mummy was stronger than Pappi because she was able to see life in shades of gray, whereas Pappi was more like me, inclined to see things in black and white. He had always sent me off to school with this: "Monique, if you don't know where you are going to, remember where you are coming from." Claudius had heard that speech as often as I had. Yet I knew that no matter what Claudius might have done, Pappi would not be able to stop himself from loving him. (*Bush noh de foh trowe bad pikin.* Bad children may not be thrown into the bush.)

They declined my offer to meet them in New York, where they had decided to go to see what they could do to assist Claudius. Mummy just asked me to pray for them. Within days, they were on their way. They did not have many tools at their disposal. In Liberia, Pappi would have known who to call and what to do. In the States the only person of influence he knew was his old friend and mentor from LAMCO, Olle Wijkström, who was now running Investor AB in America, the Wallenberg family's investment fund. Pappi had his office phone number, but had not seen or been in touch with Olle for years.

After arriving in New York, my parents went directly to some old family friends from Liberia. This generous couple, a reverend and his wife, gave them a place to stay and loaned them some winter clothing. The following morning, in coats much too large for them and Pappi in a borrowed fedora, my parents arrived at the posh Wall Street offices of Investor AB.

They took the elevator up to Olle's office. Mummy later told me that the receptionist appeared taken aback at the sight of these two forlorn-looking creatures emerging from the elevator. She asked them if they had come to the right office, and Pappi, always so proud and commanding of respect, assured her that he had, that his name was Maddy, and that he would like a few minutes with Mr. Olle Wijkström.

The receptionist buzzed Olle on the intercom and alerted him to the fact that there was a "frenzied and disoriented" couple in the outer office. But the instant she said the word "Maddy," Olle rushed out to greet his friend.

Olle had known Pappi as a strong and upright man; the Ranefelt experience many years earlier was only one of many that they had gone through together. Now Pappi must have seemed broken. Through their tears, he and Mummy explained the terrible circumstances they were in. Pappi asked if Olle could help him find a lawyer to take the case. Olle only knew corporate lawyers. Through Claudius's contacts, Pappi and Olle were eventually able to hire a defense attorney. This lawyer, however, refused to take the case without prepayment of the full fee, which was $15,000. Pappi had already forked over $20,000 in bail money, which was all that he had brought with him to America, plus some additional funds that he had wired from Liberia. He immediately arranged for an additional transfer of funds by mortgaging his dream house—an arrangement he was only able to make through a special dispensation made by LAMCO. This effectively wiped out much of Pappi's life savings. A few weeks after these events had transpired, Pappi and Mummy went back to Liberia, as there was nothing more that they could do. Pappi had to return to the restaurant, which had remained in the hands of his sous-chef, Jacob, and Mummy had to get back to the hospital. They still had tuition to pay for the rest of us.

Claudius insisted that he was innocent, but the lawyer encouraged him to plead guilty in order to avoid a lengthy trial and the possibility of a long sentence. So Claudius did and got five years.

The news crushed Pappi. He was a man who had always fixed things, but he could not fix this.

That year, 1983, was the year in which we all lost our innocence. Before then it seemed that nothing bad ever happened to me or to members of my family. The bubble that LAMCO and my parents had created around us had protected us. No longer. I was living in a brothel in Paris. The family was back in Liberia trying to deal with the tragedy of Claudius's life in America and with an increasingly uncertain and deteriorating political and economic future. The bubble had burst.

I returned to Georgetown for my senior year, and in the spring of 1984 I was accepted at the Johns Hopkins University School of Advanced International Service (SAIS) and awarded a fellowship to study for my master's degree. The fellowship finally enabled me to lighten somewhat the financial burdens that I had been putting on my parents over the years. I calculated that they must have spent $70,000 on my education by 1984. The financial help came just in time, as Claudius's troubles had wiped out Pappi's financial cushion and my two younger brothers were approaching college age and would soon be coming over to the States. The precarious situation in Liberia made Pappi all the more anxious to get us all out of the country and educated. His philosophy had not changed—education was the key to a better life. But in America a good education was also expensive.

Although my decision to go straight ahead for my master's rather than begin work pleased Pappi immensely, it was really motivated by my ultimate ambition: to work for the United Nations. My resolve had been reinforced during my earlier studies at Georgetown, where during the four years I had met many individuals affiliated with the organization, including Kurt Waldheim, the former secretary general of the UN.

Georgetown held an annual conference called the Model UN. Its purpose was to simulate various functions of the UN, with groups and individuals representing different aspects of an international issue. Given my passion for the UN, many of my classmates wondered why I did not take part in the event. But in my freshman year, I had already decided that I would wait until I got into the real UN, where I could fix the real problems, especially those of Africa. Given the UN's mandate and its prominent standing in the world, surely that was the ideal platform for me to articulate my message and join in the effort to secure global peace and economic equality. Pretending was not good enough.

When I got to Johns Hopkins I was surprised by the cynicism so many of my professors held for the UN; SAIS seemed to me to be a natural factory for churning out potential UN bureaucrats. One of my professors, Grace Goodell, was especially blunt. She said, "Monique, there is no way that you are going to spend more than five years at the UN." This worried me, because Professor Goodell knew me well. SAIS had strict requirements for each specialty, and I was always trying to create my own program. For example, I wanted to take as many economics courses as possible, which often came at the expense of what I felt were "softer" topics such as "social change," which Professor Goodell championed. I always managed to get my way, and this was perhaps a sign to her that the bureaucracy and the inertia of the UN, of which I knew nothing, would drive me insane. But who was she to challenge a dream that I had nurtured for so many years and that I had spent the last six years working toward.

"You'll see," I told her defiantly.

She just laughed. "Monique," she said, "the UN is run by a bunch of morons."

I did not believe her for a second.

Now, about to graduate from Johns Hopkins, I had no plan B, so certain was I that I did not need one, despite the fact that all my classmates and teachers kept telling me that there was no way that I would get into the UN if my father, my uncle, or my brother did not work there, or if there was no one in the organization with whom I was personally connected.

I lucked out in my initial interview, which was held at the offices of the UN in Washington, D.C. My interlocutor, the head of the recruitment division of the United Nations Development Programme, was Dutch, the son of a diplomat, and married to a Swede. As I had put Swedish down as one of the languages I am conversant in on my résumé, he decided to test me. I managed to take the discussion through the preliminaries in Swedish, after which he switched into French, in which he was bilingual. (I had put down French too.) The rest of the interview was conducted in French, and I was quite certain that I had made a good impression, and would probably make it to the next round. I did. The subsequent rounds of interviews, including one with Toon Vissers, were held at UN headquarters in New York. They were my first professional job interviews, and the UN was actually paying for my trip. It felt adult.

A couple of weeks later I received a letter that did not commit, but at the same time did not say no. So to increase my chances of getting in I enlisted the support of one of my friends, a professor at SAIS, Christian Herter, Jr. Although I did not know it at the time, it turns out that he was the son of a former governor of Massachusetts who had been secretary of state under Dwight D. Eisenhower and one of the founders of SAIS. In other words, Jr. had connections. In a casual conversation he indicated that he knew Brad Morse well—Bradford Morse, a former Republican congressman, was then the head of the United Nations Development Programme—and that he would be willing to write a letter on my behalf to his old buddy. Within weeks, I received a letter from Mr. Morse himself informing me that he had spoken to the personnel division about my application, and he wished me luck. A few weeks later I received an offer to join the United Nations Development Programme. My dream had come true. I was off to save the world.

It was April 1986. I was in a state of high excitement, because Pappi was coming to my graduation ceremony and I already had a job. Mummy and Herbert had come for my Georgetown graduation, but Pappi had once again stayed behind to work in the restaurant, promising me that when I finished SAIS, he would come to America. Finally, his sacrifices had paid off and he could reward himself with the trip. I did not tell him about the job, because I wanted to surprise him on graduation day. I was the first person in our family to receive a master's degree, and I knew that Pappi was proud of my accomplishment. I knew that he planned to take the long journey to upstate New York to visit Claudius in prison as well. My graduation would give him something to counterbalance the pain of seeing Claudius locked up in a prison.

As I was preparing for my final exams, Pappi called to tell me that he had suddenly fallen ill and was suffering from pneumonia. He said that the doctors at the LAMCO hospital had suggested that he go to Sweden for further tests. He was quite jolly as he told me he would "swing by" Sweden and get the tests over with, and then proceed over to Washington for, as he called it, "our big day." The doctors told Mummy more than they told Pappi.

In Stockholm the tests confirmed that he had lung cancer, and that it had spread throughout his body. They called me right away, telling me that he would not make it to America, and asking that I come to Sweden, quickly. Our "big day", I soon realized, was not to be. Through much of what followed, I was emotionally numb. I arranged to take my final exams on an expedited basis. Within a week I was in Stockholm with Pappi, whom I hadn't seen in three years.

He looked so fragile lying there in the hospital bed, surprisingly like the little boy he had been some 50 years before in Sierra Leone, and of whom I had a cherished picture. I immediately burst into tears.

I ran into Pappi's arms. "Pappi, you look great," I said, American-style. He was obviously not looking great. He looked tired.

Only two weeks earlier he had been getting up at his usual 4:00 in the morning to prepare for the day at the restaurant. If he had had an annual physical exam, as was normal in a developed country, the cancer could have been detected early. I knew by then that there were many people in America for whom cancer was not a death sentence. But for people in Africa, where preventive medicine is a luxury, the yardstick is unfortunately not the same. Even making it to 58, as Pappi was at the time, meant that he had already beaten the odds.

Pappi still had his wit, but he no longer had time for many jokes. It was as if he wanted his every word to have a lasting impact on me. I felt completely disoriented as I sat beside his bed, in the sanitized and impersonal hospital room. It all seemed so impersonal and alien, both the place and the situation. Mummy and Herbert, who by now was also at school at Drexel University in Philadelphia, were also in the room, as were the Swedish nurses who came in and out from time to time, telling jokes and laughing with Pappi. He already had become a favorite of theirs, and I just could not understand how they could be so cheerful around him. But then I realized that this was their job—to keep the patient's spirits up, even when the situation was grim. What was the point of being morose? What good would it do? I did not know how to feel. To me Pappi was invincible, and I could not erase that image.

Pappi looked at me quietly and said, "Monique, how are you?" He already knew that he was going to die soon. I pretended that everything was fine and would soon return to normal, but the light was out of his eyes. "Monique, I want all of you to stick together," he said. "Take care of your mother and take care of each other."

I knew this was in part an admonishment to me about Claudius, with whom I was utterly out of touch. He had not responded to the few letters that I had written to him in prison. For my part, I was still angry with him for the pain that he had caused our parents. I knew these were meant to be last wishes, but the words were far too fatalistic for me to accept. By then I already had adopted the American attitude that had so surprised me when I had first encountered it in the St. John's brochure—putting the best face on everything. I just could not imagine life without Pappi and so I did not want to discuss it, implicitly or explicitly. He was going to beat this.

For many hours we sat talking about many things. I kept asking myself, What does one say in these moments? How can one cram into hours what should be said in a lifetime? At the end of each day, Mummy, Herbert, and I went to a small, bleak apartment nearby that Mummy had been able to borrow from an old Swedish friend. I wondered how Pappi felt when we left him. What was he thinking in those hours? What does one think or feel when one is about to leave the planet, all that is familiar, and there is nothing one can do about it?

I kept thinking—and I still do today—of all the things I could so easily have done to brighten his life while he still had so much of it ahead of him. I remembered, for example, the period when I was at boarding school in England. Every single day (as I learned many years later), Pappi would walk over to our post office box, number 69, hoping for a letter or even a simple postcard from me. When he got one, he would announce the news loudly in his restaurant. But these letters and cards came once a week, at best, and were the result of the mandatory writing sessions that I had engaged in so reluctantly and even tried to delegate to Penelope Williams. He told me that he had held on to each and every one of my letters and cards over all of these years. He teased me about my standard formula: "Dear Mummy and Daddy, I hope you are well. I am."

I told Pappi the good news about the offer from the UN. He knew that this was what I wanted; I was therefore surprised by his reaction. He told me that while the news was welcome, he thought I was capable of doing much more. He asked me to never stop reaching. He challenged me to find a way to "give back" to Africa, because it could benefit from my skills. He told me that he believed that the UN represented for me a "comfort zone," and was therefore likely to stifle my professional and personal development. Finally, he let me know that he doubted that the UN would ever do much to improve conditions in Africa. I tried to argue with him, as I had with my SAIS professors, that this was not the case at all, but he shook his head, indicating that we were done talking about this subject. He recognized my stubbornness—I was his daughter after all—but he no longer had the energy or the time to spar with me. But Pappi knew what I at the time didn't, that like him I was born to be an entrepreneur, to blaze my own trail in life, and he had given me the tools and the confidence to do so.

I spent about 10 days in Stockholm with Pappi, Mummy, and Herbert. Stockholm itself, usually one of my favorite cities in the world, was a particularly grim place to be even beyond the tragic personal circumstances that had brought me there on this trip. It was in the immediate aftermath of the disastrous April 1986 accident at the nuclear plant in Chernobyl in the Ukrainian republic of the Soviet Union. Driven by the force of the winds, the resulting plume of radioactive debris had drifted northwest over Sweden, among other countries, and there was a palpable fear within the

Swedish population and the government of the palpable health and environmental impact that this and future possible nuclear accidents in the Soviet Union could have on the entire Nordic region. The irony was inescapable. Here Pappi had come all the way from Yekepa to be treated for cancer, only to find himself trapped in a city where the citizens were in a sudden panic about an epidemic of the very same ailment. Pappi told us that he wanted the chemotherapy to stop. "I don't want you to take me back home in a box," he said to Mummy. He wanted to spend his final days back home in Liberia, in his dream house, surrounded by his beautiful garden, his friends, and his family. The departure gate at Arland International Airport in Stockholm was the last place I saw him. He was in a wheelchair, all skin and bones, dressed impeccably as usual and looking dignified, even in his pain. Neither of us cried as we hugged and kissed good-bye. I waited until he could no longer see me. As he turned the corner, my tears gushed out with the force of a broken dam.

I graduated alone in Washington, a few days before I was scheduled to begin work at the UN. Pappi died about a week after graduation. Mummy and Abayomi were by his side. His final words were: "Claudius, Monique, Herbert, Abayomi."[1] Claudius, seven thousand miles away in a prison cell, was the only one denied a chance to say good-bye.

I did not go to Pappi's funeral. Sometimes I regret that decision, but most of the time I do not. I did not want to say good-bye to him in the presence of so many strangers. In truth, I did not want to say good-bye to him at all. Because I had frequently lived for such long periods without seeing Pappi, I could just simply go on pretending that he was still there. But the pain was sharp and there was something that I felt I had to do to mark the darkness and solemnity of the period, even in my solitude. I went to a record shop at Dupont Circle in Washington and bought a record with a rendition of Pappi's favorite song. I shut myself in my apartment for days, packing my bags for New York and playing the song over and over again. For the first time, I actually listened to the words.

> *O Danny boy, the pipes, the pipes are calling*
> *From glen to glen and down the mountainside*
> *The summer's gone and all the roses falling*
> *'Tis you, 'tis you must go and I must bide*
> *But come ye back when summer's in the meadow*
> *Or when the valley's hushed and white with snow*
> *'Tis I'll be here in sunshine or in shadow*
> *O Danny boy, O Danny boy, I love you so.*
>
> *But if ye come and all the flowers are dying*
> *If I am dead, as dead I well may be,*
> *You'll come and find the place where I am lying*
> *And kneel and say an Ave there for me.*
>
> *And I shall hear, though soft, your tread above me*
> *And all my grave shall warmer, sweeter be*
> *For you will bend and tell me that you love me*
> *And I will sleep in peace until you come to me.*

I probably could not find Pappi's grave today, even if I tried, as some day I must, to say my final ave. It surely has been consumed by the ravenous forest or destroyed by evil warlords as they run around the country torching anything and everything in their paths. Even the dead have not been allowed to rest in peace. As for Yekepa—as well as Pappi's restaurant, his dream house, his prizewinning garden, his collection of letters from me—the village was occupied, pillaged, and destroyed. Yekepa, the miracle in the forest, is now nothing more than bush and ruin.

My Dream Becomes a Nightmare

The United Nations was founded in 1945 in the aftermath of World War II with the following heavenly mandate:

- to maintain international peace and security;
- to develop friendly relations among nations based on respect for the principle of equal rights and self-determination of peoples;
- to cooperate in solving international economic, social, cultural, and humanitarian problems and in promoting respect for human rights and fundamental freedoms;
- to be a center for harmonizing the actions of nations in attaining these common ends.

The UN Charter decrees that its membership be open to all governments of "peace-loving" nations, from Afghanistan to Zimbabwe and virtually every strain of government in between (including Iraq, Libya, Syria, the United States, France, and Russia), regardless of the atrocities suffered by individuals, groups, and entire populations, within many of its member countries. Unfortunately, the UN is run by neither gods nor angels, making its lofty goals all the more impossible to attain even under the best of circumstances, and the circumstances are far from the best. Despite the ambitious hopes and aspirations invested in the UN in the short-lived euphoria and optimism that prevailed at the time of its founding, the sad truth is that the organization is far less than the sum of its individual parts. It is anachronistic and governed by a "least common denominator" management philosophy.

Today on its website the UN Development Programme promotes itself rather grandiosely as a one-stop shop for all the third world's problems: governance, poverty reduction, crisis prevention and recovery, energy and the environment, information and communications technology, HIV/AIDS, and the empowerment of women. But when I first joined in 1986 it modestly described itself as the coordinator of the UN's economic development activities and the largest source of international grant aid, otherwise known as free money. My first assignment with the UNDP was at its headquarters in midtown Manhattan.

As I approached the imposing UN complex, stretching along First Avenue for several city blocks, my heart climbed up in my throat. It did not matter that the secretariat building was looking a little down at the heels. What was important was that, despite its decaying façade, the spirit that had inspired the creation of this august institution still existed. The brightly colored flags, powerful symbols of global unity, were hoisted high on their staves, flapping defiantly this way and that in the wind. Images of President Franklin Roosevelt, Prime Minister Winston Churchill, and Premier Joseph Stalin came to mind, as did recollections of my high school history lessons, including a pivotal field trip I made to the

UN during my St. John's days. These men and many other forward-thinking individuals had been determined to create an institution to prevent the recurrence of one of the most tragic and devastating military conflicts in the annals of modern human history. Their accomplishment was monumental. In San Francisco in 1945 the UN Charter had been signed, and its mandate was weighty: to preserve peace and stability in an increasingly complex, diverse world. No doubt about it: I was immensely proud to be even associated with the continuing history and idealism of that vision.

Because I had decided to start work immediately upon graduation from Johns Hopkins, rather than wait for the official UNDP training program, which began three months later at the end of August, I was given a temporary assignment in the personnel department, arguably the most politically sensitive department within the entire UN. In the personnel department careers were made and destroyed. More often than not, decisions were arbitrary rather than methodical (though even the methodology of that department would make the College of Cardinals and the papal election process seem refreshingly transparent). As a result, one individual, operating on a whim or, as was more likely the case, on a personal or nationalistic vendetta, could determine whether a UN employee would spend the next three to five years of her life in the relatively splendid Bangkok or Jarkarta, or the relatively desolate Ulan Bator or Timbuktu.

My initial task in personnel was to organize and update the recruitment files; They hadn't been purged in more than a decade. This was not exactly what I had thought I would be doing at the UN, but then again, I was happy just to be there. As it turned out, the assignment gave me a lot of valuable insight into the core and inner workings of the United Nations system. It also revealed how little was left of its original idealism. There appeared to be scant correlation between a person's qualifications and his selection for the job. For example, there were the hot files, in which there were a few deserving candidates, but many more who barely met the necessary professional criteria yet were given special treatment or consideration because they knew people or because they were of a nationality that was favored at the moment. There were numerous files on exceptionally well-qualified people whose applications had never been analyzed in any serious way, and to whom rejection letters were sent almost automatically. They had the "know-how" but they did not have the determining factor, the "know-who."

Following that summer and four months in a management trainee program I was assigned to the UNDP field office in Jakarta, in January 1987. This assignment entailed an additional three months of on-the-job training. About two months into my assignment I received a letter from the personnel department informing me that my first long-term assignment was Luanda, Angola. Many of my colleagues in Indonesia expressed pity for me. Indonesia was considered a plum assignment; Angola, in the midst of a deadly and protracted civil war, was the exact opposite. But I was ecstatic. Angola was precisely why I had joined the UN. That the country was at war did not deter me. That was part and parcel of what I had signed up for. Angola seemed a place to make a meaningful difference, which the UN was certainly not doing in Indonesia, a country that from all outward appearances was running quite well on its own steam, fueled primarily by activities in the private sector.

Angola was among a handful of countries classified by the United Nations as "extreme hardship posts." This placed it in the company of Afghanistan, Iraq, Libya, Papua New Guinea, and Yemen. Assignments to such countries are typically of two years or less, and for good reason. During my eighteen-month assignment in Angola, the UNDP changed its country director four times. We had a German, a Belgian, an Italian, and a Nigerian. The one who arrived just before my departure, the fourth, died of a massive heart attack after only a couple of months on the job.

Without a doubt, part of the UNDP's problem in Angola resided in Angola's complex political environment, one that had prevailed since the beginning of the civil war in 1975 after Angola secured its independence from Portugal. It would eventually last until 2002, with the killing of Jonas Savimbi, the leader of the government's major opposition, the National Union for the Total Independence of Angola (UNITA). During this period, the fighting killed up to 1.5 million Angolans, left the country with the highest per capita amputee rate in the world, and displaced some two million more.

Until 2002, the Angolan Marxist-oriented government's need to retain its firm grip on power and quell the well-financed armed resistance movement of the UNITA rebels rendered all nondefense-related activities a distant second priority. Despite numerous attempts by the UN and other international bodies to mediate between the two sides, and even to intervene, hostilities not only continued, but intensified. Further complicating matters, Angola's domestic conflict had escalated into a full-scale international crisis because of the Cold War. Each side had a dog in the fight: The West (primarily the United States and the apartheid government of South Africa)' supported the UNITA rebels, while the Soviets and Cuba backed the Popular Movement for the Liberation of Angola (MPLA) government—including providing senior military experts, arms, and up to 50,000 Cuban troops stationed in Angola to bolster the government's own armed forces. The average Angolan thus had to endure a nightmare that persisted year after bloody year. The capital city of Luanda, where I was stationed, was insulated from the most devastating aspects of the war—much of the rest of the country was littered with the land mines that had mutilated tens of thousands of innocents. To Luanda, then, the population of migrant amputees came. Begging became their primary source of income. These men, women, and children were a pitiful sight to behold, and their futures were at best bleak and at worst hopeless. In the midst of them my UN colleagues and I lived, along with the country's elite, in a ghetto of extraordinary creature comforts.

When I first arrived in Angola, Gerd Merrem, a German bureaucrat, headed our offices. He had been in the UN system for more than twenty years in various war-torn areas, and it showed on his orange-hued brown, wrinkled, and leathery face, telltale signs of once fair European skin severely overexposed to the unforgiving and unrelenting heat of the tropics. Prior to coming to Angola, he had been stationed in Bangkok, Thailand, where he had dumped his wife for his secretary, a local Thai woman, who later accompanied him to Angola. He was now about to leave Angola under a cloud of controversy.

He and his deputy were unfortunately cut from the same cloth, though they despised and hardly spoke to each other. Jean Pierre Gernay, a Belgian, with a King-Leopold-II-in-the-Congo complex, remained in charge of us for a few months after Merrem's unceremonious departure. Gernay also had left his European wife—for a young Ethiopian woman one-third his age who seemed to have had not a clue what she had signed on for, other than to escape from a life of dire poverty. I soon discovered that this predatory pattern (old white man, exotic, young local woman) was all too common among the officials of the UN and other similar international institutions and NGOs in these countries.

I had expected and even hoped for Angola to be a professional challenge. Without a doubt it was a country crying out for help, but we were certainly not giving Angola the kind of help it needed. The fact is that my biggest challenges were more of a professional and personal survival nature than of tackling Angola's complex development problems that I thought I had been sent to do. They involved coming to terms with the Kafkaesque existence that we led as international civil servants, and reconciling my lifelong enthusiasm and idealism with the reality of our near-total irrelevance in the context of Angola's hideous and bloody civil war.

My own personal insignificance illustrates my point, and is indicative of the general futility of the work done by almost all the expatriate staff in the office, at all levels. At the age of 24, armed with my international perspective, a master's degree in development economics, four months of costly UN training, near fluency in Portuguese, and no shortage of goodwill, I was put in charge of . . . housing. I don't mean housing for the millions of displaced civilians, amputees, and other Angolan casualties of the war—we were not overly concerned with that. I mean housing for a handful of UN expatriates. My job was to take the calls from colleagues whose toilets were broken; who wanted antitheft bars on their windows; whose houses needed a fresh coat of paint; whose refrigerators, stoves, or generators had broken down; and so on, and then to try to get these problems fixed by the poorly equipped and poorly trained team of maintenance workers that the UN kept on staff exclusively for this purpose. In other words, I was to ensure that the senior expatriates enjoyed some approximation of the Western standards of living to which they were accustomed or, as in many cases, to which they aspired but could not afford in a city such as New York, Paris, London, or Stockholm. So while most of Angola lived in a quasipermanent state of blackout and with limited supplies of water, the homes of the crème de la crème (of which we were part) had 30,000-watt diesel-powered generators that spewed electricity 24 hours a day, and 1,000-gallon water tanks that were kept permanently replenished by foreign-operated private water carriers, who made a fortune catering to this highly exclusive and price-insensitive clientele.

I had access to a small commissary that sold to UN staff our quotas of essentials: basic groceries such as eggs, yogurt, powdered milk, sugar, butter, pasta, flour, bread, cheese, and of course beer—all of which were extremely difficult and at times impossible for the average Angolan to come by. Many of of the diplomatic missions and overseas-based private companies had similar facilities, and it was not uncommon for goods to be bartered. I might find myself trading fruit juice cans for a bar of Marabou chocolate, which I always craved and was available only through the Swedish embassy. As in most controlled markets, distortions popped up left and right, and people went to great lengths to satisfy their wants and needs. One afternoon my friend Sir Patrick Fairweather, the tall, charming, and aristocratic British ambassador to Angola, arrived at my office in a state of panic, in his chauffeur-driven and bulletproof Jaguar. His mission: to request that I use my quotas in the UN commissary to procure two dozen eggs for a VIP dinner he was hosting that evening.

I tell that story not out of disrespect for Sir Patrick, who I very much admired, and who was later sent by his government as their ambassador to Rome (where there were plenty of eggs to go around) but to illustrate the inconsistencies of our little cocoon of privilege. One minute he was meeting with President José Eduardo dos Santos, the president of Angola, on some important matter of state; the next he was out on the street, scavenging for eggs.

Another component of my job was ensuring that all the expensive duty-free goodies, from deluxe stereo systems to Wedgwood china to posh cars that the UN expatriates ordered from various overseas commercial establishments, arrived safely and were cleared for entry into the country by hook or, more often, by crook—literally. Crook entailed the use of an intermediary who did the dirty work (paying bribes) so as to give us, the UN, the appearance of being clean and incorruptible. Assisting me in these duties was the UNDP's security officer, a strange old German character named Gunther. Gunther was about seventy and totally certifiable. Nobody could recall how or when he had ever gotten onto the UN payroll. There was a rumor, accepted as fact, that prior to coming to Angola, he had been a mercenary somewhere in Asia. But judging from the way Gunther comported himself in the office, one was left with the disturbing impression that he did not realize he had ever left the battlefield. The slightest provocation would set him off screaming and storming around the office, ranting and raving in German. Nobody dared to reprimand him, not even King Leopold II, who must have seen in Gunther his old nemesis, Kaiser Wilhelm II, of Germany.

It is fair to say that over the course of nearly two years in Angola I had absolutely nothing to do with the development of Angola. From what I could see, no one in our office did either. Yes, the staff had endless mandatory meetings with second- and third-tier government officials. But the Angolan government and its key decision makers were far more preoccupied with defeating UNITA than with catering to the fancies and constantly changing development priorities of a bunch of eccentric and transient international bureaucrats.

We did not even have the benefit of economic clout. In the first place, the UNDP has far fewer financial resources at its disposal than its sister organizations, the World Bank and the IMF (which at the time were not operating in Angola); as a result, its ability to do good or inflict harm is limited by comparison. Second, Angola is blessed with abundant natural resources, including petroleum, diamonds, uranium, copper, and manganese. With all these sources of wealth to fuel its war efforts, the government scarcely cared about our puny contribution or advice on how to run its economy. As a result we needed the government far more than it needed us—we needed it to justify our presence and the importance of our activities in Angola. By contrast, the major petroleum companies operating the offshore drilling rigs, such as Halliburton, Shell, Elf Aquitaine, and Chevron, commanded a lot more respect and enjoyed far greater political access than we did. They came with one specific agenda: to make money. If they made money, so did the government. They came with more resources and less baggage, as the government of Angola was free to use oil revenues from their operations as it saw fit. It saw fit to purchase all the Soviet weaponry that it felt was needed to defeat UNITA, something we at the UN officially frowned upon but could do nothing about.

Despite our relative insulation from the direct atrocities of the war, there were a number of legitimate reasons why Angola was designated as a hardship post for the UN's expatriate staff. Most pressing among them was the high rate of random and violent crime in Luanda, where most of us were posted. These incidents were a by-product of the civil war that left the majority of the people in the country in economic distress and desperate for alternative sources of income.

One precaution taken by the government in an attempt to curtail the high incidence of crime in the city was the imposition of a mandatory curfew that lasted from 12:00 A.M. to 5:00 A.M. During that period it was strictly forbidden for anyone except authorized military personnel and high-ranking government officials with special passes to be outdoors. The result was as might have been expected—the victims obeyed the curfew, the perpetrators did not. Rather than reduce crime in Luanda, the curfew merely compressed the window of opportunity during which the perpetrators operated. It was during these nocturnal hours, the hours of *madrugada,* as they are called in Portuguese, that the most horrendous crimes were committed. Houses were broken into, civilian security guards terrorized or killed, whole families stripped naked, and if lucky, left alive, if not, brutally murdered. Everything that was not permanently attached to the house was fair game, from furniture, appliances, plumbing fixtures, to electronics, clothes, and cash. The booty would then be driven away, often in the victims' own cars. Even if one had had a telephone, one would have to be doubly lucky to have the phone in working order, and then for someone at the police station to pick up the call. A further miracle would then be needed for the police force to have a vehicle at its disposal to dispatch. Generally the police would ask the victims to come and pick them up, if they wanted to proceed with a full investigation of the incident. By the time victim and law enforcement were united the perpetrators might well already be over the border in Kinshasa, unloading and pricing their wares. To my knowledge, these investigations never led to the capture of the perpetrators or to the recovery of any goods. Often, it was found that the police were complicit in the affair.

Less sinister activities also went on during *madrugada*. In the city's wealthy Angolan neighborhoods, the air was filled with the exquisitely sensuous rhythms and sounds of African and Brazilian beats as family, friends, and neighbors congregated for impromptu fiestas, which involved a lot of dancing, singing, drinking, and eating. Partygoers would arrive just before midnight and dance the night away, until just after 5:00 A.M. I imagine that this was one way for the Angolans to temporarily forget the stark realities of the war. On such occasions they would recall with nostalgia the care-free days of Luanda during the colonial era, when the city was still affectionately known as the Pearl of Africa. So terrible was the more than a decade of civil war that it had dulled everyone's memories of the atrocities and indignities they had suffered at the hands of their Portuguese colonizers from the early 20th century to 1975. Having numerous Angolan friends, I attended my fair share of these events. In the neighborhoods of well-off expatriates the festivities were by comparison subdued affairs, typically formal dinners beginning at 8:00 P.M. and ending at 11:30, to give the guests sufficient time to scurry to their homes before midnight, just as the bandits were beginning their shifts. Being young, single, female, and well educated, I was automatically placed on the high-society guest list and invited to many of these events, which seemed to take place almost every night.

The unreality of those evenings challenges my modest talents as a storyteller. Imagine the most elaborate dinner you have ever attended. Now overlay that picture with a rigid and exacting protocol, dating back to the Edwardian era when kings were still kings and colonies were still colonies. Picture an enormous table on which each place setting has at least five forks, five knives, several spoons, numerous glasses for wines, water, port, and champagne, all positioned with royal precision and each governed by distinct rules of usage and etiquette. The breaking of any of these rules was a faux pas that would elicit a gentle nudge from some doyenne of the diplomatic corps, who would patronizingly dispense her superior knowledge of the proper rules of high society.

Imagine that around this table are seated a dozen or so individuals from all over the world, in their best finery and most expensive jewelry. Remember that all of this furniture, china, silver, and evening wear had to be flown, barged, and trucked in across multiple continents at great expense. In this sublime setting we talked not of the finer things in life, as suited to the sophistication of the table and the surrounding decor; nor did we reflect much upon the Angolan situation that had brought us all here. Instead we descended into the most vivid accounts possible of the latest incidences of violence perpetrated by "the locals" against us. When there was not a fresh story to tell, old ones were recycled and embellished for the benefit of new arrivals who had not yet had time to form opinions of their own on Angola.

After the elaborate meal and explicit table talk the men would retire to a separate room to smoke cigars, drink scotch or brandy, and talk about Important Things. This balkanization left me in the company of the other women, most of whom were older, career diplomat wives. Though I was often tempted to, I never did barge into that smoky room full of men, partly because I was still young and relatively insecure, but also because I knew that even if the men were talking policy or politics, we were all irrelevant anyway to the situation into which we had been thrown. This anachronistic ritual was no more absurd that the illusion of ourselves as third world development warriors. We were all just playing our parts.

The one bit of reality in these evenings was the aforementioned crime stories. They helped bond a group of disparate individuals who in almost any other situation would have never found themselves in one place, much less socializing together. The stories welcomed newcomers into the fold. But most important, telling these tales to one's peers helped dissipate some of the real fear that we all lived with, that of being the next victim.

The night of May 22, 1987, shortly after my arrival in Angola, I came uncomfortably close to being a particularly gory morsel on the dinner party circuit. I was still living in the UN's guesthouse—a transitory accommodation set aside for new arrivals or short-term UN consultants when the one major international hotel, Le Presidente Meridien, was fully booked—with two other women, Consuelo, a Spanish doctor, and Gail, a UN volunteer from the Philippines. We had all arrived recently and were all in our midtwenties. The guesthouse was located in an isolated part of the city, far away from the more luxurious residential areas inhabited by high-ranking government officials and expatriates. There was no staff. New arrivals were given a key and expected to make do.

The three-bedroom unit was located on the first floor of a three-story building that was also inhabited by two large Angolan families that we had nothing to do with. Just across the street from the building was one of the barracks for government soldiers. This is reassuring, I thought, when I first arrived. At least we will be secure. But as I walked home from the office each day, I would see them loitering or swaggering about the street, often in a drunken stupor or stoned on drugs. I would cross over to my side of the street in a deliberate attempt to feign nonchalance and avoid harassment. They just hung around all day, waiting for their turn to be shipped off to the battlefield and whatever fate awaited them.

I had been in the country for a little over two weeks. I went to bed relatively early that evening. I remember asking myself whether or not I should bother to lock my bedroom door. Since the thought had entered my mind, I decided I might as well. About two hours later I heard noises in the living room, just a couple of doors down the hall. I guessed that it was Gail and Consuelo who had come home and were having a good time. They must have invited some guests as well, as it sounded quite raucous out there. I wondered if I should just get up and join them. I decided against it and opted instead to turn the air conditioner on. At full throttle, the air conditioner droned like a power drill, and drowned the voices that were becoming increasingly loud. Soon after dosing off, I was awakened again. "What the hell are they doing out there?" I wondered. The furniture was now being moved about, and the party seemed to show no signs of ebbing. I looked at my watch and saw that it was already two in the morning. I drifted into a state of semiconsciousness but was abruptly awakened by a strange, loud sound. Not having a bedside lamp, I looked toward the door and under the slit I could see the light penetrating from the hallway. I could hear what appeared to be a heavy metal object being used to ply my bedroom door open.

I raced over to the door and switched on the light. The door was now creaking open. I yelled out, "Who's there?" and got no response, but the crowbar was pulled back. I knew that with the application of just a little more force the invaders would be in my room.

All of a sudden I heard several male voices on the other side of my door. Things seemed to be happening fast. There was of course no alarm system in the building, nor was there a telephone for me to make a call. My first instinct was to jump out of my bedroom window and into the street, even if it meant breaking a leg or two. But then I remembered that the windows were blocked by wrought-iron security bars designed to keep intruders out. I figured I was a goner, but I took a large dresser that was in the room and shoved it against the door anyway. I put on my Nike running shoes. Once they had broken into my room, I reasoned, I would make a run for it through the same door that they had entered. No matter what they chose to do to me, I was not going to make it easy for them. I wondered what had happened to Gail and Consuelo. I hadn't heard a sound from either. Could they be dead already? Every one of the crime stories about these violent break-ins that I had heard told since my arrival flashed like sharp daggers through my mind. The script was all too familiar, the outcome frighteningly predictable. I was pretty sure that Consuelo, at least, was already dead—she never locked her door and her room was nearest to the entrance. To think she had only been here for a week. Gail's room was directly opposite mine, so either they had already taken care of her, or her turn would be after mine.

By this time the men had ceased their assault on my door and were now murmuring to each other in Portuguese. I could not decipher what they were saying, but it seemed as if they were deliberating whether or not to proceed with the break-in. I decided to call out to Gail in English so they wouldn't understand and might be confused. She too was awake and at her door. She yelled back that through her keyhole she could see a group of Faplas,[2] as the government soldiers were called, with guns, standing in front of my room. I switched on my portable transistor radio and located an unused frequency, and turned the volume of the static to maximum. Then I yelled back to her, "Police! Police!" hoping that they would think that somehow we were making contact with the police, perhaps through a private radio system. This was met with complete silence, with nobody moving. The standoff lasted for about thirty minutes. I then called out to Gail to ask whether she could still see them. She said that she could not and suggested that I come over to her room, as she had a knife to protect us, the same she used to prepare her hearty Filipino breakfasts of rice and meat every morning. But I knew well that the soldiers could still be lurking in the corridor, and futhermore, I did not want Gail to stab me in a fit of panic.

We waited anxiously for three more hours in our rooms, calling out to each other occasionally to make sure that we were both still alive. At last dawn finally broke, there was movement in the streets, and we decided that it was safe to come out. We rushed to check on Consuelo, bracing ourselves to take in the grisly murder scene. Fortunately she was not there, and neither was her corpse nor were any bloodstains. It turned out that within the first few days of her arrival, Consuelo had found herself a boyfriend. That decision probably saved her life.

It did not, however, save her personal possessions and cash, all of which were gone. Except for what Gail and I had in our bedrooms, the entire apartment had been ransacked. All that remained was my stash of Swedish Marabou chocolates in the refrigerator. Africans, generally, do not have a sweet tooth.

Gail and I headed for the UNDP office, still terrified. We asked for a meeting with Mr. Merrem, who actually was scheduled to leave Angola for good the next day. He listened impatiently to our tearful account, and then laughed it off. To him, it was a tale of two hysterical young women who had been spared a brutal encounter with local thugs. Big deal.

In the fall of 1988 I got word that my next post would be Bangui, in the Central African Republic. That is how it worked in the UN, particularly at the entry level, where I was. The employee has little say in the matter; the next assignment can be Bangui just as easily as it can be Bamako or Bogotá, and you can take it or leave it because the recruitment files are filled with people from all over the world, mostly developing countries, for whom the promise of Bamako and a UN salary is like winning the lottery. I disliked the Luanda office intensely. But I concluded that Luanda was the exception, rather than the rule, and that I would see the real UNDP once I had moved to the CAR, especially because I had been told that the man who headed up the UN office there, Wally N'Dow, from Gambia, was excellent. In Bangui I would be involved directly with the organization's projects rather than the living conditions of its international staff. I would also be overseeing projects in a wide range of areas, from private-sector development (UNDP's new mission du jour) to telecommunications infrastructure and environmental protection. The job description seemed to be a little more in line with the reasons I originally had joined UNDP.

The reassignment entitled me to a paid home leave, which would be my first break since my arrival in Angola a year and a half earlier. The problem was that Liberia, already quite alien to me, was beginning to seem less and less like home. Under Samuel Doe the country was deteriorating politically and economically. It had been eight years since his bloody coup, and he had survived two coup attempts on his presidency, one of them orchestrated by his former second-in-command. He and his henchmen had pilfered the country's resources; become completely intolerant of all political opposition; banned newspapers that were critical of the regime; reinstated antilabor laws; and violated basic human rights on a massive scale. Meanwhile, the United States had reduced its support to his government substantially. The IMF and the World Bank also had suspended loans to the Liberian government, and its access to cash was severely limited. Without the U.S. financial support that had sustained him during his earlier years, when he was still of some strategic value to U.S. security interests in the region, Doe's days were numbered. Global geopolitical shifts, particularly the beginning of the end of the Cold War, had rendered him, like many other African dictators, disposable to superpower interests. I stopped in Liberia briefly to see Mummy, but Yekepa under these circumstances was definitely not the place to go for R&R before a tough new African assignment, so I went first to a friend's place in New York City.

13

Escapes from Chaos

Where the hell is Bangui? That is a question that I am frequently asked when I mention my final assignment with the United Nations Development Programme. It was certainly the question that I asked myself when I received the telegram from New York announcing my new posting. I was told by the few people who knew that Bangui was the capital of the Central African Republic, known principally in my mind for the brutality and repressive rule, and other unsavory features, of the late dictatorial emperor Jean-Bédel Bokassa. It was reported that he had given a substantial fortune in diamonds to his friend the French president, Valéry Giscard d'Estaing, who had not bothered to disclose the emperor's largesse to the French public. For his part, Giscard had helped sustain Bokassa by sending French troops to the Central African Republic and lending the regime a billion dollars. This indiscretion had caused a major political scandal in France when it became public in

1979, and was still much in the news when I was living in Marie's brothel in Paris from 1982–83. It had contributed in no small measure to Giscard's subsequent defeat by the socialist candidate, François Mitterand, in 1981. Another thought that crossed my mind at the mention of Bokassa was the popular perception that he was a cannibal. I decided that I had better read up on this place, which I understood was going to be my home for the next three to four years.

The CAR received its independence from France in 1960 under the leadership of its first president, David Dacko. Like many African-style elections, succession came by bullet, not ballot. Dacko was overthrown in 1966 by his cousin, Bokassa, whom he had previously made head of the army, a post for which the latter appeared well qualified. Bokassa had joined the French colonial army in 1939 and, like many Africans living under French colonial rule, fought for France in both World War II and the first Indochina war between the Vietnamese and the French. He accused Dacko's government of widespread corruption and promised to restore honor, dignity, and integrity to the country. Five years later, in 1971 (possibly in order to give himself sufficient time to honor this promise) Bokassa declared himself President for Life; six years later Bokassa, in his characteristic folie de grandeur, anointed himself Emperor Bokassa I and declared the Central African Republic the Central African Empire. His lavish coronation ceremony is purported to have cost the impoverished and aid-dependent nation a staggering $30 million of its meager resources and rivaled his hero Napoleon Bonaparte's own 1804 coronation bash, on which it was said to be modeled.

Rampant corruption and violence characterized Bokassa's reign from ignoble start to ignominious finish. The 1979 massacre of hundreds of innocent civilians, among them children, by his army proved to be his tropical Waterloo. He was accused of being personally involved in these murders and even of eating some of the children. While on a trip to Libya a few months after these horrific events he was overthrown with the help of the French troops that had earlier been sent to support him—Giscard had distanced himself and recovered remarkably well.[1] Rather than return home to face charges, Bokassa exiled himself to his own private Elba and Saint Helena, Côte d'Ivoire and Paris, respectively.[2] Rid of its megalomaniacal emperor, the Central African Empire became a republic again.

Bangui, the capital city, had been the jewel in Bokassa's diamond-studded crown. By the time I arrived in January 1989 the gem had lost its luster. Yet Bangui is a city that I will never forget, because of Jean Barbo, who made my life in the CAR bearable. I was extremely fortunate to have found him.

Cooking has never been one of my strong suits. Therefore, when I looked for a place to live in Bangui, I sought to hire a housekeeper who could cook as well as clean. I was then staying at the Novotel, one of two international hotels in Bangui, so I asked the hotel chef, Salé, whether he knew anyone who would be interested. A few days later Salé had managed to track down Barbo at his hut in the countryside, where he was cultivating vegetables for sale on the local market.

He was absolutely irresistible. He had an angelic face, the slightest figure, and a gentle demeanor to match. He also had no teeth, having lost all of them years earlier in an accident. Before he had spoken a word, I decided to hire him. I know that I have made fun of Linda Katz for doing much the same with Robert, our Malawian housekeeper in Tanzania, but I hit the jackpot with Barbo. I proceeded with the interview for the sake of appearances, as I felt I had to convey at least a modicum of professionalism. The discussion was more of a friendly conversation between friends, during which I probed him with questions designed to satisfy my own rabid curiosity about the CAR rather than to determine Barbo's suitability for the job. After he told me that he had worked for Bokassa I could not resist asking him whether it was true what they said about the erstwhile emperor. Barbo said it was indeed true—but hastened to reassure me that he had played no part in catering to Bokassa's gastronomic aberrations. That was the province of the sous-chefs, he assured me.

Jean Barbo, né Jean Barboza, was born in 1938 in Mbaiki, a town created by the French early in the 20th century as a military base from which their troops could suppress local anticolonial insurgencies that threatened France's commercial interests in the region. It was the Pygmy region of the CAR, but at five-foot-ten-inches tall, Barbo could claim convincingly to be no Pygmy. His father, Pierre, had worked for a Portuguese settler, Roberto Barboza, who had come to Bangui in the late 1800s to carve coffee plantations out of the jungle. As was relatively common practice at the time he gave Pierre his own name as a substitute for his African one. To make it easier on the local tongue, Jean had shortened it to "Barbo." Like his father before him, Barbo did not have a formal education and never learned to read or write, though later he did manage to teach himself how to read numbers and do rough math in order to advance in his trade. At the age of fourteen and at the request of his father, who wanted a better life for Barbo, he was apprenticed to a French colonialist to be trained as a chef. His culinary skills were subsequently honed and cultivated in a number of neighboring countries, also under French colonial rule at the time, including Zaire, Congo, and Cameroon. Barbo excelled in both cooking and pastry. Upon his return to the CAR, he was recruited immediately by the government to serve as a chef in the presidential palace and for official state functions. He was so good that the Emperor Bokassa would have Barbo prepare the meals on the CAR Air Force One. Generally, only the best chefs in the country—mostly Frenchmen—were given these plum assignments, even after independence. Barbo was therefore a notable exception.

A few months before I arrived on the scene Barbo had been laid off from his government job as part of a World Bank restructuring program that the CAR had adopted in return for a loan. For him, it had seemed like the end of the world. He was 50 years old, well above the average age of mortality (which is 42 and falling in sub-Saharan Africa), yet still in excellent health. In the Central African Republic there is no formal welfare system, neither is there unemployment insurance. With seemingly no prospects, Barbo, a devout Catholic, had resorted to prayer.

We established an immediate rapport as he set about helping me secure a home and settle into my new life. In the two years that I was there he took extremely good care of me, including mounting a 24-hour watch over me during a three-week period when, for the second time in my life, I fell dangerously ill with malaria. In addition to the massive dosages of antimalarial pills, Barbo plied me with multiple infusions of a concoction that he brewed from an esoteric blend of locally grown plants. In my fever-induced semiconscious state I was only too happy to succumb to his unconventional ministrations. I am not sure if they did any good, but they certainly did no harm.

Barbo viewed me as "white" because I did not fit neatly into his preconceived matrix, just as the Tanzanians viewed me as a *musungu*. He was amazed at all the material possessions that I had acquired at such a young age: my car, my clothes, and all the other paraphernalia that went along with my position and status. He was always looking for evidence that this abundant wealth made me happy, as he imagined it should. I did not give Barbo much satisfaction on that score. I told him honestly that it seemed to me that he was far happier than I. In material terms, he had little, which gave him a detachment and freedom from angst that I could only envy. It was the same serenity that I had seen in Ma Kema and her people.

He wondered why I was not married with children. At the time I was almost 27, and in the CAR almost all women would be married with several children by then. I told him that I was not interested in getting married, a response to which he could no more relate to than the idea of a snowstorm occurring in the Sahara. Barbo, while luckier than many in the CAR, had not had the opportunities or exposure to education that would have given him the awareness, the confidence, to question the way things are, and the means to rise above his lot. With his natural culinary talent and a little formal training Barbo easily could have rivaled the chefs in any Michelin three-star restaurant. As I pondered this, I wondered how many other Barbos were out there in Africa who would never get the chance to expand and develop their minds, who would never be able to advance to that state of awareness where contemplating the larger issues of life supersedes the constant daily grind of merely surviving. The waste was incalculable.

The year that I went to the CAR, 1989, was the year in which Claudius was released from prison. For him, back then, the world was circumscribed by his crime: He was 29 years old and had no choice but to go back to Liberia, where he began the slow and painful process of rebuilding his life. Much had changed in our family. Pappi was gone, and both Abayomi and Herbert were studying in America, Abayomi at the University of West Virginia and Herbert at Drexel University in Philadelphia. Mummy had retired from the LAMCO hospital and had taken over the restaurant, which she was running on a full-time basis. Claudius was determined to carry on where Pappi had left off and assume some of the responsibilities that he felt he had neglected in his youth. He helped Mummy at the restaurant and also started his own business, a video rental shop, importing American movies that he would drive down to Monrovia to pick up through a supplier there. We were all glad that he was back in Liberia, because he would take care of Mummy if the political situation there deteriorated. It deteriorated much quicker than any of us had imagined.

On Christmas Eve 1989, Charles Taylor and rebels from his National Patriotic Front of Liberia (NPFL) movement invaded Liberia from neighboring Côte d'Ivoire with the intention of overthrowing Samuel Doe and ostensibly handing power back to the people. Taylor was not unknown in Liberia. He had been a procurement clerk in the Doe government in the early eighties, after the execution of William Tolbert, then subsequently he was accused by the government of embezzling $1 million from the state coffers. He managed to escape prosecution by fleeing to the United States, whereupon he was captured and held as a federal detainee in the Plymouth County jail in Massachusetts, awaiting INS extradition to Liberia. On September 15, 1985, he escaped again, allegedly with the aid of a hacksaw and some bedsheets, only to emerge four years later at the Liberian border fresh from a stint at al-Mathabh al-Thauriya al-Alamiya (World Revolution Headquarters), a secret service guerrilla training camp run by Libyan dictator Muammar el-Qaddafi. Taylor was supported by troops from Burkina Faso and reinforced by about 150,000 additional fighters, mostly members of the Gio and Mano tribes, recruited in my home region of Nimba, who for years had suffered oppression at the hands of the Doe regime.

Many of the recruits were children, some only 10 years old, forcibly enlisted and so besotted with drink and drugs that any inhibitions or traces of compassion that might interfere with carrying out the brutal orders their leaders were about to give them were quashed. These soldiers, known as the Small Boys Unit, were too young to know who they were fighting, much less why. They were told to kill their fathers and their mothers, so that Taylor would be their sole parent—Our Father, as they called him. Much later, when Taylor ran for office, these same children ran around shouting the following political ditty: "You killed my ma, you killed my pa, you have my vote." Within months the invading coalition degenerated further into ethnic rivalries between the Mano and Gio. The Gio took on a new leader, Field Marshal Brigadier-General Prince Y. Johnson, and formed a splinter group called the Independent Patriotic Front. Overriding the differences between the insurgents was a shared hatred of President Doe and all those associated with him, in particular the Krahn and Mandingo.

All of these events were having a major impact on the inhabitants of Yekepa in Nimba County, where Taylor and his rebels had entered the country to launch their insurgency. At the time of the invasion the governments of Liberia and Guinea had been close to reaching an agreement that would allow LAMCO to extend its mining operations into Guinea, using the existing infrastructure, notably the railway and the port, in Liberia. To the Yekepans this was a long-awaited sign of hope. The hope, however, was short-lived. When Taylor and his troops invaded the country they began a reign of terror that inched closer and closer to Yekepa each day. The most gruesome stories that made their way to LAMCO were those about the Mandingo, whom the rebels accused of having been granted special privileges by the Doe government because of their importance to the overall economy.

They were now being massacred brutally and hacked to death with machetes by the rebels in areas where the government no longer had control. These *included* the many villages along the road that we used to travel on our trips to Monrovia, *including* Fofana Town, which was torched once all its remaining residents had either fled or were eliminated. For its part, the government was not only unable to protect its people, but actually had resorted to killing those they felt had aided and abetted the invading rebels. As the future looked increasingly dangerous, LAMCO strongly advised its expatriate staff to return home, possibly for good, despite the agreement reached on the iron ore deal.

Claudius began to worry deeply about Mummy's safety. She was half Mandingo and half Americo-Liberian, which made her doubly a target. So in March 1990, while fighting was raging throughout Liberia, he loaded her into a car with just one small suitcase in her possession and drove her across the Guinean border, the closest and safest border crossing. From Guinea she could travel back into Liberia through another point of entry that would get her most directly into Monrovia, one of the few places the government still held. Mummy spent the first night in Guinea at a refugee camp and the next day she was about to board an open truck for the ride to the capital when a Guinean Mandingo approached her. "I remember one day I came to your restaurant to buy ice cream for my children and I did not have enough money, but you gave me a cone for each of my children, anyway," he said. He offered Mummy a ride in a much more comfortable taxi that was going all the way to Monrovia.

Even so, it was not an easy journey. All along the route the passengers had to bribe their way through various checkpoints manned by armed soldiers. At one point they had to descend and carry their possessions across the fragile suspension bridge—one of those known as monkey bridges in Liberia, handmade from materials of the forest—over the Lofa River, notorious for its dense population of crocodiles, because the vehicle might collapse the bridge if it was too heavily loaded.

Claudius remained home in Yekepa, hoping that the advance of Taylor and his troops eventually would be thwarted by the government or perhaps by ECOMOG, a West African peacekeeping force that had been sent to Liberia in an attempt to negotiate a cease-fire among the warring factions. He wanted to protect our property—our home and our restaurant and his new video business. He invited the restaurant staff and their families to stay at our house, and many gladly accepted. Most of them lived in the suburbs of Yekepa, where they were more vulnerable to marauding attacks.

A few days later Mummy reached Monrovia, but she had not escaped. Within days Monrovia was on fire. Sporadic fighting erupted throughout the city, as looters brazenly assaulted homes and shopping areas and dead bodies were left to rot on the street in the sweltering tropical heat. Unable to obtain an American visa, she had few options. Fortunately I was in the Central African Republic, and that was how she came to buy a one-way ticket to Bangui. For this, at least, I can thank the UN, as they had unwittingly stationed me in one of the few countries in the world where a Liberian citizen did not need a visa. I was in Senegal on business when my boss, Wally N'Dow, received a call from the airport in Bangui from Mummy, who had arrived with her one little suitcase, as if out of nowhere. The office located Barbo, whom I had given a few days off, and he immediately took charge of everything.

Doe was by now holed up in the executive mansion, and his troops were increasingly out of control. In July 1990, in one of the most widely reported stories of the Liberian civil war, they killed about 600 innocent civilians who had taken refuge in Saint Peter's Lutheran Church in Monrovia. The United States had a contingent of marines, as well as a navy task force, off the Liberian coast at the time; they were there to rescue about 60 American citizens from the U.S. embassy in Monrovia. They had no instructions to intervene on behalf of Liberians.

Many in Liberia believe that Doe was a personal witness to the hideous slaughter in the church. Journalist Mark Huband provides an eyewitness account of the atrocities that transpired on the night of July 29, 1990:

> *They made me strip off my clothes to let me inside. I saw women with their heads smashed to pieces, with babies still tied to their backs. I saw the bodies of people who had tried to escape hanging from the window frames. I saw people draped over the altar, who had been butchered with knives and shot with machine-guns. The floor was thick with blood, and there were bodies huddled together under the pews where people had tried to hide. The crucifix had been thrown to the ground and the*

ceiling was riddled with bullet-holes. And then outside, in the school buildings, where there had been people sleeping, everybody was dead. People had been killed where they lay on their mattresses. Everywhere dead people. There must have been hundreds. Six hundred I counted, around six hundred, or maybe more. And there were people who survived and jumped over the wall and went to houses across the road. And I talked to people who said they saw the soldiers going into the houses and finding these people and then taking them down the road to the beach. I don't know what happened to them then. Then they made me leave the area.[3]

It was not Taylor but the rebel faction led by Prince Johnson that got to Doe first. The president was tricked into leaving the executive mansion to attend a meeting at the headquarters of ECO-MOG. Doe was captured and subsequently killed by slow and savage torture, a process that was videotaped and circulated throughout the world. To the reggae strains of "By the Rivers of Babylon" his ears were cut off and other parts of his body dismembered while his drunken and stoned torturers interrogated him, trying to extract from him the numbers and codes to bank accounts he was believed to have in London and Switzerland.

The death of Doe only served to plunge Liberia further into chaos. Claudius remained in Yekepa even as most of the LAMCO expatriates left. Many of the Liberians, especially the working-class ones, had nowhere else to go. During a lull in the fighting Claudius decided to make the trip to Monrovia to pick up a shipment of videotapes that had arrived from the States. It was the last time he ever saw Yekepa. When he arrived in the capital he received an urgent phone call from one of our family's friends in Yekepa who was on his way to Guinea. "The NPFL have occupied your house, they have stripped it of everything, the marble tiles, the bathtubs, the furniture, the roof, everything," he told Claudius. "They killed your dogs and the restaurant has been completely looted, and the employees have fled for their lives. Don't come back because they will kill you. Claudius, just don't come back." He then described in detail the horrors that Yekepans were witnessing, as all that LAMCO had taken decades to build was ripped apart and destroyed in days—homes, hospitals, schools, tennis courts and pools, the electrical and water plants, communications facilities, the railroad tracks, everything. The rebels in their savage brutality did not care that they were destroying their own country. All that mattered to them was that they were in charge and that they were feared. There was no thought of protecting or preserving anything for the future.

To this day, none of us knows what happened to our local employees; sometimes I almost do not want to know. I think especially of Jacob, Pappi's sous-chef, who had been with us from the beginning. Jacob would be an old man now, but I don't know where he is, or even if he is. Many of the local employees of LAMCO were killed. Those who managed to escape had to build new lives from nothing in a foreign country, usually in neighboring Côte d'Ivoire or Sierra Leone, just when they thought they would be preparing for a comfortable retirement on their generous LAMCO pensions. They live in refugee camps, often as unwanted and unwelcome guests, dependent on the intermittent goodwill and charity of others.

In the weeks and months following the death of Doe, everyone who could left Yekepa. Families with their children who had been living a normal life in the secure cocoon of LAMCO were being forced to abandon everything, often with nothing more than the clothes they were wearing. Claudius, trapped in Monrovia, began the long walk (there were few vehicles in the streets) to the border of neighboring Sierra Leone, where he found members of Pappi's extended family who helped him. His goal was to start over in Sierra Leone. But less than a year later, in 1991, the war in Liberia spilled into Sierra Leone, beginning a brutal civil conflict that lasted from 1992 to 2002, leaving 50,000 dead, more than 100,000 intentionally mutilated with axes and machetes, and more than 2 million civilians homeless. The country was now more dangerous than it had been when the Fly-Catcher had first made his appearance there more than 200 years earlier, and the odds of survival were even worse; but where nature had once been the prime perpetrator, man had taken over with a vengeance.

Claudius applied for and received political asylum in Europe. This is how he began anew just as I was entering Harvard Business School. Our family had lost everything it owned and was scattered around the globe, like many other Liberian families—the lucky ones, that is. In Europe Claudius studied textiles and apprenticed himself to a well-known fashion atelier in Italy. Today, he has a successful business. He is married and has two beautiful children.

Mummy stayed with me for a few months in the Central African Republic, and through my U.S. contacts in Bangui she was able to secure a visa to come to the United States, where she applied for and eventually was granted political asylum. She settled in Philadelphia, living with Herbert, who was out of school and working. Abayomi, too, was completing school not far away in West Virginia where he was studying agricultural sciences at the University of West Virginia—so we were all safely out of Liberia.

Eventually Mummy was able to find work and move out on her own, but it was far from an easy road. First she took a job as a home health aide, many steps below her former position as a head nurse. This was difficult and menial work, which paid her only enough to get by, but a job that she never complained about. She considered herself far more fortunate than many who had been left behind in Liberia, or who had found the individual-oriented life in the United States too difficult to endure without the support and security of friends and family. She immediately began investigating what it would take for her to work as a registered nurse again and learned that she would have to take the state board exams and meet numerous other daunting eligibility requirements. At the age of 60, Mummy started from scratch.

Never one to run from a challenge she took nursing courses at the University of Pennsylvania, and then Kaplan courses to prepare for the RN exam. She passed with flying colors. Even today she recalls her terror of taking that exam, on which so much depended. She now works as the unit manager of the Pennsylvania Center for Rehabilitation and Care, a part of the University of Pennsylvania Health System. She has a good life now, but it remains difficult for her to speak about Liberia. The memory is too painful.

Back then it seemed that all of Africa was either on fire or about to be—Liberia, Sierra Leone, Angola, the Congo, Zaire (now the Democratic Republic of Congo), Rwanda, Ethiopia, Eritrea, Sudan, Chad, Cameroon, Mauritania, Senegal, Nigeria, Somalia, Djibouti, and Uganda, just to name a few. In Bangui too there was trouble, due to the fallout from chronic political instability and economic distress. Over the next decade the CAR would degenerate into a series of coups and countercoups and interventions by a round-robin of players, a number of African countries, France, and the UN, each either taking sides or attempting to instill peace at various stages of the conflict.

The wave of instability in the CAR began with a series of antigovernment protests that were triggered by the growing popular demand for political and democratic reforms, and by the same series of economic measures that had resulted in Barbo's layoff. These measures were part of the standard one-size-fits-all World Bank enhanced structural adjustment program that had been subscribed to by the CAR government. The program consisted of a series of harsh fiscal and monetary policies, including major cuts in government spending, particularly in the provision of basic social services to the population, including education, health, and housing. They also included massive reductions in the number of people on the government's payroll. The proponents of these so-called stabilization programs argued that they were necessary to ensure that the CAR could continue to service its external debts, which were going to be rescheduled by its major creditors if the country stayed this course of economic reform. These reforms would enable the CAR to secure additional loans from the World Bank and the IMF, much of which would be earmarked automatically for payment of interest and principal on earlier loans from these and other foreign institutions and governments, rather than to deliver needed social services. The Lord giveth, the Lord taketh away.

The effects of the draconian measures taken to cut government costs, services, and subsidies were felt immediately at the street level in Bangui, where they caused real pain to everyday citizens and fomented major civil unrest. Unlike Barbo, most of the people had not found alternative employment, and their living conditions were deteriorating further day by day. The experts argued that in the long run the benefits would trickle down. The outrage pouring into the streets of Bangui could not afford to hold out for the long run and its spurious windfall was in response to the shortcomings or outright deception of these trickle-down policies and promises. The truth was that only the costs seemed to trickle down, while the benefits coagulated at the top—especially when applied within the context of a nondemocratic and unaccountable government such as that running the CAR.

These protests were common in countries all over the world where the World Bank and IMF structural adjustment programs were applied. Indeed, they had become such an integral part of the programs that it is a wonder that the World Bank and IMF do not incorporate a low-interest antiviolence module into their programs, including funds for the governments to buy guns and other "antiviolence" ammunition to equip them to deal more effectively with the menace of these unruly, disaffected, and disenfranchised people. They were merely the collateral damage of these precision-guided adjustment programs to which Laputa habitually turns a blind eye. Once they have ignited the spark, or launched the first salvo, the Laputa experts check out of their five-star hotels and bolt back to the safety and security of their deluxe bunkers in Washington, D.C.

I was fortunate to escape the worst of the protests, when hundreds of civilians were killed in the streets of Bangui, but I did not have the option to bolt, at least not one day in 1989 when I was returning to the capital after a brief trip to Nairobi. As the Air France jet prepared to land at Bangui International Airport, the captain informed us that widespread rioting and looting had broken out in the streets of the city and that a state of alert was in effect. This sounded ominous. I decided that the best course of action was to remain on board and head directly to Paris, the plane's next destination. But Air France refused to allow any passengers who were not European or U.S. citizens, or in possession of French visas, to stay on the plane.

As I made my way through the airport terminal, where angry mobs were lurking in the corridors, I realized with a sinking heart that the UN hadn't sent a driver to pick me up, as was the custom. There were no phones in the terminal, so I could not call anyone. Who was I going to call, anyway? Nobody in his right mind would have ventured out to the airport at this late hour and under these precarious circumstances. The only alternative was to join forces with other disembarking passengers and find strength in numbers.

We found a driver courageous enough to venture into the city, and as our minivan made its way out of the airport and down the road toward Bangui's city center—a narrow strip of tarmac, shrouded in darkness—all hell broke loose. Suddenly, the van began rocking from side to side, jolting under the impact of what sounded like heavy stones or bricks. Throngs of angry people lining the road closed in on us, screaming epithets. Sounds of smashing glass, followed by sudden and unnatural flares of light, told me that we were being showered with Molotov cocktails.

I knew that if the van were disabled we would be dragged out and lynched. I suddenly became rational about, and even detached from, my probable fate.

Most of my fellow travelers alternated between screaming and crying. One by one the windows shattered in upon us, leaving us exposed to the next round of pellets. I stayed quiet, crouched in my seat with my head to my knees, protecting myself as much as I could with my Samsonite suitcase, which I held up against the window frame. The rocks continued to hit their targets (not me; definitely my suitcase) except, mercifully, our driver, who somehow managed to plow the van through the murderous horde. I felt as I had in the incident in Angola, as though Pappi were watching over and protecting me. The bus then headed directly to the Bangui hospital, where the critically injured among us were taken in.

It was the events of that night, along with the disintegrating political situation in the Central African Republic and my continuing frustration with the UNDP and its immediate cohorts, the World Bank and the IMF, and their modus operandi in these countries, which convinced me that it was time to leave the UN. Around this time, though, I was offered a posting to Windhoek, capital of the newly independent state of Namibia, a choice assignment, I was told. After 105 years of German and then South African colonial rule, and 24 years of guerrilla warfare waged against the government by the South West African People's Organization (SWAPO)—many of whose leaders I had met while I was stationed in Angola, as the UN had special programs for them there—Namibia finally had won its independence, making it among the last countries in Africa to do so. Interestingly enough, my erstwhile faculty supervisor at Georgetown, Chester Crocker, had been the principal architect of the "constructive engagement" approach to the numerous issues in southern Africa at the time, which included as a goal Namibia's independence.

Namibia was said to be a beautiful country. The UN was opening a brand-new office there and needed a lot of talent. I also understood that the competition for the new positions was intense, so I knew I was lucky to have been selected without having even applied. I was therefore tempted to take it. However, my boss, Mr. N'Dow, felt otherwise. He said that I was too valuable to the UNDP office in Bangui to be released.

The frustration of being detained against my will in Bangui provoked some serious soul-searching on my part. I reflected upon the four years that I had spent in the service of the organization. In the Central African Republic my activities, though more directly related to the UNDP's core projects, still had not convinced me that the organization was making any difference to the long-term success of the CAR. Despite all of the development aid that had been poured into the country over the decades, the people did not seem any better off; on the contrary, they were getting poorer. Worse yet, nobody in the international community or in the government appeared even casually preoccupied with this inconsistency. During my tenure there, we saw an endless parade of well-paid experts and consultants sent by the UN's various specialized agencies: the Food and Agricultural Organization (FAO), the World Food Program (WFP), the World Health Organization (WHO), the United Nations Industrial Development Organization (UNIDO), the International Telecommunications Union (ITU), the World Bank, and the IMF. Upon their arrival these experts and consultants would check into either the Sofitel or the Novotel and make the obligatory round of meetings with me or other UN generalists responsible for their paychecks, and with government officials and various other local and international staff connected to the projects on which they were working. Emphasis was placed much more on quantity than on quality of delivery. There was little or no incentive to bring a project to fruition. On the contrary, any project that ended, successful or not, would reduce the number of lucrative consulting contracts available to the large cadre of international experts dependent on the UN system for their livelihoods. It was like an addiction. Numerous spurious reasons were invented therefore to ensure that projects were rarely completed or terminated. The government often was complicit in these schemes; the expert could easily connive with the government official responsible for supervising the project to guarantee its renewal. The official's judgment and objectivity could be influenced by his access, say, to a project car, a good salary, furniture for his office, special allowances, training, trips abroad, and other perks associated with an internationally financed venture—all of which trumped the poorly paying government position he would have to return to upon termination of the project. The government official therefore would send an official letter to the UNDP representative, requesting the project's extension and attaching a document—which had been totally prepared by the international consultant but appeared to be the work of the government—presenting the justification for it. As the government was the final arbiter on the use of proceeds allocated to the country by the UN, the approval for the project extension would generally sail right through all official channels. Meanwhile, no fewer than 10 other international and bilateral organizations would be financing similar projects, for example, designed to increase the private sector contribution to the economy of the CAR. Nevertheless, during my two years in Bangui I did not see one private company created as a result of Laputa, Inc., despite the fact that entrepreneurship was our mantra.

The few entrepreneurs of any significant scale who did flourish did so in the face of overwhelming odds and steered clear of Laputa and its ilk. The bureaucrats, not the industrious entrepreneurs, dispensed and determined the use of Laputa's money.

It was while I was bedridden with malaria that I read *Gulliver's Travels*. I could not help but marvel at the striking parallels between certain activities observed by Gulliver on the island of Balnibarbi and those that I had observed in the UN, first in Indonesia, later in Angola, and finally in the CAR:

> *Lord Munodi, Gulliver's host in Balnibari and its capital, Lagado, treats Gulliver well. For instance, he gives him a tour of the extremely bizarre island. Other than Munodi's own estate, which is thriving and fertile, the land is completely eroded and barren. Gulliver questions Munodi about this contrast. Munodi explains that about forty years before, a group of Balnibarbian inventors and promoters visited Laputa, the flying island that hovers over Balnibarbi to learn innovative concepts in architecture, agriculture, and manufacturing.[4] They came out of the clouds and returned to Lagado, on earth, where they established the Academy of Projects to implement the theoretical schemes and blueprints that they had brought with them from Laputa. Nor surprisingly, most of their plans were never completed, and those that were, never worked. It was a total disaster for the island. By contrast, Munodi's fields were bountiful because he followed the customs of his ancestors. He acknowledged one exception, in which he was forced to replace his perfectly functional mill, in favor of one that was built halfway up the mountain. For the new mill to work, the water first had to be driven uphill and then downhill. The bubbles were supposed to give the water more "vivacity." The project was a total failure.[5]*

Swift's analogy encapsulates the dilemma that exists when the so-called experts have no personal stake. The truth is that in most of the developing countries, long before the arrival of the experts, it was entrepreneurs, and not governments and politicians, or the development institutions, that were the primary drivers of the economy. Moreover, market forces prevailed, not so much as a result of policy but of practice and practicality. For the most part, these entrepreneurs went about their businesses and the governments remained satisfied, so long as they were compensated adequately from taxing the businessmen's activities. They had no choice because, unlike the dawning of the age of Laputa, Inc. 50 years ago, there were no sources of "free money" available to them, which made them dependent on and beholden to the industriousness of their most enterprising people. With the arrival of development institutions on the scene, in partnership with inept and frequently illegitimate governments, a new player has been added and the roles have been reversed. The long-standing symbiosis between government and the private sector was destroyed. Now it is the alliance between governments and the large development institutions, not business, that is driving, or more accurately, stalling the economies, especially in Africa. As a result, the people have been economically and politically disenfranchised. Even where other countries—the former Soviet Union, all of Eastern Europe, and even China—have come to recognize the importance of the private sector, the Laputa charade goes on.

One can only conclude that the UN, World Bank, IMF, and other institutions like them have from the beginning been ill suited to the task of economic development and have tried to compensate for their shortcomings by growing bigger and bigger, adding new specialized agencies and more money in the misguided perception (or deliberate ruse) that because of their sheer size, internationally sanctioned oligopoly on development aid resources, limited accountability, and the apparent lack of alternatives, they are the only show in town. But if one takes stock of the reality today it is clear that there are players in the global community—the global corporations and entrepreneurs especially—far more adept at fostering economic growth than the inefficient international bureaucracies and autocratic third world governments.

Throughout my tenure with the United Nations Development Programme there was a near continuous attempt to broaden our mission and mandate and reinvent the organization for the benefit of the gullible tax-paying Western public. For a while we were the champions of the environment, then we were the go-to guys for entrepreneurs, then the savior of women and children, then the Terminator of the scourge of poverty, then the guarantor of perfect health for everybody by the year 2000. Just as the organization seemed to be running out of viable themes, along came HIV/AIDS, giving us and all the other Laputans a new lease on life. While I am all in favor of a clear sense of organizational purpose, and for the elimination of the aforementioned ills, the UNDP and its kind are poverty chameleons, constantly changing strategy and focus to justify their own upkeep, rather than to attain any legitimate goal or target. They know only too well that once a problem is solved, the party will be over.

My argument is that, given the choice, the vast majority of the people living in poverty, almost four billion, would choose to be run not by their governments and the UN but by a global corporation, as economic security always trumps nationalism. How else can one account for the massive immigration from developing countries to developed ones? Unfortunately, most people living in poverty throughout the developing world, and in Africa in particular, do not have that choice. For a while, some fortunate Liberians had a choice. They chose the corporation over the government, and as a result the citizens of Yekepa were far better off than most of the citizens of Liberia. LAMCO in Yekepa is where my argument begins; the UN in Bangui is where it ends.

I should not make it sound as though leaving the UN was an easy decision for me. It was not. I had prepared for what I thought would be a lifetime of service within that organization. My goal had been to help promote economic development in emerging market countries—a goal that I still regard as noble. But just as my college professors had predicted, I was no match for the bureaucracy, political infighting, and almost maniacal resistance to substantive change. My path to success in the UN was not to come up with a viable solution to economic development but to strive for mediocrity, to blend in and go with the flow. That way I would be assured of slow but steady professional advancement. I would become a Toon Vissers. My ascent within the organization would be a function of my age, nationality, and sex rather than of my performance. On a set timetable I would move through a series of mandatory steps within a defective and archaic system of job classifications. Even if I had been willing to climb this ladder, I knew that I would find disappointment further up.

So shortly after I learned that I would not be posted to Namibia, I sat in my Bangui living room munching on some of Barbo's miniquiches and pizzas and decided to apply to business school. For me, Harvard was the only option, and Harvard was by far the best known of all the business schools in the world. I also was attracted to the case study method of teaching for which Harvard was famous. The opportunity to actually study and analyze real-world business problems and experiences was appealing.

As usual, I had no plan B. Either I would be admitted to Harvard, or I would remain in Bangui, a Lord of Poverty, as Graham Hancock in his book of the same name so accurately labeled us.

Fortunately, I did not need a Plan B. With the sale of my personal effects, the proceeds from my UN pension investments, and a fellowship from Harvard I could scrape together the $100,000 that I estimated the two years at business school would cost me. My UN colleagues were astounded. I was burning my rock-solid bridge to lifelong employment and financial security for the unknown. They thought I was crazy. I had never felt more sane.

14

Back to School

In going from the United Nations to Harvard, I felt like I had leap-frogged from the Dark Ages to the Age of Enlightenment. How refreshing and liberating it was to be in an environment where creative thinking and self-expression were encouraged.

As at Georgetown and Johns Hopkins, many of the friendships that I formed at Harvard tended to be with other international students or first-generation Americans. Among them were Côme; Peju Onafowokan from Nigeria; Joe Massoud, an American citizen whose parents came from Egypt; Mehir Desai, an American whose parents came to America from India; Barbara Schmidt-Rahmer from Germany; Lan Tu, from Vietnam by way of London; Eytan Glazer, from Israel; José Leal from Brazil; Shannon Fergusson from America; Miwa Matsuo from Japan; and Waleed Iskandar, whose family had immigrated from Lebanon when he was a teenager.

Like Côme, Waleed would have a profound influence on my life in the next eight years. We met in a second-year class, Management in Developing Countries, a subject we both felt we knew all about. I used to tell him that he was my brother, a reference to the substantial Lebanese population in Liberia. Almost every Lebanese person that I have met in the world has a Lebanese, friend, cousin, or uncle who lives or has lived in Liberia. Waleed had penetrating, expressive eyes, and when I first met him he wore his hair tied back in a ponytail and had a Californian's "Where's the surf?" attitude. But he had traveled all over the world—Africa, Asia, the Middle East, Europe, and America. Often the two of us would get to class before the professor arrived and Waleed would tell me all about what party he was going to or throwing, which consulting project he was working on (in addition to the heavy school load we all carried), and when he would be able to get out to Western Mass. to do some waterskiing, another passion that we shared. He seemed to inhabit a different stratum than the rest of us, somewhere between earth and sky. He could be intensely serious and private, and extremely fun-loving and extroverted, all at the same time, without it appearing at all contradictory. For that reason, and because he always could make my spirit soar whenever I was with him, no matter what my mood. Like Côme, Waleed was planning after graduation to return to the Monitor Co. where he had worked prior to coming to HBS, but he also planned to travel to Africa. Tanzania was not on his itinerary; at least, that is what we both thought at the time.

Even in the first year at HBS, graduation loomed in our minds. I realized that, given the plethora of newly minted MBAs entering the U.S. job market every year, my contribution to the American economy in a field such as management consulting or investment banking would be marginal. Anyway, there were many students far more qualified and eager than I for such occupations. By contrast, with an HBS degree and my background, I stood a decent chance of making a major difference in the lives of tens if not hundreds of millions of those less fortunate than I have been. The choice was simple—at times I think even preordained. All of my activities during my two years at Harvard were directed toward making a difference upon reentering the real world. Every course I took, and every contact that I made brought me closer to that objective.

As I have said before, I focused my efforts on my emerging vision of a new kind of company. I was going to build the first continentwide telecommunications and media company in Africa. I immediately began putting together a team to assist me in the formulation of a preliminary business plan, which we would carry out as a field study. This warrants some explanation. Although HBS is famous for its case method, students learn in other important ways. One of these is the field study, in which a team of students, in the middle of the first semester of the second year, puts together a proposal for a field-based, independent study to be conducted during the second semester. The team then has to find a professor who is willing to approve the proposal and supervise the field study.

To fund the field study I used what was then an unconventional approach for an HBS student. (Though by the late 1990s, in the middle of the dot-com frenzy, this approach became almost commonplace.) I raised a total of $100,000 from four major telecommunications companies, including G.E., Motorola, Lockheed, and Sprint, and from my former employer, the United Nations Development Programme. I sought the UNDP's involvement not only because I needed the additional cash, but also because I figured it might facilitate access to government decision makers in emerging market countries.

Our team still needed a supervising professor. I had been told that Professor Howard Stevenson would be an excellent choice. For any faculty member to agree to sponsor a field-study team was a significant time commitment. And Stevenson wasn't just any professor: He was the guru of entrepreneurial studies at Harvard, an accomplished scholar, teacher, and writer, and according to local legend about his business ventures—the Baupost Group and numerous personal investments that he made—he possessed the Midas touch. For all these reasons and more, he was in great demand by other field-study teams. I submitted our proposal to him anyway, even though I figured that our chances of getting him were slim to nil. In that same semester—the fall of 1992—I had taken a course called Entrepreneurial Management, which was one of the few classes on entrepreneurship being taught at the Harvard Business School at the time. It had been designed and was being taught by Stevenson. But he rarely called on me in class, and this was a problem that went beyond ego massaging. As I have described elsewhere, class participation was an important part of the HBS grading system and, equally important, I desperately needed to ward off the cold call.

During the early part of the course, while the general framework was still being established, certain student comments based on historical patterns allowed the professors to communicate a predetermined number of important teaching points that would be critical to future directions that the course would take. An out-of-left-field comment could throw the entire discussion off course, and it was often difficult for the professor to get it back on track. I soon came to suspect that rather than setting me up for a cold call, Stevenson was afraid that my UN background made me a sort of wild card. Unlike the course Management in Developing Countries, which even included "alien radicals" from Harvard's Kennedy School of Government, most students in this class came from fairly traditional business backgrounds; the majority of them were American and had spent several years after college working at consulting firms, investment banks, or consumer marketing companies. Their comments in class, while astute and to the point, tended to be predictable, rarely venturing into terra incognita.

Indeed, my suspicions were stoked when I "looped" Stevenson's course. In HBS parlance, that means I passed, but barely. I was absolutely convinced that Stevenson had looped me because I was different, because he did not like me. How could I have not aced the final? I thought cockily. After all, I was just about the only one in the class who was actually going to do a real start-up. What did he know, this genius who himself had graduated from Harvard as a Baker Scholar and from Stanford with distinction in mathematics?

Given this history, the prospect of his accepting our field-study proposal now seemed even more remote. I told myself I was grateful for this; who needed the aggravation, anyway? But I was in for a surprise. A few days later I received a note from him indicating that he would be glad to supervise the field study. My biggest challenge now was to figure how best to get him to back out of advising us. I certainly did not want to be looped by him twice, and getting looped in the field-study course would have been a double whammy, because it counted for double credit. The two other members of my team were worried too. They did not want their geese cooked along with mine, if it turned out that Stevenson really did have it in for me.

I found another professor who enthusiastically agreed to supervise our field study. He promised to speak to Stevenson about the switch. Stevenson stood firm. As it turned out, this was one of the luckiest breaks I have ever had.

My unfolding vision for the trans-African communications network that I planned to build consisted of telephones, television, and other communications services for hundreds of millions of people, many of whom had never before had access to such services. I was not thinking small; Harvard had taught me to think big.

From the first-year students I chose my five interns for the summer while my field-study teammates and I were working hard to complete our project and overcome Stevenson's skepticism. At the end of a field study, the team makes a presentation to the supervising professor. My suspicion that Stevenson did not like me had not changed during the semester, and I was eager to finish and finally get on with my life and my plan. On the day we presented to Stevenson he began the whole exercise with a skeptical, "So, do you still think it's a good idea to invest in Africa?"

When we were getting up to leave, I asked him if I could speak with him alone. My two teammates left, but waited anxiously outside. Since they were both potential Bakers, they worried that Stevenson's animosity for me might affect their grade. After their exit I asked Stevenson flat out if he did not like me. Before he could respond I told him what a tremendous effort it had taken to put this work together. I confided that I would have appreciated it if he had looked at me just once during our closing discussion. Then, uncharacteristically and uncontrollably, I burst into tears.

Poor Howard! The world-renowned authority on entrepreneurship makes time in his crowded schedule for a field-study finale and winds up instead with an *opera finale*, worthy of Verdi, and staged right in his office. He ran to the door, closed it, and nervously handed me a box of tissues. My team must really be panicking now, I thought. I pulled myself together, and he sat down and leveled with me. He said he was mostly worried about me. He knew that for my two teammates this had been only a field study, whereas for me it was clearly so much more. Because of his experiences in the business world he already saw what I could not yet see. It was going to be a long and difficult road, he told me, and he suspected that I was still very much alone. He also knew that my immigration status would change now that I was no longer a student, that I did not have a work permit, and that I faced a host of other daunting and complicated hurdles that did not even seem to have entered my mind. Rather than having it in for me, he said, he was thinking of ways in which he could help me.

"The first thing you'll need," he said, "is a good lawyer." He recommended that I contact his friend Dick Floor, a partner at Goodwin, Procter & Hoar, one of Boston's most prominent law firms. Floor was also an occasional lecturer at HBS and, Stevenson said, he was successful enough that he might be able to help me without running up huge legal bills. He also would probably be able to put me in touch with a good immigration lawyer when I needed it. My teammates and I wound up getting high passes from Stevenson. But even if we had looped, I would not have cared; I was already looking beyond that small triumph to the challenge of turning our rudimentary business plan into a real company. I had learned in the infamous entrepreneurial management course, from Stevenson himself, all about Fred Smith, the founder of FedEx. Smith submitted the business plan for FedEx to his Yale business professor. He received a C– and was told it was impossible, and even if he could do it, he'd never make a profit.

A few days later, with the assistance of Dick Floor, I incorporated my company as African Communications Group. Several years later, when there was high demand to take our services to Asia, Latin America, and Eastern Europe, the company name was changed to Adesemi, after my namesake, Mamma Ade.

I now needed to make critical contacts in the financial community, especially in the venture capital industry, to start lining up some additional seed money for when I returned from Tanzania with the business plan. But where was I to start? I had no track record in the telecommunications industry, only a skeleton of a business plan, and no management team. One person came to mind—William Draper III. Bill was one of the early pioneers of the U.S. venture capital industry, creating (among other partnerships) Sutter Hill Ventures. In an indirect sense he had been my boss during my employment at the UN. His friend and Yale classmate, President George Herbert Walker Bush, had in 1986 appointed Bill chief executive of the UNDP, to replace Bradford Morse. Our tenures at the UN had overlapped almost exactly. He had tried to make the UN more corporate, to make it more fiscally responsible and managerially astute, and had encountered enormous internal resistance in the process. Over the years we had gotten to know each other, and we continued to stay in close touch.

When I informed him that I was interested in starting my own business, Bill immediately put me in touch with his son, Tim Draper. Tim is also a graduate of HBS and a talented investor in his own right. He later would invest in such firms as Hotmail, acquired by Microsoft; TRADEX, acquired by ARBA, for $6 billion, and Four11, acquired by Yahoo. He became one of Silicon Valley's most successful and high profile venture capitalists. We talked about ACG. He told me that he viewed it as a "flyer," but that he was willing to bet on me. Tim was somewhat familiar with Africa, and was reasonably aware of both the risks and the potential rewards. He proposed that he invest $50,000 in the company in exchange for a 25 percent stake. I agreed in general terms; after all, a post money valuation of $200,000 sounded good enough to me, and I knew that there was a lot more where that came from, which could make my life much easier down the road. I asked him to put our tentative agreement in writing. Within days he sent me an investment proposal, outlining the terms that we had agreed upon over dinner. All seemed to be in order.

But, as I would learn again and again when putting new deals together, nothing went smoothly. I sent a copy of Tim's proposal to Dick Floor for review. Dick told me flatly that I should not accept it, because it was still far too early to settle on a valuation for the company. I felt terrible about this—having already given Tim what I felt was a "handshake" agreement—but Floor reassured me that these things happened all the time in the venture capital industry. Dick and Tim then talked it over, and when Tim called me back, it was clear he had not enjoyed his conversation with my lawyer. He said that Dick was acting more like a concerned father than a lawyer (which I secretly found reassuring). I told him that I would think about it a little more and get back to him. I called Stevenson to tell him of my dilemma. "Listen to

Dick," Stevenson advised. So I contacted Tim and confirmed that the deal was off.

Tim was a little annoyed, but seemed to understand my position. He reassured me that there were no hard feelings.

By the end of the semester, not only was I dealing with lawyers and venture capitalists, I was also in almost daily contact with the UNDP office in Tanzania. I wanted to hit the ground running. We attended to the final predeparture logistics, including making airline reservations, securing passports, and applying for visas. Most painful of all was subjecting our bodies to a full arsenal of shots, boosters, antimalarial pills, and all the other medical precautions that the Harvard doctors could come up with once they realized that we were determined to go to Africa despite their dire warnings about the ravages and dangers of the tropics. In June we headed for Tanzania, my summer of truth, and eventual redemption at the hands of Côme Laguë.

Part IV

Adesemi
and Beyond

15

We Are in Business

September 1993. Now that I had run the gauntlet of U.S. Immigration and Customs at Logan airport and was back in the States free and clear, I had to turn to the suddenly urgent matter of where to live. I really had not given much thought to what I would do once I got in, because I had not been at all sure that I would get in.

I again pulled out my precious HBS class directory, and this time I called another classmate and friend, Barbara Schmidt-Rahmer, who I knew had taken a two-bedroom apartment and a job with Coopers & Lybrand in Boston. I was hoping that if Barbara hadn't found a roommate yet that she would have a cheap room to rent out. I was right. I moved into the spare bedroom, got my own telephone line, and hooked up a simple Panasonic thermal fax machine, my beat-up IBM laptop, and a tiny, portable Kodak dot matrix printer. My 9-by-12-foot abode, located at 23 Haskell Street, within shouting distance of HBS, became the temporary World-wide Headquarters of African Communications Group, Inc.

I got straight to work, and was in constant contact with Côme, who was back in Toronto working for Monitor. He insisted that I get an AOL address. Email was the new thing, and we agreed that it was the most efficient and economical way for us to communicate. He told me that he would work for Monitor during the day and dedicate his evenings to ACG. If we raised the money to launch the pay phone project, Côme would quit his job and join me.

Together we finished the final sponsor report in about four weeks and sent it out. Then we began putting the finishing touches on the business plan. It was October 1993, and for the next three months I was constantly in touch with Tingitana, our partner in Tanzania, checking on his progress in securing important technical concessions from the Tanzania Posts and Telecommunications Corp. and updating him on my fund-raising efforts. Through my HBS contacts I began with the who's who of VCs in Boston: Advent International; Burr, Egan, Deleage & Co.; Greylock Venture Capital; Highland Capital Partners, and others. Their plush offices, decorated in rich velvet curtains, thick Oriental rugs, and oil paintings, had all been meticulously selected to convey a sense of wealth, sophistication, and establishment. The typical conference room was fitted with a heavy oakwood table surrounded by large overstuffed burgundy-leather chairs, evoking images of a passing era. The floor-to-ceiling windows in these offices afforded spectacular views of the Boston skyline and harbor. But despite the aura of civility, no samosas or tea in fancy china cups were served here. There was a cool, almost impersonal efficiency with which the meetings were conducted, in stark contrast to my business meetings in Tanzania.

For the venture capitalists in Boston, even California was long distance. I can only imagine what was going through their heads as I spoke to them about a wonderful pay phone opportunity in Tanzania, "a country located in East Africa," as I often had to explain.

"Isn't that where Idi Amin came from, the guy that used to eat people?" one venture capitalist asked me.

"No," I corrected him. "Amin was from Uganda, and he was a cruel dictator, but as far as I know he never ate people. You must be confusing him with Emperor Bokassa of the Central African Republic." I did not elaborate further on my intimate knowledge or dubious connection to that tiny bit of trivia, although I am sure it would have made for a very interesting story in their otherwise insipid annals.

Whenever the discussion deteriorated to this level and we were no longer talking about pay phones, I realized that they would not be writing me a check. "A pay phone business in Africa? Whatever happened to plain vanilla deals?" one of them asked me incredulously. "Isn't this something that the World Bank should be doing?"

Those were difficult days. It was before the Internet boom, so there was little information that I could get online, and there were mornings when all I could do was turn on the TV and watch some of the appalling but strangely fascinating talk shows. Sally Jessy Raphael one day featured two brothers who were so hairy that they looked like apes, but they had managed to attract two very normal-looking girls. Like the people on these shows, I seemed to be living in a parallel universe, isolated from reality. I do not know how I kept going, other than pure persistence, which I have always had in abundance. I was running so low on cash that Côme sent me $1,000 to keep both the opportunity and me afloat. Barbara told me I could wait to pay rent until we were funded. One day, with nothing but time on my hands, I walked into Rebecca's Café at Harvard Square and sat down for a cup of coffee. A couple of minutes later in walked Waleed Iskandar.

As expected, he had returned to work for Monitor and was based in their Cambridge headquarters offices, but he was traveling a lot, mostly to Eastern Europe, which was now all the rage with consulting firms and investors now that the Cold War was over.

After I told him my whole saga, he said, "How much do you need?"

I responded to what I thought was a rhetorical question. "Six hundred K," I said, using the numbers from our revised business plan.

"Maybe I would be interested," Waleed said. "Let me take a look at the business plan." I looked at him in amazement. At school he was fond of wearing tattered jeans and T-shirts; he certainly had not given me the impression that he had two copper pennies to rub together, much less several hundred thousand dollars. I practically sprinted home and called Côme.

I later found out that Waleed already had made a few small investments in developing countries, so he knew the type of market opportunity it was and the risks involved. After about a month and some very probing questions on the financials and the nature of the market, Waleed called to tell me that we should begin drawing up the legal documents for his investment. I could hardly believe it! On a cold Saturday morning in January 1994, a lawyer from Dick Floor's firm, Waleed, and I met at the Boston Plaza hotel for a closing breakfast. We signed the documents and Waleed deposited $600,000—$200,000 of his own money, an equity investment, and a $400,000 loan to the company, from members of his family—into a corporate account that I had opened. Waleed, Côme, and I were now the official owners of African Communications Group, Inc.

Côme immediately gave notice to Monitor, and I moved the ACG headquarters and our limited office paraphernalia to a two-bedroom apartment on the first floor of a three-family townhouse in Cambridge. A couple of years later, with a little bit of negotiation with the landlord and some creative construction, a hole was made from my unit into the townhouse's unfinished basement and we transformed it into an additional two offices and a conference room. This would serve ACG well for an additional five years. But for the first year and a half we had only my apartment to work in. The kitchen doubled as an office for our newly hired assistant, and the extra bedroom served as an office and a bedroom for Côme, who was winding down his work with Monitor and preparing to move to Cambridge.

Waleed's investment in us had another profound effect on my life. ACG was now considered a well-capitalized company, and Waleed and Côme, as major shareholders of that corporation, were free to sponsor me for a special working visa that would allow me to come and go freely from America and eventually to sponsor me for my green card. The latter took five years and a long and tedious process, but they supported me all the way. With a green card I would be eligible to work in the States and not risk deportation to Liberia, even if ACG were to flounder. The green card was also my first step toward citizenship. What Côme and Waleed did for me went beyond business. They were truly amazing friends.

Now flush with more than half a million dollars, my immigration nightmare in a manageable state, Côme and I were finally in a position to take our first trip back to Tanzania. Almost five months had passed since I had left Tanzania. I called Tingi to give him the good news: that we were finally financed; that Côme had joined me full time; and that we were coming back to launch ACG Tanzania with him. But instead of shouting for joy, he asked me how much money I had raised, and on what terms. I was perplexed, because all of this had already been signed and agreed to in the memorandum of understanding that we had signed prior to my departure. Why was he asking me this? I wondered. I had an awful feeling that after months and months of all my hard work, and of of rejection and humiliation by one VC after another, Tingi had double-crossed us or would try to change the terms, which would jeopardize the financing that we had just secured. I sensed that something was terribly wrong, that Tingi was not being honest with me. I shared my suspicions with Côme. I told him that I had noticed that Tingi was no longer returning my phone calls promptly, or with eagerness, and was being increasingly evasive.

"Perhaps the phones aren't working well, or maybe he hasn't gotten your messages," he suggested. "Maybe he is sick or traveling." Deep down I felt that there was indeed something very wrong. Yet Côme had left his job, the funds had been invested, and at the very least we needed to figure out whether or not we still had a deal and an opportunity.

We agreed that we should proceed with our trip to Tanzania to assess the situation fully. I offered to go first.

I arrived in Tanzania at close to midnight, this time with no official UN support, as we were now operating as a private company. However, since the local UN office felt that it had been involved with the start of this initiative, and it was in Tanzania's national interest that it be brought to fruition, it agreed to give me some limited support for a few weeks. This included accommodation for a couple of nights, until I could make my own arrangements, and the temporary use of a vehicle.

I was told that I was going to stay at the house of the head of the UN office. As it turned out, the entire house had been locked up during his prolonged absence and I was going to be staying in a room in the basement. The room had no curtains, no screens, and nothing but the bed and a satellite phone on the table beside it. I could not get over the irony. Here I was, deep in the heart of Africa, surrounded by armed security guards staring at me through the heavily barred window, with a satellite phone on the bed stand because it was easier for the UN to get through on one of those than to rely on a regular telephone.

I had brought sheets and towels with me, which I hung over the windows to keep the guards from peering in. Unfortunately this left me with no covers, no pillow, nothing—only lizards, roaches, and mosquitoes for company. I turned on the air conditioning, hoping that it would keep away the bugs. The sound of it was like a car revving up in my bedroom. It also was extremely cold, with the temperature dropping to what felt like 40 degrees. I put on my jacket and started to cry. What in the world was I doing here? I was voluntarily going back to this? I picked up the satellite phone and called Côme in California, where he was visiting Charlene. I was prepared to abandon everything. But when he answered the phone, his voice sounded so certain and reassuring that I didn't have the wherewithal to back out; I realized that I was no longer in this alone, and that now, more than ever, I needed to be brave and practical. I was only too happy to see the morning come so that I could begin my now urgent search for alternative accommodation. But first I needed to find Tingi. After some hide-and-seek, I managed to get him to meet me for lunch.

"So, Tingi," I said, smiling to conceal my inner turmoil, "how are you? Is there something wrong, because I have had difficulty reaching you."

"Monique," he asked sheepishly, "did you really raise six hundred thousand?"

"Yes, Tingi, I told you that I would come through for you."

When I told him that under our investors' terms he was to retain 25 percent of the company, as we had originally agreed, his face fell. He confirmed that he had broken our agreement and raised money from a new venture capital fund, the Tanzania Venture Capital Fund, Ltd. (TVCF), set up in 1993 by a British government agency, Commonwealth Development Corp., and that he was not in a position to extricate himself from that commitment.

I could not believe this. We had worked with him for almost nine months and he had stabbed us in the back. Moreover, he had given up far more of his company for far less money. Tingi had made a stupid mistake.

I called Côme that evening to tell him what had happened. I was afraid that he would give up. He suggested that we try to convince Tingi to reverse his position. But I said that I was no longer comfortable working with Tingi, as I didn't trust him anymore. If we decided to walk away from the deal, we would have to dissolve the company, return the money to Waleed, and concede defeat. I therefore suggested that we work it out upon Côme's arrival—assuming he still wanted to come. I did not know how many more rabbits I had left in my hat, and I was certain that Côme was counting on me to pull out a few more.

Côme is a man of his word. "Monique," he said, "I have made a commitment to you, and I intend to keep it." That was the end of the story. Never during all the years of Adesemi, through all the ups and downs that we went through, did Côme ever lead me to believe that he regretted his decision. On the contrary, by the end of it all, Côme's commitment to Africa sometimes would even trump mine.

I am a dreamer, Côme is a pragmatist. While this combination created challenges; and at times tension, our divergent personalities were absolutely critical to the successful partnership that we built. So in that situation, I did what I had to do. I dreamed.

"Côme, why can't we do this on our own, even bigger and better than Tingi? We have more money, more know-how, more know-who." I knew that if I could give Côme this assurance, he would go about figuring out the practical ways in which we could or could not achieve that vision. After spending so much time on the business plan, Côme already had become quite the expert on pay phones and marketing, and he had absolutely no doubt that he could "beat Tingi's ass," as he put it. Having crafted the business plan, he knew all the strengths and weaknesses of Tingi's business better than Tingi himself. His competitive juices were flowing, and this is when Côme is at his best. It is also the time when I know that I have to step aside, clear away any obstacles, and just let him focus.

All we needed to do, we told ourselves, was demonstrate that we could provide better service than the utterly decrepit public pay phone service that was available locally. By the end of our conversation we had managed to talk ourselves into thinking that Tingi actually had done us a favor. Nevertheless, we did not kid ourselves into thinking that this would be a slam dunk. On the contrary, if each of us had had to make the decision separately, we probably would have abandoned the project. But together we felt invincible. We soon embarked upon a relentless campaign to persuade the Tanzanian government to issue us the necessary operating licenses that would enable us to meet the pent-up demand. This would put us in direct competition with the government's own fledgling pay phone operations, and with Tingi's as well, which now went by the name Jupiter Communications. We soon discovered that despite Tanzania's official eagerness to attract foreign investments, for the most part it was interested only in those investments that could personally benefit certain high-level officials in the form of kickbacks. As it turned out, the investment climate in Tanzania was paradise for unscrupulous investors and sheer hell for the rest of us.

Our struggles with the authorities in Tanzania lasted for the entire duration of Adesemi's presence in there, nearly seven years. It is difficult to convey the weariness we suffered from battling the government's impediments to our activities and operations. Côme and I were compelled to spend days at a time sweating outside dingy, cramped, and stuffy antechambers with broken air conditioners, trying to maintain some semblance of dignity and decorum in the face of these deliberately orchestrated waiting periods. The irony of all of this was that with less than a 1 percent telephone penetration-density in Tanzania, the government should have been beating down the doors to have companies like ACG investing in the country to provide a service that the government clearly had demonstrated it was incapable of providing. With little else to do while we waited for an audience with some reluctant government official, we were obliged to waste many tedious hours reading outdated and obscure technical or propaganda magazines from all corners of the globe that had been left by foreign visitors attempting to sell the government one useless technology after another. Once we finally made it into the office of the government official, nine times out of ten, and after much sycophancy and kowtowing, we would discover to our utter dismay that our host, despite his elevated title and position, was not only ignorant, discourteous, and conceited, but had no real power or authority. Shortly after these meetings some low-level intermediary would inform us that with the appropriate "inducement," our host might be favorably disposed to lean upon the person with the actual power to grant us our wish.

The uncertainty and whimsical nature of the political and regulatory environment were the primary reasons we ultimately decided to limit the scope of our operations in Tanzania. The regulatory body was neither independent nor competent. What was even more appalling than the government's recalcitrance was our discovery that as U.S. taxpayers, through our contribution to the World Bank, we were in essence subsidizing our own competition. This was because, subsequent to ACG's investment in the pay phone business, a segment it had neglected completely for decades the Tanzania Telecommunications Company Limited (TTCL) (formerly TPTC had suddenly experienced an epiphany. After more than 30 years in business—as a monopoly, no less—TTCL now saw ACG's activities and market popularity and discovered that there actually was an opportunity to make money in the pay phone business, a segment it had neglected completely for decades. It therefore went to its sugar daddy, the World Bank, for help. Aware of the flagrant market and regulatory inequities that existed in the Tanzanian telecommunications sector, because even the president of the World Bank himself, Jim Wolfensohn, a Harvard Business School graduate, had personally but ultimately unsuccessfully intervened on our behalf to at least try to level the playing field, the World Bank provided Tanzania with a favorable loan to launch an identical public pay phone network to compete directly, and unfairly, against ACG's. As soon as it launched its network, TTCL began a deliberate strategy of predatory pricing in an unsuccessful but aggressive attempt to drive us out of the market. TTCL controlled the regulatory framework, and had what amounted to free money from the World Bank.

ACG's protestations to the World Bank and the U.S. government, who also challenged the Bank on our behalf, through the Overseas Private Investment Corp., from which ACG had purchased political insurance risk, were met by the bank's usual smorgasbord of impenetrable bureaucrats, who claimed either ignorance or impotence and sometimes both, even in defiance of the U.S. government, its largest shareholder. It turned out that the World Bank's official policy of private-sector development in Africa was little more than froth and wind, except for when its own private sector development arm, the International Finance Corp., stood to benefit as an investor. Not content with the highly lucrative development aid business it has carved out for itself, the insatiable World Bank also created the IFC to corner the market on lucrative private sector investment opportunities that come its way as a result of the inside edge and insider information it enjoys as a key adviser and lender to governments, even when such ventures may be inimical to the economic interests of the government in question, or better served by third-party investors. This type of behavior would be prosecuted aggressively by the Securities and Exchange Commission, the Federal Trade Commission, the Federal Communications Commission, or any equivalent regulatory body in a developed country. But the World Bank operates in a universe of its own, free from the probing and prying of the watchdogs that are essential to an efficient and effective capitalist system. Imagine the U.S. economy with each of its federal regulatory commissions having an investment arm. The FCC could invest in AT&T and Worldcom, the Food and Drug Administration could invest in Monsanto or in ImClone, or the Securities and Exchange Commmision could invest in the New York Stock Exchange. Well, that is precisely the kind of cozy setup that Laputa has successfully orchestrated for itself, and, despite this deliberately rigged handicap, it still manages to fail abysmally. Laputa preaches competition, but it certainly does not practice it. In spite of it all, by 1995 we had successfully begged the bare minimum of operating licenses from an array of government functionaries to launch the first phase of our network, and set about raising a new round of capital to bring in the required technical and managerial expertise to build and run the business. After far too many rejections to count, and once again on the verge of bankruptcy, we struck gold.

This second round of capital investment, for $1 million, was led by Landmark Communications, a media company based in Norfolk, Virginia. We had been introduced to Landmark by Howard Stevenson, by now my trusted friend and the Obi-Wan Kenobi of ACG. Howard, who had been our fourth board member (after Waleed, Côme, and me), also sat on Landmark's board of directors. Landmark was willing to put $750,000 into ACG, provided that we raised another $250,000 elsewhere. We discussed this with Waleed, who agreed to pony up the capital needed to secure Landmark's $750,000 commitment. Howard also made an investment at the same time and participated in all subsequent rounds of ACG financing as well. Of course the more we raised, the more we needed, especially as we began to staff up for the launch.

Identifying well-qualified managers for Adesemi's operators in Tanzania was no easy feat; we were a start-up, which carried not only the typical baggage of limited cash and uncertain survival, but also the not so typical baggage: that our employees be willing to carry theirs on flights to Tanzania, as opposed to Boston or San Francisco. Howard advised Côme and me, upon reviewing the bios of a couple of our managerial candidates, "At least resist the urge to pick up any warm body you come across." At times even Howard's very basic counsel proved difficult to adhere to, and on more than one occasion we found ourselves in the unfortunate position of jamming square pegs into round holes. Without a doubt the most extreme example of this tendency was the selection of our first marketing director, a southern belle whose only prior experience in marketing had been selling real estate in Little Rock, Arkansas. The U.S. ambassador to Tanzania, who was also from Little Rock and a strong supporter of ACG, had recommended her to us. She was eager to come to Tanzania, which by our somewhat desperate recruitment standards automatically made her 50 percent eligible, and she had political connections in those days of the Clinton administration. It soon became clear, however, that the synergies between selling upscale real estate in America and pitching a complex telephone service to first-time users in an emerging market did not really exist, no matter how much southern charm, which she oozed, was being applied. She was the first that we let go when her contract expired.

Fortunately, we made some great initial hires. I had not forgotten Jean Barbo! Since I had left the CAR in 1991 Barbo had been working on his farm and running his snack bar. Côme and I asked him if he would consider coming to Tanzania to manage the guesthouse where we and other ACG consultants stayed while in Dar es Salaam, as this was a far cheaper arrangement than putting everyone up in a hotel. Barbo, never one to shy away from an adventure, moved to Tanzania immediately, putting his retirement on hold and accepting a five-year stint with us.

There came a time when Côme acknowledged that, having never built or run a public telecommunications network before, he had reached his limits on the technical side of our business and that it would be wise to bring on board someone with the requisite background in this area. This is when I contacted Gunnar Mathisen, a Norwegian, who became our chief technology officer. Gunnar was a godsend. He had run the telecommunications network for LAMCO in Liberia when I was a child, and was a good family friend. But I had not seen him in years. I managed to track him down in Saudi Arabia, and convinced him to return to Africa. The first thing that Gunnar told us was that because of the deficiencies of the Tanzanian telecommunications infrastructure, our network would have to be wireless. This was an incredible break, as it would give us maximum independence from the TTCL infrastructure and increase the reliability of our service. The bad news was that to complete the first phase, which consisted of a modest network of 400 pay phones, we would need an additional $3.5 million, given the specifications of the cutting-edge technology that Gunnar had researched extensively and recommended.

Out of necessity, Côme and I became nearly full-time fund-raisers for the venture, and were constantly on the lookout for new, complementary opportunities even as we sought to raise the additional capital for our network in Tanzania. This was to leverage our existing investment. With the highly qualified team that we had in place, especially our technical talent, led by Gunnar, there was a lot more we could do than build and operate a modest-size pay phone business in Tanzania. One day in 1996 I came across an advertisement in *The Economist*. The government of Ghana was privatizing its national telecommunications company, Ghana Telecom, and issuing a second national operator (SNO) license. Management and ACG's board of directors agreed that securing such a license would be an asset for ACG and improve its future fund-raising prospects. This was because winning the SNO license would enable us to establish a foothold in a second country. It also would give us the opportunity to provide a broader range of services to our customers, including private and commercial telephone service, and international access—the most lucrative components of telecommunications services in these countries. Moreover, the SNO in Ghana would be the first of its kind in Africa, and winning it would establish ACG as a major trendsetter on the continent.

In light of the large scope of the project and the expected complexity of the proposed network, we decided to form a consortium to bid on the SNO license. Our consortium came to consist of the Western Wireless Corp. and the Ghana National Petroleum Corp. (GNPC). Western Wireless (later renamed VoiceStream) was a leading provider of wireless communications services in America and had an impressive track record. We were introduced to the company by one of our existing investors, who also happened to be a major investor in Western Wireless. GNPC was our local partner (we had been introduced to its chief executive by one of our suppliers) and a significant player in the local Ghanaian economy with plans for diversification into the telecommunications industry.

The government of Ghana had chosen globally recognized firms to manage the privatization process. CS First Boston was retained as the government's financial advisers, and the New York–based law firm of O'Melveny & Myers was hired as its legal counsel. Fortunately for all concerned, the World Bank was not involved. This provided us with reasonable assurances that the bidding process would be fair and transparent, unlike most other opportunities that had come our way during our three years in business. Had the World Bank been part of the process, we surely would have lost out to IFC, which would have elbowed itself into a winning position using insider information and other standard strong-arm Laputa operating tactics.

We won the license and automatically became a founding partner, although a minority shareholder, of one of the largest telecommunications transactions on the continent. With well-established and deep-pocketed partners like Western Wireless and GNPC, we seemed to have entered the big leagues.

Along with the acquisition came the greater responsibilities and complications inherent in all business partnerships, where the players have different objectives. We had had a shotgun wedding, and reality soon set in. Western Wireless's sole role in the bidding process had been to write the check to pay for 50 percent of the license. Although the ACG team had led almost the entire bidding process, including the technical, financial, marketing, and political components, identifed a well-capitalized and politically influential local partner, Western Wireless wanted to assert control over the new venture. There was little we could do to resist, even though we tried. Western Wireless, part of a publicly traded company, was infinitely more capitalized than ACG was, and had far more extensive industry experience, even though it lagged ACG in the area of pay phone operations, something the company had never run before. This is why we attempted to secure a concession from WW that would at least allow us to run the pay phone operation within our winning consortium. Soon Western Wireless was putting its own people in charge and relegating the ACG team to the role of silent shareholders. In an attempt to salvage something from the hard work we had put in, we attempted to negotiate an arrangement with Western Wireless where we would be responsible for at least the portion of the market we knew best, and in which it had no experience itself: public pay phones. But now that it was firmly in control, Western Wireless was not interested in conceding an inch—the company already had our technical know-how in this area, which we had provided in the spirit of the partnership and with the tacit and explicit understanding that this would be the province of ACG.

Still, despite our disappointment with the Ghana partnership, four years after the incorporation of ACG we had a lot more to show potential investors than just a concept. With the financing from Waleed, Landmark, a few angel investors, and some supplier credit, we had successfully installed a state-of-the-art and highly functional wireless local loop network, with 400 public pay phones in Dar es Salaam, and were processing over 50,000 calls per day, which translated into annual revenues of approximately $1.5 million. We also had a 10 percent stake in the Ghana SNO, valued at $2.5 million. But we had far higher aspirations. In response to growing customer demand, we planned to extend our service, first throughout the country, and next across the continent and beyond, to preempt potential competitors.

Most exciting of all, though, we were poised to introduce what would become our signature service: the virtual phone service, the first of its kind on a wireless platform in the world.

The virtual phone was a seamlessly integrated platform of wireless public pay phones, electronic voicemail boxes, and beepers. It offered the subscriber a low-cost but highly effective alternative to basic telephone service, which was beyond the economic reach of the overwhelming majority of the people in Tanzania, Ghana, and other countries that we would target eventually. Instead of having to wait years and years for a telephone to be installed in his home, a customer could simply go to the post office or to any one of the numerous retail establishments we contracted with throughout Dar es Salaam to market our product, and for less than $25, and no monthly fee, he could buy an Adesephone™, a self-contained and attractively packaged personal communications system that included a beeper and a telephone number that was linked to his personal electronic mailbox. The package also contained a number of little extras, such as a starter set of business cards, an address book, and a pen to enable the customer to begin exchanging phone numbers immediately with family, friends, and business associates. Once the customer called the toll-free customer service number listed on the package, he was immediately in business. Calls would go into the subscriber's voicemail box, a message would be left, and his beeper would go off, alerting him that he had a message to be retrieved. Nine times out of 10, the message would be both sent and retrieved through Adesemi's public pay phone network, generating revenues on both ends of the call. This system may have appeared rudimentary by Western standards, but to someone who has never had a telephone, and whose only alternative form of communication is to send a messenger on foot or by vehicle, it was indeed revolutionary and a godsend. It democratized communications. Think of the stranded travelers along the road near Fofana Town, or traders all over the continent trying to figure out where they could get the best prices for their commodities, and what a difference an Adesephone™ could make in all aspects of their lives. The virtual phone service was targeted at people making between $200 and $1,000 a month, a global potential of 4 billion people. Simple as the concept was, it belied the complexity of the high-tech backbone on which we were building the service, as well as the extensive marketing it would take for a successful launch in Tanzania and other countries. It was going to be an ambitious and costly undertaking.

This meant raising more money—at least $7 million, but $10 million would be a lot better. We had to turn to deep-pocketed investors. Côme and I, sometimes accompanied by Waleed, who had a lot at stake in ACG, flew far and wide—to Seoul, London, Amsterdam, Johannesburg—before we found HarbourVest Partners right in our own backyard of Boston. HVP is primarily a "fund of funds," with over $14 billion in capital under management. It rarely invested directly in companies, but made an exception with ACG. Although our operations were in Africa, our headquarters were in Cambridge. Moreover, we made a compelling business case with our Tanzania and Ghana successes. HVP committed to investing $3.5 million, provided that ACG found an additional institutional investor that had experience and operations in Africa to invest the remaining amount. Having HVP, which commanded tremendous respect and credibility in the global private equity market, as a potential investor in ACG significantly facilitated our effort to secure the rest of the capital. To meet HVP's conditions for financing, we secured the balance from development finance institutions, notably the Dutch Development Finance Corp. (FMO) and the British Commonwealth Development Corp. (CDC). Both of these were fully or partly government-owned entities of the IFC kind, and they had extensive experience working in developing countries all over the world.

When ACG had first entered Tanzania in 1993, CDC was in the process of creating a small venture capital fund, the Tanzania Venture Capital Fund, to invest in entrepreneurial ventures. This was the very company for which Tingi had jilted us. In backing Tingi, CDC had never dreamed that ACG would soldier on, posing a threat to one of their first and most promising ventures, Jupiter Communications. The head of the new venture fund—an employee of CDC—had sent a highly defamatory letter with baseless claims about ACG to the United Nations office in Dar es Salaam and, I'm told, to the Tanzanian government as well in an attempt to block our license application and intimidate us from entering the market. The CDC rep was persistent, but ultimately unsuccessful, and within a couple of years, because of our superior technology, better financing, marketing, and overall management, we had captured an unassailable share of the pay phone market, just as Côme and I had predicted when Tingi left us at the altar. Jupiter still had fewer than twenty-five phones, compared to our 400. Even with the highly subsidized loan from the World Bank, TTCL had been unable to challenge our position.

So in an attempt to salvage its Tanzania pay phone investment, CDC fired its managing director and approached Adesemi with a request that we acquire Jupiter. We declined, not seeing any salvageable value in Jupiter. In what can only be described as "if you can't beat them, join them," CDC decided to invest instead in ACG. Where they had once been vilifying us, we were now their belle of the ball. Perhaps this history should have served as a cautionary tale, but we needed CDC's money. FMO, which worked closely with CDC on deals around the world, wanted in on ACG too. For both CDC and FMO, the prospect of being in bed with the powerful and prestigious HVP was intoxicating, as was the ability to have a stake in our high-profile Ghana SNO holding, both of which would look impressive in their fancy brochures and PR materials. In the end, CDC and FMO provided a loan guarantee and a loan to our local subsidiary in Tanzania, in the amounts of $3 million and $1 million respectively, against which we secured the entire virtual phone operation in Tanzania, the book value of which was approximately $5.5 million (net of depreciation). They also invested equity into ACG. CDC invested $4 million and FMO, always playing the role of second fiddle, kicked in $2.5 million. Their equity and loan investments, combined with HVP's, infused ACG with $14 million ($10 million in equity, $4 million in loans). The value of the company had increased from $800K when Waleed first made his investment in 1994, to $20M after HVP/CDC/FMO had completed their investment. More important, we had succeeded in attracting the type of deep-pocketed investors that we needed to fuel our planned growth and international expansion. We used the proceeds of the equity investments and the loans to further expand the network in Tanzania, to launch the virtual phone service, and to develop new country expansion opportunities. We knew we were fortunate to have HVP on board; we thought we were lucky to have CDC and FMO on board, at least until we actually started working with them. Once again I had been seduced and duped by glossy brochures.

In this period I also had another brush with greatness in Africa, bolstering my theory that in far-flung places you meet real stars. One morning in March 1997, while going through some documents in our U.S. headquarters—still in the basement of my apartment in Cambridge—I received an urgent phone call from our managing director in Tanzania. He informed me that he had been alerted by the U.S. embassy in Dar es Salaam that Hillary Clinton was coming to Tanzania. The embassy was in the process of preparing her agenda, Mrs. Clinton had expressed a desire to visit a successful U.S. company during her visit, and the embassy had selected ACG. Because I was the president and CEO of the company, it was more or less obligatory that I be there to welcome her to Tanzania and to our operations.

I left Boston for Tanzania with less than 24 hours' notice. By the time I arrived in Dar es Salaam early Sunday morning, the Secret Service had already completed a thorough security sweep of our office premises. With barely a moment to put down my suitcases, I staggered through the rehearsal drill with members of Clinton's advance team, representatives of the embassy, and of course the security guys. We went through every detail of the planned visit: who would stand where; who would say what and when; what to do if somebody, meaning the First Lady, suddenly needed to attend to nature's call; and so on.

A few minutes before her arrival, and to our immense surprise and delight, we were told that Mrs. Clinton was going to give a speech encouraging U.S. companies to follow ACG's lead and take advantage of the open investment climate in Tanzania and other parts of Africa. She was, of course, not up to speed on our endless trials and tribulations with the government and its almost fanatical resistance to any form of competition that threatened the government's own activities in the private sector.

The visit to our offices went off flawlessly, including the symbolic telephone call that Mrs. Clinton placed from one of our wireless pay phones in Dar es Salaam to our offices in Cambridge, where Côme was waiting anxiously by the phone. We had hoped to record his end of the conversation, but the normally calm, cool, and collected Côme had been so starstruck that he had forgotten to turn on the tape recorder. No great loss, however, as the entire visit in Dar es Salaam was videotaped. We knew that we couldn't have put together a better promotional piece for any price: The First Lady had endorsed ACG.

By 1998 we had built up a significant amount of momentum. We had 75 employees worldwide, revenues of nearly $2 million in Tanzania, a 10 percent share of revenues of $15 million in Ghana, had launched a global marketing campaign, and had several new potential acquisition prospects in Africa and Asia. That year we changed our name to Adesemi, to reflect the broader global markets we were now going after. *The Wall Street Journal,* the *Financial Times, Success* magazine, *Wired,* and several other publications wrote us up in glowing terms. A Harvard Business School case on the company had been written already, and the case was further updated to record our progress. Côme and I were invited to speak at several major business schools where the case was taught and about the experience of starting up Adesemi. All this publicity and the inherent merit of the virtual phone system led to a flood of inquiries from people and companies in India, the Philippines, Brazil, Russia, and Côte d'Ivoire, among other places. They all wanted to know if we could replicate our virtual phone service in their countries. After five years of 16-hour days living in cramped apartments, and with no social life to speak of, Côme and I began allowing ourselves to believe that Adesemi might succeed even beyond our most ambitious dreams.

Many days of a start-up are calamities waiting to happen. The likelihood of this increases exponentially for a small company operating in a turbulent region like Africa.

On August 7, 1998, at 4:30 A.M., I was out for my daily run along the Charles River. I treasure this time of the day, when I am entirely alone with my thoughts. As usual I had my Walkman strapped around my waist and was listening to the BBC news. As I approached mile 12 or so of my run, the reporter announced that there had been an explosion, apparently caused by a bomb, at the U.S. embassy in Nairobi.

I was shocked. Africa has had more than its share of plagues and maladies, but by and large, terrorism was not one of them.

I thought immediately of Côme and our local staff, relatively close to the scene in neighboring Tanzania. By now, seven hours ahead of us, they surely would have heard this terrible news. As I approached the end of my run, there was an updated news bulletin:

A second bomb had gone off, this time at the U.S. embassy in Dar es Salaam, less than a mile from Adesemi's offices. I now tore home and immediately switched on the TV. CNN crews were already at the scene of both attacks.

I knew that Côme was supposed to be at the office that day, because he was scheduled to lead the new director of the Tanzanian Communications Commission, a regulatory agency set up in 1994, on a tour of our office and operational facilities. This was an important event for Adesemi, since the director held, at least on paper, enormous sway over telecommunications licensing issues in Tanzania. We therefore were attempting to make our best possible impression on him in the hopes that he finally would do his job and settle the numerous outstanding issues between Adesemi and TTCL.

Just as I was about to pick up the phone to call Dar es Salaam, it rang. Côme was on the other end of the line. I breathed a deep sigh of relief. He reassured me that everyone at the office was fine, although, like everyone in Tanzania, they were all shocked and horrified at this assault.

Just as the tour for the new TLC director had gotten under way there had been a loud blast. Several of the windowpanes on one side of the office had blown out of their frames. Momentarily disoriented and trying to gather their wits, several Adesemi employees, Côme among them, assumed that the detonation must have come from our telecommunications equipment. Not the best of timing, Côme remembered thinking. The TLC director was amazingly unfazed. Given the deplorable state of telecommunications in Tanzania, he had no doubt witnessed more than his share of system breakdowns and blowouts.

But through the broken windows, off in the distance, they saw a thick plume of smoke billowing from what appeared to be the U.S. embassy. Bad news travels fast in Africa with or without a phone, and reports of a bombing reached our offices very quickly by word of mouth. The scope of the attack in Tanzania: 12 killed, 300 injured.

After my conversation with Côme, I prepared a release for the Tanzanian press expressing our sadness and condolences to the people of Tanzania. The statement was soon picked up by the major international newswires, and our Cambridge office phones began ringing off the hook. For the next several days there was an endless parade of television reporters and camera crews outside my apartment, requesting interviews with Côme. As the only Bostonian on the scene, he was their local peg.

Exciting at first, the drill soon became trying and tedious. One by one the reporters asked me to show the viewers exactly where Tanzania was. They would then ask me to pinpoint on a Dar es Salaam map that we had the precise location of Adesemi's offices in relation to the U.S. embassy. Whenever Côme was conferenced in, his voice was accompanied by a mug shot that we had given to the reporters. This image was intermittently switched with that of one of our wireless pay phone booths, which we kept in our Cambridge office for demonstration purposes. Some of them wanted to know if Côme would consider remaining in Dar es Salaam to assist them in covering the story. But he was more interested in coming home than in boosting local television ratings. Moreover, this was not exactly good public relations for Adesemi, with investors who were already weary of turbulence in Africa. Several of our key equipment suppliers, having heard the news of the bombing incident, called to express their condolences—and, more importantly, to inform us that they would no longer ship products to Tanzania until they had received 100 percent payment up front.

When Côme flew home, he was greeted by an impromptu press conference that began right there at the international arrivals terminal of Logan airport. A reporter asked if we thought that Tanzanians had been responsible for this crime. We explained that this was highly unlikely, given that Tanzanians are generally a peace-loving society with positive feelings toward America. Côme went a step further. He took advantage of this unexpected and somewhat overwhelming media opportunity to emphasize Adesemi's ongoing commitment to Tanzania. Only 36 hours removed from this traumatic event, which would probably have left more seasoned entrepreneurs understandably jaded and discouraged, he found the right words to tell a television audience the truth about a faraway land and people that he had over five years come to know, admire, and respect.

In November 1999 Côme was selected by MIT's *Technology Review* magazine as one of the 100 top entrepreneurs under 35 for past and future potential to make a significant contribution to technological innovation in the next century. During the award ceremony, in which he was the runner-up to the first prize, he was distinguished as a "techno-Samaritan," skilled at developing and applying cutting-edge technologies with a social mission. I am certain his words at the airport that day in August were heard.

Business is about two things: people and money. Good people and good money are neither easy to find nor to manage. In my experience, senior managers are the most difficult of all to manage—especially within the context of a constantly evolving and high-pressure environment of a start-up. New people are constantly being added to the core team, often upsetting an already fragile balance of egos. Goals and targets are perennially shifting. These and more are the normal growing pains of any start-up, but Adesemi's were more complex because of the international nature of both our management and our operations. A few months after the embassy bombing, our Boston staff had doubled to about 10, and after six years in my basement, we finally had graduated into some commercial office space. These changes, combined with other operational challenges we were facing, led to strained relations between Côme and me. Things had come to a head when Adesemi faced the critical decision of whether to expand our operations beyond Dar es Salaam into the other major cities of Tanzania, as we had planned originally, or whether we should look at opportunities in other countries, where the regulatory climate was more advanced, the markets were more efficient, and there was less political interference. Team members went both ways: I felt that our license stipulated that we had to keep our expansion plans in Tanzania and might jeopardize our entire operation by failing to live up to our obligations. But TTCL, with whom we had the license, had not lived up to its obligations; therefore, one could argue, we too had no obligation to Tanzania except within Dar es Salaam. Côme was on that side of the argument—he wanted to go into other countries.

Before long Côme and I were at loggerheads on this, and it had turned into something between us that went beyond the immediate debate. On the eve of our departure from Boston for an important series of meetings with the regulatory authorities in Tanzania over the issue, we screamed at each other—Côme has probably raised his voice three times in his life—and accused each other of disloyalty and worse. Côme canceled his trip. "You can go on your own, and when you get back I'm not going to be here," he said. I went to Tanzania alone, but I was a wreck the whole time. The advantage of being in business with a close friend is that you can count on each other even during the worst of times, and in our five years of business together, Côme and I had seen the worst and survived it. The flip side is that when you have such a terrible fight, you don't know who to talk to without feeling that you are betraying that friend. We certainly could not talk to each other about it.

He was still there when I got back, but the rift went on for some time and affected morale at the company. In addition, we had obligations—to our investors, to our employees, to our customers. We had to solve this problem.

We needed help from someone with basic common sense, compassion, and decency. As soon as I phrased the problem this way, a solution came instantly to mind: Barbo. I spoke to Côme about it, and he agreed with me, although he did not suspect my ulterior motive.

Barbo had done such an astounding job in Dar es Salaam that we had promised him that at the end of his career with Adesemi we would bring him to the United States for a visit. He had one more year to go before he would retire, but we expedited his retirement party by bringing him to Boston in early 1999. I felt that his services were urgently needed.

During the next six months Barbo, through a combination of his calming and caring presence, restored the personal and professional bonds not only between Côme and me, but also among Adesemi's staff. Shortly after his arrival we created a lunch pool. Each of us contributed $20 per week to the pool. Barbo would make fresh croissants and other delicious French pastries in the morning, followed by lunch at one o'clock. We were the envy of the entire building, as the rich aromas of fresh bread and other delicacies wafted all the way to the bottom floor and seeped out into the street. We stopped eating stale sandwiches and yogurt, isolated in our individual offices. Now with the entire team eating together in the intimate and cosy dining room of our newly renovated office, we had the opportunity to get to know one another a lot better, and to discuss both work and recreational topics. In addition to the bonding opportunity these daily lunches provided, numerous new ideas were generated and presented for open discussion by everybody from the CEO to the receptionist. Fridays were looked forward to with particular zeal because it was buffet day, on which Barbo would concoct masterpieces from the leftovers of all of the goodies we had had during the week. I am not exaggerating when I say that within two months of Barbo's arrival, the team unity had been fully restored and was in many ways even stronger than it had ever been.

I am by no means suggesting that what every company needs to overcome its Human Resources Management problems is someone who is functionally illiterate with no significant business experience and no academic credentials. What I am saying is that I believe that the solutions can often be found within the organization, rather than through a third party.

Barbo did not come to Boston believing that he was on a mission to save us. I suspect that he did not even know that there was a problem to be solved during his half-year stay. What he quite coincidentally created was the context for us to identify and resolve our problems. As we convened for lunch each day, we were drawn at first to Barbo's excellent cuisine. The team spirit that emerged was a serendipitous by-product.

One day, when his early fascination with the big buildings, giant supermarkets and shopping malls, glowing city lights, and all the other symbols of modernity had begun to wane, Barbo looked at me sadly and said: "Mamma, the people in the street, they don't say 'hello.' " He had seen for himself what I had tried to explain to him, probably unsuccessfully, in Bangui; that the cars, the houses, the clothes, the money did not make one happy. After almost six months in America he was aching to return home to his village where, as he explained to me, when the people see you, they smile and they say hello. They take good care of each other, he explained. Just as he had done so unwittingly for us during his brief stay. I could see the pain in his eyes, and I knew that it was time for Barbo to go home. Progress, I have learned from people like Ma Kema and Barbo, is an extremely delicate balance and usually comes accompanied by a very hefty price tag. For all its horrors, miseries, and calamaties, maybe in partial compensation for, and to help its people deal with them, Africa remains the one place on this planet where one can still find Eden. As Greene so aptly put it, "Love . . . stripped of all its trappings."

16

The End

By January 1999, after almost six years of research, development, and testing in Tanzania, numerous fits and starts, and nerve-wracking vicissitudes, Adesemi had successfully completed the full build-out of its integrated virtual phone network. We were now looking forward to providing our growing customer base with yet another service: Internet access at our public kiosks. We had even identified a U.S. company, ITXC Corp., to partner with us in this effort.

All the while Adesemi continued to be plagued by numerous regulatory and administrative obstacles in Tanzania, which we finally had concluded was no El Dorado. Our board of directors voted for the company to expand the Adesephone™ concept to other countries because the government had not met several key obligations to us, and still had a long way to go on the path of capitalism, where market and regulatory conditions were infinitely more favorable than they had turned out to be in Tanzania, despite its urgent pleas for international investors. We already had conceded Ghana to Western Wireless, where we remained a silent partner. But over the previous year we had done significant due diligence in a number of other countries, including Côte d'Ivoire in West Africa and Sri Lanka in South Asia. We had reached agreements with existing pay phone operators in these two countries to acquire majority stakes in their operations, expand, and introduce the virtual phone system and public Internet access. The majority of the board was in favor of the expansion.

Beyond the desire for more favorable, or at least predictable, regulatory and operating environments, another motivation for expansion beyond Tanzania was our belief that it was only a matter of time before the larger and more established global telecommunications players focused their sights on the same emerging market countries that we were targeting. So we had to move quickly. Our goal was to introduce the Adesephone™ service in at least 25 countries within five to seven years. By successfully executing this ambitious strategy, Adesemi would position itself for either an initial public offering or to be acquired by a global telecommunications or media company. Both were perfectly desirable exit strategies for our investors, a just reward for all the early risks they had taken.

Côte d'Ivoire and Sri Lanka were particularly attractive for a number of reasons. The per capita GDP in each of these countries was almost six times that of Tanzania. The market and financial prospects looked very promising, because we had negotiated standard revenue-sharing agreements with the TTCL equivalents in these countries, something that TTCL had absolutely refused to do, limiting the upside potential of our investment in Tanzania. This time we had resolved all potential regulatory hurdles before we had committed any capital; we had learned our lesson in Tanzania. Finally, it looked as if six years of work were about to pay off in a big way. Côme, Waleed, and I, the original partners in Adesemi, were ecstatic.

Here's where the concept of good money versus bad comes into play. To finance the acquisitions in Côte d'Ivoire and Sri Lanka, and similar ones in three more countries in the next two years, management and the board of directors decided to raise between $15 million and $20 million in new equity. We also agreed that it would take us approximately one year to raise this amount. We already were hearing a refrain from potential investors that we had approached: "Come back when you are operational in three or four countries." In other words, they wanted scale. The board voted to do a "bridge" round— business jargon for the money that gets you from here to there—of $6 million among the existing investors. The bridge capital would enable Adesemi to expand immediately into Côte d'Ivoire and Sri Lanka, and by doing so increase the valuation on which outside capital could be raised approximately one year later. HarbourVest and Landmark agreed to put up their pro rata shares, which amounted to several million dollars. So did the majority of our early individual investors—the angels. Not all of Adesemi's investors were so savvy. While potential new sources of equity wanted the company to grow before considering investing in Adesemi, CDC and FMO wanted us to scale back, which would have made Adesemi less, rather than more, appealing to new investors.

Despite the adverse market and regulatory conditions in Tanzania, they wanted us to focus exclusively on Tanzania. In this way, their loan to the Tanzanian subsidiary, which was as important to them as the equity stake they held in the holding company, would be better protected. FMO promptly declined to participate in the bridge round. Initially CDC said "yes"; after a few months it shifted to "yes, but"; almost a year later, after all the legal documents had been drawn up and dispatched for signature, it said "no."

After its initial decision in January to participate in the bridge round, CDC dragged its feet, declining to make its pro rata investments in Adesemi until we recast the company into a mold to its liking. Each time we met CDC's new requirements, it was like opening a Russian Matrioshki doll: always one more doll inside, each more insignificant than the previous one. Given the intensity and frequency of the interaction between management and CDC, we soon began to feel like one of its departments, rather than a separate company. We were asked to renege on contracts that we had signed with partners and longtime suppliers. CDC took the view, based on its dealings elsewhere, that these local partners and equipment suppliers could be squeezed.

Such unscrupulousness and insensitivity shocked not only Côme and me, but the rest of our mostly buttoned-down board members as well. We considered ourselves to be a credible company with high integrity. We were certainly not accustomed to being instructed by a board member to shaft our already cash-strapped local partners, with whom we had built a bond of trust and signed binding contracts. Who exactly were we in bed with here?

This was the first time that CDC had invested in a U.S.-based company, and it was also probably the last, because whereas they could get their way with desperate entrepreneurs in far-flung places such as Dar es Salaam, Abidjan, and Colombo, the deep-pocketed sophistication of Boston was a different story.

We refused to comply with CDC's order. "Well," the CDC board member said, "then we're going to have to cut costs by radically reducing your staff."

It was as if the agency wanted us to apply one of Dilbert's core principles: Just keep cutting costs and soon you won't have to do anything to be profitable. The problem was that we could hardly afford to do nothing. We had services to deliver and complex telecommunications networks to build and run in extremely tough markets. Evidently CDC had hoped that we could use our "profits" from the Tanzanian operation—which were only paper profits, especially as we had to service the staggering CDC and FMO debts—to create a $100 million company without any further investment. For almost a year the CDC had had almost our entire staff at its beck and call. We had been catering to its each and every whim, even when it distracted us, as it so often did, from running the business. Its true Laputa colors were showing; even its brief flirtation with smart money, as represented by HVP, could not tame the beast within. Like Swift's projectors of Laputa, CDC was almost maniacally obsessed with the conceptual rather than the real world, and with the infinite number of "what-if" scenarios that it could construct, the most important being, "What if Adesemi never raised a penny again, would the company still survive?" Like the bankers rather than risk takers that they are, they wanted a 100 percent guarantee.

The irony is that we were raising the bridge capital to expand while CDC was saying it would only participate if we contracted. It was an inherent contradiction. But no matter how many scenarios CDC concocted, the result was always the same: Adesemi needed more money if the company was to grow. This conclusion was already apparent to our experienced and successful venture capitalist investors from the day that they decided to proceed with the bridge financing. They understood that the only way to grow was to put more money into the company, and to use that money in ways that would increase the value of Adesemi and enable us to raise further rounds of capital on much better terms for the investors.

CDC, on the other hand, expected to reap a bountiful harvest without planting any seeds. The agency had a formula for investing in emerging market countries, one that it had been applying for almost 50 years, from the time it operated as the Colonial Development Fund, when the overriding government philosophy was to make the colonies pay their own way, and even more important, pay more than their own way by contributing to the British coffers, therein contributing to the development of Great Britain with the minimum amount of investment. CDC applied the same investment theory to projects ranging from fishing to mining to telecommunications. It was a one-size-fits-all approach that I recognized only too well from my days at the UN. In its boundless arrogance it gave absolutely no credibility to the views of our experienced venture capitalist investors, despite the fact that the venture capitalists were accustomed to giving returns of 25 percent to 35 percent to their investors, a range that even in their worst years crushed the astonishingly mediocre 8 percent that CDC typically returned to the British government.

More unpalatable to CDC was that it was not a majority investor, a position it was not used to being in in its dealings around the world, which kept the organization from being able to throw its weight around. The CDC was quite unaccustomed to negotiating or even interacting with equals, let alone with entities that were more successful or more financially sophisticated. Like most development institutions, CDC prefers dealing with the cash-strapped, subserviently timid, local entrepreneurs and governments of the third world. They had erroneously, though totally in character with their unparalleled arrogance, interpreted HVP's earlier insistence that an organization with local operating knowledge be brought on board as a condition of its investment as HVP's surrender to CDC's superior knowledge and wisdom on all matters third-world-market related. It didn't even dawn on them that in less than 12 months HVP had already far surpassed them in this category as well.

I'm sure the CDC has its own view of these events. My view is that for whatever reason, the CDC spent almost an entire year trying to destroy both the vision and the spirit of Adesemi by trying to make Adesemi (and us, the staff) conform to its rigid and outdated perception of the developing world. CDC became the enemy within.

Adesemi had obtained full investment commitments from HarbourVest Partners, Landmark Communications (which had even agreed to take up the FMO's pro-rata share), and all the angels, in the amount of $5 million, conditional upon CDC's contribution of $1 million, less than its pro rata share of the $6 million of bridge capital. Adesemi had just had its best quarter in Tanzania. Not only that, the entrepreneurs in Côte d'Ivoire and Sri Lanka had complied with all of our conditions, and the suppliers had extended extremely generous terms to us for the new equipment we planned to purchase for our expansion into these two new countries. If CDC did not put its $1 million in, Adesemi would fold.

For a rational investor the choice would have been simple: You already have $4 million in the game (it is a sunk cost), $6 million is required for you to have any chance of recovering that $4 million, of which a number of other players have put up $5 million. It was a no-brainer. But CDC, like the experts of Laputa, was not rational and could not think in practical terms. It was as if they were on a mission to prove themselves right, even if it meant cutting off their nose to spite their face. Moreover, they were arrogant enough to believe that the other investors would cave, and ultimately put in the $6 million and let CDC get a free ride. What it did not understand was that there was no way that Adesemi's management and the other investors would tolerate any infusion of cash when we all knew CDC and FMO legally could, and based on past behavior very likely would, oblige Adesemi to pay off all or a substantial part of their $4 million debt to our subsidiary in Tanzania, rather than allow it to be used to expand our operations into Côte d'Ivoire and Sri Lanka.

We had long known that CDC was difficult to work with. It had taken the other major investors six to eight months to complete their due diligence and initial investments in Adesemi, whereas it had taken CDC over two years. We had known that CDC played rough; we had had our own experience with that when its local Tanzania Venture Capital Fund had tried to squelch the nascent ACG in Tanzania in 1994. But we had not believed that CDC intentionally would mislead its own partners. Despite its track record, we all figured that CDC would come to its senses before the do-or-die day, which was approaching rapidly, as the company was running out of cash. It was now June, and October was the drop-dead date.

For the next four months we soldiered on, as CDC wanted us to run more scenarios, mostly involving radical staff cuts, hoping that as our cash reserves diminished, so would our resolve. CDC wanted Adesemi to scale back to a two-person operation, Côme and me, and for us to move the office back to my basement. Finally, in October 1999, after we had met what CDC insisted were its final demands, the agency imposed a new set of conditions, followed by yet another, each time turning the screws tighter and tighter, until it dropped the bomb. By now, as CDC was well aware, Adesemi was out of cash. The agency would not make the $1 million investment; as a result, Adesemi would not get the $5 million that was already committed conditional on the CDC investment. Adesemi would fold.

Even CDC was surprised at how quickly Adesemi died; it had accomplished this within a little over a year of its entry into the company as a shareholder. Still, the company expected the process to drag on for months, or even years, keeping its myriad committees and subcommittees at work. What CDC didn't understand was that in America, unlike in many third world countries, everyone had options—alternative start-up opportunities or jobs in corporate America. The other investors in Adesemi had lost all their money, but it was the local employees and our customers in Tanzania who were going to suffer the most.

But unlike CDC we did not intend to devote another minute to fruitless scenarios. We were purposeful, methodical, and swift. As quickly as possible after the financing fell through, our board met in Boston on October 21, 1999: Black Thursday, we called it. Fewer than 25 percent of the investors showed up in person, so disgusted were they (as some of them later told me) at this nonsensical turn of events. Some of the absent investors participated by phone; a few opted not to participate at all. They had other more important things to do than listen to CDC on its soapbox. Howard, however, at my request came to the meeting, to provide moral support, which the entire team desperately needed. Howard had been there since the beginning; I needed him there at the end. Adesemi's lawyers were also present, now joined by a bankruptcy attorney. The CDC board member arrived from London. The mere sight of him made me want to throw up. It was typical that he would find the time and money to come all the way from London for this. I am sure he enjoyed Boston's finest hotels and restaurants during his stay.

From his opening comments it was clear that the CDC was still under the impression that Adesemi's management and the U.S.-based investors would capitulate, invest the additional $1 million needed, save the company, and give CDC a free ride. But it was not to be.

Instead, the U.S.-based investors took the necessary votes to proceed with the liquidation of the company. Those investors present then walked out, and those who had been conferenced in hung up their phones, leaving the stunned CDC representative to deal with the havoc that his institution had wreaked. Côme and I spent the next few hours with the bankruptcy attorney and the CDC representative in an attempt to arrange an orderly wind-down of the operation. We made a modest request to CDC to fund this effort. They declined, but offered to place security guards at our offices in Tanzania to protect what they now viewed as CDC's assets, as Adesemi was now in default of the CDC and FMO loans to the subsidiary. CDC had carefully crafted the loans to ensure that theirs had precedence over the FMO, so for all intents and purposes, FMO had lost its $1 million loan to the subsidiary. We did the best we could with almost no resources, an experience we were all too familiar with from our earlier days. As Howard had once said of one particularly distressing period during the early days of the company, when I had had to chase him down in Bombay, where he was on a business trip, and ask him to wire us funds to keep the lights on in my apartment and pay the phone bills: "I never saw a company operate on fumes for so long."

CDC's actions were particularly disappointing because its corporate mandate is precisely to catalyze private investments in emerging markets. With its conduct with Adesemi, it had achieved precisely the opposite. But the people at CDC had never really practiced risk in these markets. They confused business risk with country risk, which was something that had not been clear to us prior to working with them. The American venture capitalists had demonstrated that they understood the concept of risk, even in the context of the African market, and that patience was necessary to achieve long-term success. For CDC, the concept of risk is very narrow.

After Adesemi's close, CDC moved expeditiously to seize the entire Adesemi operation in Tanzania. It also wasted no time in going after our minority stake in our Ghanaian operation, eventually forcing Côme and me out of the liquidation process. In closing, the CDC representative turned to me and said, "Monique, you know, this isn't so bad. We close telecom companies all the time at CDC." He seemed to say it with a certain amount of pride.

After the CDC representative left the building, we breathed a collective sigh of relief. It had been all that we could do not to kick him out immediately after the meeting was concluded. But he had just hung around, as if it were just another day in the office. Côme and I immediately called a meeting of the Boston staff and informed them of the pending liquidation. I can truly say that they were stunned. They knew that we had been hovering on the brink, but it just did not seem rational that CDC would not invest the $1 million to save the $40 million that had already been invested in the company ($15.6 million directly into Adesemi plus $25 million raised for the Ghana SNO)—$4 million was their own! With the exception of Barbo, whose life experience gave him some perspective and who really did not understand the magnitude of what had just transpired anyway, we were all very shaken.

As we sat despondently trying to console one another, one of my colleagues, Robert Keter, from Kenya, said that the entire debacle reminded him of a Swahili proverb, which, given that Swahili is the principal language in Tanzania, seemed a fitting analogy: *Nahisi ya kwamba mtoto amepokonywa uhai wake kabla hajapewa nafasi ya kugundua uwezo wake.* "A child has been robbed of her life before she has had the opportunity to realize her potential." I told him and the others that I disagreed. I said that I felt Adesemi's potential was still out there, that this was a mere setback, and that each and every one of us still believed in it and had an obligation to fulfill it, in our own ways. We had been compelled to show the courage to let go when it became clear that our current course was untenable. The wind had shifted, I told them, and now we needed to plot a new course, each in our own individual way. I knew that some of us would continue the journey, others would embark upon journeys of their own, but with important lessons learned. The magic and the pull of a start-up are those rare and precious moments when the company experiences the opportunity to dramatically alter people's lives. Adesemi had accomplished this in no small measure. We had made a significant contribution to Tanzania's telecommunications sector. We had created many new jobs, and won many loyal customers, who were extremely sorry to see us go. Most important, though, we had the immense satisfaction of knowing that despite the numerous obstacles and setbacks during our six years in East Africa, we became known in Tanzania as "the company with phones that work."

In its postmortem on Adesemi, CDC prided itself on having saved other less capable investors (in its opinion) from throwing good money after bad. In a perverse way, they were right, but for all the wrong reasons. There were other forces, far more powerful and pervasive, working against our interests. Adesemi would have eventually foundered on some rock.

I should point out that just as Adesemi was closing its doors, CDC was engaged in yet another of its periodic makeovers. This time, under the new name CDC Capital Partners, it was positioning itself to the global financial community as a venture capital corporation with an excellent track record in emerging market countries, and attempting to raise capital not only from the British government but from private institutions as well, in competition with seasoned venture capital funds. In this new packaging it actually went back to the Adesemi investors that it had "saved"—as new sources of financing for its own development agenda. Côme and I took some comfort in the fact that our former investors roundly rebuffed CDC's advances.

Doing business in Africa is not for the faint of heart. It requires persistence, innovation, determination, and patience. This is because doing business in Africa is akin to sailing in turbulent seas, with little or no navigational assistance, no lighthouses or beacons, no gale warnings, and flimsy lifeboats.

But the real problem, as Pappi certainly would have told me, was that Adesemi was building a house from the roof down. Our business model was solid—it was just that there was no foundation for it within the general economic context in which the goal was being pursued. Such adverse forces block the effectiveness of even the most sound business models and concepts. They are also why the efforts of entrepreneurial companies such as Adesemi ultimately are limited in their ability to affect the overall economies of the countries in which they operate. Just a month after Adesemi's close there was a military coup in Côte d'Ivoire, where a few months earlier we had been planning on making our next investment. We had concluded, you see, that next to Tanzania, Côte d'Ivoire was probably the most stable and secure place to do business in Africa. Had Adesemi survived and committed the $3.5 million that we had planned to invest in Côte d'Ivoire, our directors and investors would have had major cause for concern. In Ghana the company continues to operate, run by Western Wireless, but under tremendous constraints, including threatened penalties and threats that its license will be revoked for failure to meet certain service obligations, such as the provision of 40,000 telephone lines stipulated in the SNO license. One of the company's executives was incarcerated, and the chairman of the company, who also happens to be the president of Western Wireless International, was on at least one occasion thrown out of the country.

Many private companies can and do survive and even thrive in this type of highly volatile environment. But they are firms that for the most part are impervious to the instability of these markets, either because the rewards are so high for both the company and the government—as in the case of petroleum, diamonds, and other natural resources—that the investment of time and money justifies the costs, or because the time frame for their return on investment is relatively short. Alternatively, they are firms or individual entities that are simply unscrupulous and have no qualms whatsoever about taking advantage of institutional vacuums and the bountiful opportunities for collusion with corrupt officials they create, ultimately shafting millions of citizens as a result. Adesemi, in the business of infrastructure development, fortunately was in neither of these categories.

Moreover, very few of the aforementioned types of companies provide lasting benefits to the host country unless the proceeds generated in the form of royalty payments or taxes paid to the government are put to effective use and trickle down to the broader economic base, which, as has already been demonstrated, it really does. The only exception to this is when, as in the case of LAMCO, the companies have strong business reasons and incentives to invest in local people and infrastructure, a task that they would be ill-advised to leave to the government. But even in such cases the broader environment is fraught with risks that are difficult to contain, as LAMCO eventually discovered. Governments change abruptly, and market forces are distorted by poorly articulated and inconsistent policies, or by policies that exist without ever being enforced. Such structural and institutional deficiencies are ideal breeding grounds for corruption, inefficiency, chaos, and exploitation and, as can be expected, all of these occur in shocking abundance, often in the name of poverty alleviation and economic development. There is very little incentive for, and even less pressure on, the governments and the international development institutions to make the bold changes necessary to bring about the stability necessary to attract long-term economic growth. This is the reason countless businesses have come and gone in Africa in the past half century without making a dent. Some have made money, others have lost it. One thing is clear: The continent has suffered huge losses in terms of the opportunities squandered.

Nevertheless, there are numerous historical precedents to which one can readily turn for guidance and inspiration, beginning with the early European charter companies. The activities of these formidable agents of change, despite the long-term adverse political, economic and social consequences that frequently accompanied their rule, notably massive exploitation, brutality, excessive taxation, and other intolerable acts inflicted against their fellow man, were often in accidental harmony with the long-term local economic interests of the occupied country. This is because even though they rarely applied their profits to the benefit of the colonies themselves, charter company management and colonial administrators were obliged to make at least a minimum amount of investment in local infrastructure in order to exrtact the full economic value of their investments in these countries. Many Africans today lack even this modest windfall.

By contrast, local infrastructure investments during the colonial era, and similar investments by certain multinational corporations like LAMCO in Liberia, stimulated the industriousness and growth of various local groups and individuals (the Mandingo and Pappi among them), who built corporate entities, many of which continued to thrive long after independence. In some cases these entities have even outgrown and outlasted some of the corporations on which they were modeled, for example, certain Marwari business groups in India, like Birla, Duncan-Goenka and Dalmia, among others, and the Chaebols of Korea, such as Samsung, Daewoo, Lucky Goldstar, and Hyundai. In any event, both the economic and the political components of the charter company and colonial models, for all their deficiencies, were far more conducive to economic development and national prosperity than the welfare or aid-driven strategies prevailing today that are colonial in everything but name and (at times) degree of physical brutality inflicted.

In building Adesemi we were in some way unwittingly emulating the experts of Swift's Balnibarbi—we were building a house from the roof down. With its operations based primarily in Africa, Adesemi was built upon what was inherently a very tenuous foundation. Given our limited resources, we were unable to shield ourselves long enough to stave off the inevitable tumble. Even LAMCO, with its vast resources, couldn't accomplish that, because its sovereignty was very limited.

17

Life after Adesemi

On Black Thursday, with Adesemi on the brink of filing for bankruptcy and creditors soon descending upon us and threatening legal action, the board of directors voted to give Côme and me the power of attorney and the authority to wind down the company's operations and fend off the creditors. As together we were owed close to half a million dollars in back pay that we had deferred in order to keep the company going, the board also voted that we would be responsible for recovering the proceeds resulting from the sale of our one remaining asset, the Ghana venture, which was at the time valued somewhere between $1 million and $3 million. Côme and I would be entitled to a small percentage of the amount we negotiated.

For the next week the entire Adesemi team in Boston pitched in to help dispose of the property, such as furniture, office equipment, and supplies, and to clean up the company files. Then Côme and I began putting in place mechanisms to ensure the orderly closing of the company and to keep Adesemi's principal outside creditors, mostly our suppliers, who collectively were owed $1.69 million, at bay. Côme and I convinced almost all of them to accept our plan to sell our ACG Telesystems Ghana holding and give them a prorated share of the proceeds, and I spent much of my time trying to identify potential buyers for our shares in the company. The best by far, and the least complicated, was a written offer that I received from our former partner, the Ghana National Petroleum Corporation. GNPC would purchase our Ghana shares for $1 million. Rather than plunge the company into bankruptcy and have the courts decide what to do, we had successfully found a way to at least partially compensate our outside creditors to the tune of 60 cents on the dollar. I contacted our attorney, Dick Floor, and asked that he communicate this development to all the shareholders.

I waited a couple of weeks and heard nothing back. It was only accidentally, through a slip of the tongue by one of the firm's junior associates, that I learned that the firm had been working with CDC and two disgruntled early investors on another plan to sell the Ghana holding. In my opinion, the firm should have told Côme and me about that, since at that point we were the people the board had elected to wind things down. But no one discussed anything with us, including the fact that CDC and the investors had engaged the services of a Mark Noonan at Alouette Capital. As Noonan himself was perfectly happy to acknowledge, while he had some experience in telecommunications, he knew nothing about Africa. Yet he was confident that he could handle the Ghana sale within a couple of months and had already been in touch with potential buyers.

CDC and the investors called a board meeting. The purpose was to override the Black Thursday vote that had been taken when they desperately needed Côme and me to salvage what was left of the company, rather than putting matters into the hands of the bankruptcy court. Côme and I were guided by the principal that it was our duty to protect all the creditors, and we did not think that allowing Noonan to handle the Ghana sale would in fact benefit everyone. However, Côme and I had no money to retain a lawyer to fight. There was no way that we could prevent the vote from being held. We were basically screwed.

On June 13, 2000, a shareholders' meeting was called to revoke Côme's and my authority to act or negotiate on behalf of Adesemi. Only Waleed and Howard Stevenson voted to keep us in charge of the recovery process. They had been with us from the very beginning, and despite the heavy personal financial losses that they each had incurred, they stood by us to the very end, not only out of loyalty, but equally important, they felt that we stood the most realistic chance of successfully selling the company. So far it turns out that they were right.

The board deliberately turned down the $1 million for ACG Telesystems Ghana that Côme and I had negotiated from GNPC, and in doing so denied all of Adesemi's creditors the opportunity to recover at least a percentage of their claims. Those who had voted for Côme's and my ouster then voted to give Noonan the responsibility of selling the Ghana asset. In return, he would be guaranteed a percentage of whatever amount he was able to realize on the sale.

The putsch did not end there. Immediately after the company's closing, Côme and I had negotiated successfully with a third party to take over our office space. In return, we were able to charge a premium that enabled us to share approximately $4,000 per month that we used for the ongoing management of Adesemi's remaining assets. The shareholders instructed us to transfer these monthly payments immediately over to Noonan. Their victory was a Pyrrhic one, because they had absolutely nothing to gain—only Mark did— but the schadenfreude they had in ensuring that Côme and I were completely shut out was, I suppose, adequate compensation for their efforts. At this writing, almost four years later, Noonan has still not sold our Ghana holding and thus has not collected a single penny for our shareholders. Given the problems that the company is facing, it would appear that the only person who has profited so far is Noonan, who gets to bill his hourly rate for his efforts. Ultimately, GNPC rescinded the $1 million offer that Côme and I negotiated. CDC did come away with a consolation prize, however: Our Tanzania wireless pay phone operation, which in less than two years sold to a cellular operator for a song and a dance, but not before much of the value had been run into the ground. So ultimately our predictions on the CDC spurious investment logic proved true—but they deal with "free money," so it really doesn't take any skin off their hides.

My closest and most regular contacts in those days were Côme, Waleed, and Howard. Côme, always far more practical and less emotional than I, went almost immediately to work for another of our HBS classmates at a dot-com company. He had not completely given up on telecommunications in Africa, however. During the final twelve months at Adesemi he had worked very hard on the Internet service we had wanted to offer at our public kiosks and had done the numbers that proved that the business could be a winner—yet even this had not convinced CDC. He and Robert, who had joined the company in 1998 and with whom I ran my first marathon in 1999, decided to pursue the opportunity in Kenya, provided that Robert could first secure the necessary operating licenses. A couple of months after Adesemi's closing, Robert returned to Kenya and spent many months trying to obtain a VOIP (Voice Over Internet Protocol) license that would allow him to provide telecommunications services between Kenya and the rest of the world. Côme and Doug Fox, one of Adesemi's technical experts, provided respectively the financial and technical backup for the license applications. They called their new company CDR, for Côme, Doug, and Robert.

I felt very much alone. I was even envious of Côme. How could he have gone on without me? All the others at Adesemi had moved on too. Adesemi had been my family, my baby; I did not know what else to do. After all, it is not every day that one gets to live out one's dream—and then watch it tank. Seven years down the drain: I had failed, spectacularly. The numerous accolades, the *Wall Street Journal* article, the *Wired* magazine and *Boston Globe* press, Hillary Clinton's plug, all of these events that had stood out as the high points of our achievements meant absolutely nothing. Finding a normal job would have been the most practical option, but it just was not in the cards for me. I would have felt like a caged animal. Howard recommended that I just do nothing for at least a month, but doing nothing is absolutely against my nature.

I also turned to Waleed for guidance. As a percentage of his net worth, Waleed lost more than any individual investor involved in the financing of Adesemi, yet he never said a recriminatory word to me, even as he saw over half a million of his own and his family's money evaporate. We had become close during the two final years of Adesemi. No matter where he was—he was working in several of Monitor's offices in Europe and traveling constantly—we were in touch; my address book was filled with his phone numbers. During this time something tragic happened in his personal life. He had been working in Monitor's Turkey offices, where he had met a woman there named Mirel Sayinsoy. Each time we spoke he told me their relationship was getting more serious. One day he called to tell me that he and Mirel were taking a year off to travel around the world. During that time he was sure he would find out if he had found his life partner. A couple of months into their trip, Mirel fell ill and was admitted to a hospital in London, where she was diagnosed with leukemia. Waleed dropped everything and focused all of his energy and resources on her. He did extensive research on the disease, and used his knowledge and contacts to ensure that she was treated by the best doctors and at the best medical facilities. He moved her from the hospital in London to Texas, which we believed had the best hospital for treating her cancer. For many months, through the challenges and trials of the exhausting chemotherapy treatments, Waleed was at her side. Mirel, a beautiful, bright, and cosmopolitan woman, was gradually losing all of her hair and rapidly gaining weight. Waleed's attachment to her seemed to grow ever stronger. He told me that he had fallen in love. All I could think about was that if she had to be ill, how lucky Mirel was to have someone like Waleed.

One morning during CDC's nine-month siege of Adesemi I returned from a meeting with our lawyers, and received a call from him. He was crying. "Monique," he said, "Mirel died early this morning."

I began to sob too. He did not deserve this. He was kind, compassionate, and giving—he had done everything right.

I offered to fly down to Texas, but he told me that he preferred to be alone, and that members of Mirel's family were on their way from Turkey to carry out her final rites. I called him periodically during the weeks that followed, thinking how difficult it must have been for him. I could not help but remember my own feelings when Pappi died, and therefore understood his need and desire to be alone.

A couple of months later, on July 4, 1999, I met Waleed in New York. He had some friends with a boat there. We would spend the evening on the river watching the fireworks, and the rest of the weekend just hanging out in Manhattan. Waleed knew the city well and took me from one amazing shop to another. "These were all of Mirel's favorite places," he told me. He said that after her death he had gone out and bought all her favorite perfumes and surrounded their apartment with the scents and the hats she had bought and collected after losing her hair. He had immersed himself in the full experience of the loss, in the beauty of everything that Mirel had stood for in his life. I could not help but think of the guys that I had cared for who would have run away even in the best of times, much less in a situation as dire and stressful as Mirel's illness and death.

As Waleed talked about Mirel, I felt overwhelmed with the need to tell him how much I loved him. But I did not because I was afraid that he would take it the wrong way. Now I wish I had.

Not long after, Waleed packed up his belongings at his home in Texas and prepared to move on to the next phase of his life. He went to London and joined the Monitor offices there. I was sad to see him leave, but I told myself that he was always only a phone call or an email away.

It was the summer of 2001, and it seemed that everyone connected to Adesemi had moved on but me. Less than ten months after Côme went to work for Learning Brands, the dot-com venture, it imploded. But Côme's other initiative, CDR, was gaining momentum in Kenya and ready to start services in Nairobi. Côme, who had married Charlene Li in 1995, also was preparing to move to the West Coast to be closer to her family.

Howard was gradually reducing his teaching responsibilities at Harvard, working on a new book, and taking over the challenge of launching Harvard Business School's first major capital campaign. I had exhausted my unemployment benefits and was rapidly running out of cash. By now I knew that with the fate of Adesemi in the hands of Mark Noonan, I would never see any money owed to me by the company. Howard knew of my predicament and made a no-interest loan to me to give me time to get back on my feet and figure out what I wanted to do next.

The problem was that I still had no idea what I wanted to do. I had spent the past seven years trying to change the world for the better. How could I fill the gaping void that I was left with or replicate the thrill of building something from nothing?

Worse yet, I was utterly disillusioned with Africa, believing that things would certainly not change in my lifetime. I certainly didn't have the wherewithal to topple the likes of the World Bank or the

UN. Because of Adesemi's high profile, I was still invited to speak at numerous international development conferences, including the World Economic Forum, but I avoided most of them. Who would want to hear my naysaying? When I did speak at these events I felt increasingly like some sort of libertarian, completely out of sync with those who tend to gravitate to and feed on the problems of the third world at these venues. The people who do have a shot at changing the continent, the entrepreneurs, the global corporations, are never there. They are viewed as the enemy. One day, in the beginning of September, I called Waleed to check in. He was on an island in Greece in the middle of a party, judging from the noise in the background. He told me that he was planning his wedding for the following summer! I knew that Waleed had been seeing someone in London for over a year, and they were planning to marry in the summer of 2002. He told me he would call me when he got back to London, in a week or so.

A few days later, on September 11, I remember waking up a little after 8:30 A.M. It was a glorious day in Boston. As was my habit, I turned on National Public Radio. Soon I heard the announcer telling us that a plane had just flown into the World Trade Center. I switched on the cable news and saw the image of the plane with its nose protruding through the prominent landmark, against the backdrop of the clear blue sky. Trying to fathom this accident, I then watched as the second jet crashed into the second tower.

Did one plane make an error and then another exactly the same one? What are the chances of that? I asked myself. I quickly called Côme, who at the time was still in Boston. "Do you see what's happening?" I asked.

"No," he said, "what?" I just couldn't explain it. I told him to switch on the TV.

"It's terrorism," he said, without a second's hesitation. We stared in disbelief at what we were witnessing. The next person I called was Howard. I knew that he was on his way to New York and

I wanted to stop him. I called his wife, Fredericka, to make sure that he was OK. She told me that she too was concerned and had been trying to reach him.

I spent the day like the rest of America, glued to the television. I thought of all the people like myself who had left our countries of origin to search for the American dream and the security inherent in it. I felt an overwhelming sense of a loss of innocence. I thought that given there were so many HBS students at work in the Wall Street area, chances were that I might know someone who worked in the towers. Thankfully, as the day progressed, HBS classmates kept emailing, accounting for people who had been in the area, and all the news was good. By noon I felt a sense of relief that at least nobody that I knew personally had been a victim.

On Wednesday evening I received another email that had been compiled by a consortium of business schools. It directed me to a site that provided information on the whereabouts of individuals by school and by class. I did not go to the link, but I forwarded it to Côme, in case he wanted to take a look.

Half an hour later the phone rang.

"Monique," Côme said, "did you visit the site?"

"No, why?"

"Monique, Waleed was on board American Airlines Flight 11, but I just checked the flight list and his name is not on it."

Côme suggested that I call Waleed's family. With great dread, I picked up the phone and called his parents in Southern California. His father answered.

"Joseph, Joseph, tell me . . ." I could not even ask the question.

"He's gone," Joseph said.

I think I doubled over at his words as all the air was sucked out of me. "Monique, where are you?" he asked me. I told him that I was in Cambridge. He must have been in shock, because he then made polite conversation with me. "What are you doing in Cambridge?" he asked. "Aren't you supposed to be in Africa with the company?"

I then realized that Waleed had not told his parents about the demise of Adesemi almost two years earlier. I took a deep breath.

"Didn't Waleed tell you?" I asked.

"Tell me what?"

"Adesemi was liquidated well over a year ago."

"You mean all the money's gone?" Joseph asked quietly. It was yet one more shock to him on that day, one that would have been significant but now paled in comparison to what he was now struggling to comprehend.

"Yes," I whispered.

It was a most horrible way to find out that Waleed had never told his family about the fate of Adesemi. In the months that followed the closing of Adesemi, I often had asked Waleed if he had told his family about the company's fate, knowing that this would be a very difficult discussion for him to have with them. Waleed always told me that he was waiting for the right time. Eventually I stopped asking. Knowing Waleed, my guess is that he was hoping to make back the money through alternative investments that he had or would make, in which case the loss to his family on the Adesemi investment, or at least the full extent of it, may never have had to be known. Things had not worked out that way. Waleed, in the prime of his youth, with everything to live for, had no reason to think that he did not have yet another day to do all that had to be done, to tidy things up and smooth them over. To make amends.

Next to Pappi and Ma Kema, I had never lost anyone that I was so close to. I was practically numb. I opened my PDA and went directly to his name—Iskandar. I had always loved the ring it had to it. All his contact numbers through the years—Boston, Moscow, Seoul, Istanbul, London . . . I had never wanted to delete them. They were the tapestry of our friendship. Where could I reach him now? I called his number in London, knowing that his voicemail would pick up, and I would hear his kind and gentle voice, as if he were still with us. But no matter how many times I hit the redial button it was not enough. I reached for my little tape recorder, inserted a cassette, and registered what I felt would be my only live memento of Waleed, one that I could hold on to forever, just as he had told me he would do with the picture of Mirel that he kept in his wallet. I called Côme several times a day in the week that followed, still trying to come to grips with the reality and the incomprehensibility of the situation. Côme and I decided it would be fitting to establish a fellowship at the Harvard Business School to remember Waleed and his ideals. But we were stopped before we could even get it started. "Thank you, but at the family's request, we will handle all memorial arrangements," we were told by Monitor. The Iskandars had delegated to the company the responsibility of arranging a memorial service for Waleed's friends in the Boston area.

I was in a manic, frantic state in those days. I felt that I was being denied the opportunity to help my friend, to thank him for all that he had done and meant to me, and I vented my frustration with Côme over and over again. While I was locked up in my room crying and staring at Waleed's picture and going over the numerous memories and experiences we had shared, he seemed to be taking everything that had happened in stride, which made me crazier: How could he not be equally distraught and outraged, given all that Waleed had meant to us. We spoke several times on the phone, and as usual he was the practical one. He suggested that we begin putting an email message out to our classmates to inform them of the planned memorial service. He volunteered to take the lead, and soon he had drafted a message for me to look at. I told him that I thought the whole matter was just too impersonal and cold. For someone as warm and caring as Waleed, how could we leave this in the hands of a company?

"Monique," he finally said, impatient with my self-absorption, "this is what the family wants, and Monitor has the resources to coordinate everything."

Meanwhile I had spoken to Waleed's best friend, Nikos, who also worked for Monitor in London, and he had told me that he was not planning to come to the ceremony in Cambridge. This further deepened my consternation. "How can this be a memorial for Waleed," I moaned, "if even Nikos is not coming?"

There was silence on the other end of the line. Finally, Côme said, "I don't know."

I went ballistic. I accused him of not caring about Waleed and forgetting that Adesemi would not have happened if it had not been for him. I reminded him of how Waleed had constantly stood by us even during the worst of times. "It is now our turn to do something, even if it means asserting ourselves to make it happen," I said.

I accused Côme of being disloyal. It was a very low blow, and he responded in kind. After we hung up he immediately sent me an email informing me that he had finally had it with me, and that henceforth we would go our separate ways. He wished me the best of luck.

It is indicative of my state of mind at the time that I was happy to receive Côme's email. I wanted nothing more to do with him, with Adesemi, with anything that linked me to the past. Waleed was gone, and now everything else that had linked me to him was gone as well. Côme and I attended the memorial service separately. We avoided each other.

Of the original Adesemi four, Howard was the only one I had left. He knew I was adrift, and he kept encouraging me to write it all down. That is what I did. I wrote about all that had happened to me since I had started Adesemi, and when I was not writing, I ran. I had run my first marathon in 1999, the Boston Marathon, with Robert Keter, the Kenyan Adesemi had hired and who was an accomplished 800-meter track runner. My objective was to finish with a respectable time. With Robert's help I did; now I was an avid long-distance runner, accustomed to logging about 100 miles a week.

I discovered that there was an opening at the Harvard Business School in the external relations office. They needed someone to help with fund-raising. I had never done fund-raising in the non-profit world, but I had been successful raising money for my own ventures and knew that I could do it. I applied for and got the job, expecting to remain there for about a year. I would use the time to figure out what mountain to climb next.

Around this time, still grieving, I met a man through my running named Ilus Nilson. Ilus was beautiful, with the physique of an elite marathon runner and a kind, gentle smile. After I had run my first three miles with him I liked him—a lot. Like me he had spent much of his life in boarding schools, away from family. Like me he seemed to crave companionship and solitude at the same time. Indeed, normally I am a solitary runner, and Ilus was the first person whom I felt completely in sync with as I ran and, more important, we encouraged each other to do better. He was a much more technical runner than I, and suggested that I apply more technical discipline to my running. I took his advice to heart. I tended to rely almost exclusively on passion and emotion, and in turn urged him to infuse these traits into his own training regimen. At the end of our first run together, I felt that I had found a soul mate.

I was convinced that this was a new beginning for me. I invested much of my own emotion and self-worth in trying to make Ilus all the things that Côme and Waleed had represented to me, and more. Less than three months later, he sent me a succinct email, informing me that he wanted absolutely nothing more to do with me and wishing me the best of luck for the rest of my life. This news was delivered on the evening that I was about to take an important trip to Latin America on behalf of HBS. During that trip I visited Brazil, Argentina, and Chile. I sat in my hotel in Chile, the final leg of the journey, thinking that I would just stay in Latin America for the rest of my life. I have always found travel to be an excellent means of escape. So what if I didn't ever return to Boston, I thought. Nobody would really care. As I lay on my bed at the Hyatt Regency in Santiago, contemplating whether or not I should get on the plane to return to Boston that evening, the phone rang. It was Howard. My assistant obviously had reached his assistant with the message: Monique is in trouble.

"Howard," I said, "do you think I am a loser?" This was not the first time that Howard had heard this question from me.

"No, Monique," he assured me, yet again, "you are not a loser." Howard had seen me go through many tough times; if he thought this was something I could overcome, then I probably could. He assured me that I would get over it and convinced me to come home to Boston.

When I did return to Boston, however, I was so depressed that for the first time in over six months I picked up the phone and called Côme. I needed to get back to the person I had been before Ilus, and I knew that reconciling with Côme was a big part of that. When I heard his voice, I realized how much I had missed him. No apologies were necessary. We picked up where we had always been, and Côme gave me the assurances that I needed to believe in myself. It was his old habit. It was why Waleed had given me his numbers all over the globe, so that when I suffered a professional or personal setback, he would be there. I am a lucky person to have had and to continue to have such great friends in my life. Naturally, Côme and I found ourselves talking about Waleed again, since this is where we had left off. I told him that the Iskandar family had established a scholarship in his name at the Harvard Business School, but that the total amount contributed to the fellowship to date was low—according to HBS regulations, the fellowship endowment needed a total of $250,000 to be activated, and the fellowship fund was nowhere near that figure. I decided to dedicate my next Boston Marathon to Waleed, and to use the opportunity to raise money for his fellowship. Côme was my first sponsor, Howard my second, and Rupert Murdoch was my third. I am not sure if I will ever again accomplish the time that I did in the 2002 Boston Marathon. I ran a blistering 2:48:38, erasing a full 15 minutes off my previous best time and catapulting me into the elite ranks of the world of female marathon runners. It was as if I were running on the wings of Waleed. He was certainly on my mind throughout the entire course, as some of my sponsors had given me specific financial incentives to run a faster race so as to maximize the amount of money that I would raise for the fellowship. As soon as I got home, Côme was calling to congratulate me. Now living in San Francisco, the techno-Samaritan had monitored my entire race progress online.

In the years since the closing of Adesemi, there have been some encouraging signs of change in ways the Western world deals with the numerous problems of Africa and the rest of the developing world. It has been the recognition by certain high-profile business personalities that a new and fresh approach is needed. The most prominent of these of course, by sheer force of the resources at its disposal, but also because of the prominence of the individuals behind it, is the Bill and Melinda Gates Foundation. This is one of the few instances in which a major and internationally prominent businessman (George Soros is another), rather than a politician or international bureaucrat, has focused his attention, people, and resources on the problems of the third world through an independent vehicle. And he has done so by trying to shore up one of the pillars of economic development: health care. Yet he has done this as a philanthropist, not as the astute, shrewd, "take no prisoners" businessman that enabled him to build one of the most successful and dominant companies in the world.

If we are to save the lives of hundreds of millions of children through improved vaccines and medication, as the Gates Foundation aims to do, we also have the responsibility to give them the promise of a better life. If not, all we are doing is saving them from one disease or another, only to watch them die from poverty, or be condemned to live in ignorance and servitude, deprived of the most basic political, social, and economic human rights. What we need are long-term solutions that view Africa as a potential new consumer market, rather than as simply a massive social welfare project. Only corporations, not do-gooders, can look at Africa in this manner. Bill Gates needs to look at Africa and see not just vaccines, but Windows. Steve Balmer, the CEO of Microsoft, should be as excited about Africa as Bill Gates is; until then, the continent will remain a sideshow. There are signs of encouragement that corporations are interested in playing a more active and innovative role in economic development, outside the debilitating sphere of influence of Laputa, precisely because of its market potential. In April 2003, while speaking at Columbia University in New York, the chairman and CEO of Coca-Cola, a major global corporation with an especially high profile in Africa, Douglas Daft, made the following remarkably forward-looking statement:

> *Today, we are in the midst of a change in world history in which businesses, NGOs, and even individuals—or, as New York Times columnist Tom Friedman calls them, "super-empowered individuals"—are playing ever-increasing roles on the world stage, and having a more decisive impact on events than ever before. Events over the past few years have turned upside down assumptions and conventional wisdom that became accepted through hundreds of years of history—from the establishment of states as the primary actor in international relations to the presumed importance of nationalism and patriotism. . . .*
>
> *[T]he problems we are facing are larger than any nation and no longer just matters for politicians and diplomats to solve. Business must step up and play the important role it can. It used to be that large international businesses were symbols of exploita-*

tion—of people . . . of the environment . . . and of developing nations. . . . But business must be a medium of healing, . . . building understanding, . . . improving peoples' lives. . . . I believe the leaders of the largest and most international businesses, including the Coca-Cola Company, need to seek ways to focus and combine our efforts to confront those most threatening issues. I want to see us come together and create working groups of companies. Each group would be dedicated to playing a larger role in attacking one specific problem: combating disease, . . . fostering international understanding, . . . eliminating hunger, . . . or reducing conflicts. I am talking about the companies in those working groups each dedicating resources, personnel, and expertise to formulate and organize, in effect, business plans to address these key problems. They will design and implement programs that will make a real difference to the world, not in 25 or 50 years, but over the next decade, or before it is too late.[1]

In my own private life, too, I see signs of growth and hope after a few difficult years, and in part I can again credit both running and Côme with coming to my rescue. Because of my performance in the 2002 Boston Marathon, I was invited to participate as an elite athlete in the 2003 Boston Marathon, which was the 107th running of the event. In other words, instead of running with 20,000 runners of the marathon as I had in years past, I was invited by the Boston Athletic Association to join the roughly 50 or so elite runners in the field and receive VIP treatment. I had run four prior Boston Marathons, but running the event as an elite runner, as I discovered, is an entirely different experience.

On Sunday morning, the day before the marathon, I attended the mandatory elite runners' briefing session at the Copley Plaza Hotel, not far from where I had signed the initial ACG investment documents with Waleed some ten years earlier. Most of the athletes arrived with their coaches and managers and others in their entourage. I felt somewhat like an imposter, as though I had gotten there under false pretenses.

The organizers described the strict rules that applied exclusively to the elite athletes—the real contenders for prizes. In other words, as a member of the audience, I had a legitimate shot at winning the $80,000 1st prize money. Among the restrictions was that female runners were not allowed to have a male pacer; we were entitled to have our own special drink bottles positioned at various stations along the course route; and we would be subject to random drug testing post race. I don't know what kind of drugs I would have had to take to give me even a remote chance of winning $80,000.

Monday was the big day. In prior years, as a member of the general herd, I had spent the four to five hours before the race start freezing cold or sweating with heat, waiting in long lines to get coffee, food, or to use the portable potties. The elite area was an entirely different experience. We were in the warmth of a church, where we had comfortable places to rest, warm up, eat, and drink, and automatic access to bathroom facilities. We still had three hours to while away, though. So I decided to make the best of it.

In the elite field, the Europeans and Americans for the most part all meant business, and had on their game faces (APPROACH AT YOUR OWN PERIL), unlike the Kenyans, who were totally relaxed and enjoying themselves. I therefore gravitated toward them. I spent the time talking about Kenya with a particular group of Kenyan athletes sponsored by Fila, the Italian sportswear company. About an hour before the start of the race they invited me to join them for a warm-up. One of them, Robert Cheruiyot, the tallest in the group at about six-foot-three-inches, which was unusual for a marathon runner, and extremely handsome, with an electrifying smile, was kind enough to hang back from the rest of his teammates and run with me. As we did our laps, he told me about himself. He was 24 and lived in the Eldoret region of Kenya, where he also had a farm. Boston was his second marathon. Upon hearing this, I thought, "Boy, are you in for a rude awakening," thinking of the notoriously hilly course. Yet he was very modest: "I just want to do well, and finish," he said. After our warm-up we returned to the waiting area, exchanged contact information, and continued our conversation.

To the utter amazement of the so-called running experts calling the race, not to mention my own immense delight, my new buddy, Robert, came out of nowhere and won the 2003 Boston Marathon. I won my own first trophy in Boston that year as well, though nothing to the tune of Robert's accomplishment.

But I will remember Boston 2003 most especially because it helped me reach an important decision: that I could never turn my back on Africa, even if I wanted to. As I quoted the Roman lyricist Horace earlier: *Patriae quis exsul se quoque fugit?* "What exile from his country has also escaped from himself?" The close interaction with the Kenyans, the way that they had automatically adopted me and welcomed me into their fold, brought back some very important memories of what Africa means to me. The sheer physical beauty of the Kenyan runners, their graciousness, their strength, and their elegance reminded me of my love and dedication to Africa and the need to keep fighting on behalf of its economic development.

Ilus also was back in my life, and I was able to share the experience with him. I felt that I had been given a second chance to do things right with him, no matter where that leads. Taking a lesson from my old friend Barbo, I am finally getting some perspective on things. As he had said to me on the eve of his departure from Boston just after the close of Adesemi three years earlier: "Mamma, *tu vas réussir encore mieux qu'avant*" "Mamma, don't worry, you are going to succeed even more than before."

With my renewed hope for Africa, it was totally natural that Côme would be the one who would come up with the first opportunity for me to get involved again. Shortly after the marathon he gave me a call. CDR's operations in Kenya were in full force and he was running the entire operation from his home office in San Francisco. Doug worked out of Boston, and Robert was on the ground in Kenya. Côme was calling to tell me that they wanted to do something socially beneficial for Kenya and had decided to build a school in the Rift Valley region of Kenya, the place from which Robert and most of the world-class Kenyan runners come.

CDR planned to help build a new facility for a local school, the Ngererit School. The school had been founded in 1961 but had fallen into significant disrepair. As Côme explained, the goal of the project was to enable the school to return to its original core mission: to help young girls and boys in the community achieve their potential so that they can go on to lead responsible, productive, and fulfilling lives.

Would I be interested, Côme asked, in helping to raise the capital necessary to pull this off? What appealed to me, beyond the chance to give young boys and girls the opportunity to learn at home without having to go far from family, as my brothers and I had had to do, was the opportunity to demonstrate that corporations such as CDR actually do contribute to development in third world countries. The $750,000 Ngererit project would accommodate 1,000 primary and secondary school students annually. I was determined that athletics, entrepreneurship, and other extracurricular activities would play as big a role as academics.

Côme sent me the original project plan for the school and I began working on it. It was just like old times. He and I could put together the best of plans when we worked jointly, and as we emailed revised versions back and forth, I felt myself being gradually sucked in, just as he had been with ACG when I had interrupted his safari a decade before.

As I write these pages, several corporations already have expressed their interest in helping fund the school, as have a number of individuals and entities that I know through the HBS network. So far so good, but experience tells me that small companies like CDR are particularly vulnerable to the whims and vicissitudes of the business climate in Africa, and the question is will CDR as a business survive the additional two to three year period required to accomplish this goal? A lot more needs to be done, and in a more systematic way. As Douglas Daft said, corporations need to come together.

Despite the known obstacles, I am back in the business of trying to transform a continent, albeit this time, applying the lessons that I learned through Adesemi and a lifetime of observation and practice of entrepreneurship in Africa. I, too, agree with the noble UN Millennium objectives to eliminate poverty, disease, and ignorance. Who wouldn't? I can practically hear the Stradivari in the background. But let's be realistic. If we continue to rely on Laputa, Inc. rather than experiment with more effective agents of change, it will indeed require a millenium, if not more, to achieve even half of these objectives, and we might just as well resort to my "Modest Proposal." I have no way of knowing what the future holds. But of the following I am absolutely certain: that the cure to many of Africa's woes lies in business, in the entrepreneurial spirit that is alive and well there, and definitely not in more development aid to irresponsible governments and their agents, Laputa, Inc.; and that we cannot and must not be deterred by the enormity and complexity of the challenge that lies ahead.

Come, my friends.
'Tis not too late to seek a newer world.
Push off, and sitting well in order smite
The sounding furrows; for my purpose holds
To sail beyond the sunset, and the baths
Of all the western stars, until I die.
It may be that the gulfs will wash us down;
It may be we shall touch the Happy Isles,
And see the great Achilles, whom we knew.
Tho' much is taken, much abides; and tho'
We are not now that strength which in old days
Moved earth and heaven, that which we are, we
are,—
One equal temper of heroic hearts,
Made weak by time and fate, but strong in will
To strive, to seek, to find, and not to yield.

—*Ulysses*, Alfred, Lord Tennyson

Epilogue

It has been almost fourteen years since Charles Taylor launched the civil war in Liberia. In the aftermath of Doe's assassination, the fighting persisted. Repeated efforts by the association of neighboring West African States, ECOWAS, failed to bring about a lasting cease-fire, and the country was divided into areas controlled by warring factions. The capital and an interim government backed by ECOWAS initially were protected by the presence of a regional peacekeeping force, but they were unable to resist the continuing onslaught of Taylor's NPFL. By 1996, Taylor controlled the lion's share of the country's more than $421 million in diamonds, gold, iron ore, and timber trade. Likewise LAMCO, which actually resumed operations for a while, had to pay taxes to the NPFL, as it also controlled Liberia's shipping facilities. The NPFL signed additional agreements with European companies to exploit natural resources—diamonds, gold, timber—that would keep funding its bloody campaign.

After seven years of fighting, an agreement finally was reached to hold elections in Monrovia in 1997. Former U.S. President Jimmy

Carter was back in Monrovia, this time as a private American citizen, to oversee the fairness and regularity of the mostly foreign-financed election process, along with several hundred other international observers. Charles Taylor and his National Patriotic Party were voted into office by a landslide, 75 percent of the voting population. Many voted for him because they understood that had the election gone to any of his opponents, full-scale fighting would have resumed. All they wanted was peace. The war had resulted in the loss of between 150,000 and 200,000 lives and the internal and external displacement of about half of Liberia's population. Many of them fled to refugee camps in neighboring countries such at Côte d'Ivoire, Guinea, and Sierra Leone, all of which are countries with substantial economic and political problems of their own and that can ill afford the massive influx.

Among the primary victims of the NPFL were the Mandingo people, because of their alleged ties and affiliation with Doe. The Mandingo in villages throughout the country, including Ma Kema's beloved Fofana Town, were killed mercilessly, shot to death with guns or hacked with machetes, with no mercy given to children, women, or the elderly. Their properties were seized, the women were raped, and the bodies of all were left strewn like animals wherever they happened to be when they were killed. In some cases their heads were hoisted upon sticks as symbols of victory. But the Mandingo villages were not the only targets. Warlords roamed the country aboard stolen vehicles, dressed in everything from ballgowns to masks to bathrobes, sporting blond and gray wigs, shower caps, or baseball caps on their heads, and brandishing AK-47 rifles.

Taylor promised the people of Liberia that he would bring peace and restore to them everything that they had lost, provide every Liberian child with a computer, every home with water and electricity, reestablish the U.S. dollar as sole legal tender in Liberia, and suppress all remaining rebel groups. Instead, he appropriated for himself and his henchmen all that the Liberian people had lost. "Business" in Liberia consists of a spectral web of arms deals, political payoffs and smuggling by an international cast of characters lifted from a twisted Le Carré novel. These include, according to the UN, a Dutch hotel owner who "organizes the transfer of weaponry from Monrovia into Sierra Leone"; a Ukrainian-born Israeli and Taylor confidant involved in "organized crime, trafficking in stolen works of art, illegal possession of firearms, arms trafficking, and money laundering"; and an erstwhile South African colonel, hired to train Taylor's Anti-Terrorist Unit, who also "acquired the gold and other mineral rights for two concessions on behalf of a Bermuda-based holding corporation . . . a company in which Charles Taylor and some of his relatives hold interests." Even the American televangelist, Pat Robertson, was actively involved in this unsavory and Kafkaesque business environment created and sustained by Taylor to perpetuate his reign of terror over the Liberian people. Robertson is the founder and president of Freedom Gold, Ltd. a company incorporated in the Cayman Islands, that was granted the right by the Liberian government to engage in exploratory mining operations in Liberia. It would appear that God and Gold are not such strange bedfellows after all.[1]

As for Yekepa, the hospitals, the doctors and the nurses, the teachers have disappeared or left. The houses, shops, and gardens have vanished. The central market, where the women of Lola and hundreds of other entrepreneurs came daily to sell their wares, has disappeared, the merchants having been massacred, mutilated, or forced to flee. Illiteracy, malnutrition, diseases, and the medicine man have returned. Like the fabled city of Atlantis, Yekepa has sunk back into oblivion, consumed by the forest out of which it so miraculously sprang. And Laputa, Inc., continues to muddle about the margins.

The United Nations High Commission for Refugees (UNHCR) began operating repatriation programs in 1998, returning up to a quarter of a million Liberians from neighboring countries. Unfortunately, there was little to return to—the country's infrastructure had been reduced to rubble. There were few schools, few hospitals, few industries, and few agricultural projects that had survived the years of turmoil. Roads were laced with land mines. People were sick and starving, with no place to call home. The newly installed Liberian government was soon engaged in armed conflict with neighboring Guinea, which was now experiencing armed incursions from both Sierra Leonean and Liberian rebels. Liberia, Sierra Leone, and Guinea were now therefore all in various degrees of instability. By 2002, Liberian forces had also entered Côte d'Ivoire in an attempt to destabilize and support the overthrow of the government there.

Internally, Taylor's government was challenged almost from the beginning. In 1999 a major internal threat emerged in the form of a rebel group called the Liberians United for Reconciliation and Democracy (LURD), which later spawned the Movement for Democracy in Liberia, which was the result of internal division. Despite a UN embargo on diamond exports from, and arms sales to, Liberia, proceeds from the country's national resources continued to be channeled to Taylor's acquisition of arms to fight off the insurgents.

Yet within the first six months of 2003, the rebels, mostly from the LURD, had captured much of the Liberian territory, advancing closer and closer toward the capital city of Monrovia. Whichever of the warring factions wins, the people of Liberia will lose, because these are equal opportunity tyrants. However, the world grows increasingly numb to what is happening in Liberia—after all, in a year of bad news from Iraq, Afghanistan, and the Congo, there is only so much outrage and shock to go around. Thus many of the atrocities in Liberia are most faithfully reported by humanitarian groups rather than by the general press.

On June 4, 2003, the Special Court for Sierra Leone, a joint tribunal of the United Nations and the government of Sierra Leone, announced that Liberia's President Charles Taylor had been indicted for war crimes, crimes against humanity, and serious violations of international humanitarian law during Sierra Leone's decade-long civil unrest. Because of the way that international law generally works, however, asserting noninterference in the internal affairs of individual states, he faces no charges for what he has done to the millions of people in Liberia, yet that same month civilians were once again fleeing to the unstable countries that border Liberia because they had nowhere else to go. The killing and the torture resumed and even escalated beyond what had become almost normal levels, and the rebels once again warned all civilians to leave the capital city of Monrovia, which they were approaching for the final showdown. As usual, foreign nationals were told to evacuate the country. French embassy officials in Abidjan said 534 "evacuees" (code for Westerners) were taken out by military helicopters in early June to a French warship anchored off the Liberian coast. Even Ghana was preparing to send a warship and several planes to rescue its own nationals. The United States urged all of its citizens to leave the country, and Robertsfield was jammed with civilians, mostly members of the large Lebanese business community in Liberia, trying to leave the country on chartered flights, as most of the major commercial carriers had already suspended operations to and from the country. Meanwhile, Secretary General of the United Nations Kofi Annan, presumably speaking for those who cannot simply hop on a plane, urged all parties in the conflict to protect civilians.

As I listened to the news on the night of June 25, 2003, I learned that rocket-launched grenades had been propelled into the U.S. embassy compound in Monrovia, where hundreds of terrified Liberian civilians had taken refuge. To my astonishment, the BBC was conducting a live interview with none other than Eric Boateng, the kindly Ghanaian who had been the interns' and my liaison in Dar es Salaam in the summer of 1993, who was now trapped in the embassy compound. Eric was explaining the deadly plight in which he and the others had found themselves as the rebels and Taylor's troops moved toward the final showdown. The distraught men, women, and children inside, some so young that their parents were transporting them and the wounded in wheelbarrows, were all frantically pondering their next moves, and their choices were growing more limited by the minute, like a gruesome and twisted "reality" version of the game we used to play at Leelands: "Port, Starboard, Deck." But while at Leelands the exercise was confined to the safety of our gymnasium, and our flight was artificially generated by our coach, here reality was the coach, and there appeared to be no safe harbor—not port, not starboard, nor deck.

As this was going on, the government of France was reminding the United States that France had gone in to "fix" Côte d'Ivoire, its former colony, and the British were reminding the United States that Britain had gone in to "fix" Sierra Leone, its former colony.[2] In what would appear to be a patent admission by the entire global community that the ties of colonialism still bind, despite the decades of freedom and independence rhetoric to the contrary, Britain and France, and even the Secretary General of the UN, Kofi Annan, argued that given its historical ties to Liberia, it was naturally the job of America to save Liberia, its own renegade province. But the United States, mired in Iraq with its soldiers under attack every single day in what had morphed from a conventional to a guerrilla war, and trying to put together a "roadmap to peace in the Middle East," and to keep Kim Jong Il from blasting us all to bits, told the Africans to sort out the Liberian problem themselves. But the pressure continued to mount on the U.S. government, and in light of an imminent trip to Africa by President George Bush, it appeared that change was in the air, and that the United States might intervene in the latest act of the well-intentioned but horribly failed drama that it had started almost 200 years ago. I could not ignore the irony of it all: The Iraqis calling for America to get out; Africa, France, Britain, and most of all, rank-and-file Liberians calling for her to get in. So, after almost half a century of pretense, the veil finally has been lifted on what has been apparent to just about anybody who dares to be honest. Colonialism is alive and well, and when convenient, as in the cases of Côte d'Ivoire, Sierra Leone, and Liberia, it is sanctioned even by the UN that once condemned it; when not, as in the case of Iraq, where significant amounts of oil reserves are at stake, it is reviled, again by the same UN.

So rather than continuing to castigate the concept of colonialism, as political correctness and cheap rhetoric would have us do even as reality endorses and even embraces it, why not revive the institution, but give it a more equitable and contemporary face. With a few rare exceptions (King Leopold II comes to mind) even European imperialism was not as bad as what is happening in Africa now, as more and more Africans have sadly discovered. Without a doubt, colonialism had major structural and ethical flaws: I saw how it treated Pappa Larry and even Pappi in Sierra Leone; I saw how it treated the indigenous people of Liberia and hundreds of millions of people all over the world. Yet because of the ugly race factor, which is inextricably but erroneously linked to colonialism, we have thrown out the baby with the bathwater. This seriously flawed logic has caused colonialism to be judged far more harshly than the most unspeakable atrocities that have been and continue to be inflicted by Africans on Africans. Perhaps a more enlightened colonialism is the answer—one that looks beyond the historical concept of nation and reflects the harsh realities of today: that a group of people thrown together into one geographic area does not a nation make. Perhaps it is time for the world to take a serious look at viable alternatives and precedents to nation building, such as Jardine Matheson in Hong Kong, Thomas Stamford Raffles in Singapore, and such as LAMCO in Liberia. But let's take it a step further. Why not let the people in developing countries be shareholders in these charter companies, and the Western public, rather than giving "free money" to Laputa, Inc., through their taxes, could invest directly in these companies, under an equitable and rigorously enforced regulatory framework of course, and even secure tax breaks as a reward for part of their risk. At least this way their money will not be thrown into the bottomless money pit of Laputa.

Acknowledgments

To my dear mother, Julia Maddy, and my brothers, Claudius, Herbert, and Abayomi for your love and the innumerable sacrifices you have made on my behalf.

To Jean Barbo, for your friendship, loyalty, and wisdom, not to mention your excellent cuisine. To Mary Katherine Barkley Jeston, for nurturing and encouraging me at a critical juncture in my life, when I was placed in your care. To Nmano Carlbo, for always being there for the Maddy family. To Elise Schanke for years of kindness and nurturing. To Bill Draper III, for being my number one cheerleader. To Ann Epstein for keeping me sane, literally and figuratively. To John McArthur, aka "the Intellectual Venture Capitalist," for all those early morning breakfasts during which you always dispensed good, sound, advice—not to mention many invaluable contacts. To Father Thomas King, for introducing me to the unity of knowledge, and to all things Pierre Teilhard de Chardin. To Joff Masukawa, for putting up with me through all seasons, but most especially the summer of 1992. To Barbara Schmidt-Rahmer, for providing Adesemi with its first worldwide headquarters, and for listening to my countless hours of analysis of matters of the heart—especially when it was broken. To Joe Massoud, for always reassuring me that I am smart even when I do stupid things and for directing and producing the high drama and entertainment up in the sky deck—you gave me more than my money's worth. To Cihan Sultanoglu, for being the sister that I never had. To Dot Wyndoe, for your pragmatism, your indomitable Aussie warmth and wit, and your steadfast grace under pressure.

To the memory and spirit of Waleed Iskandar, for the priceless gift and privilege of having known him, learned from him, and called him a friend. To Côme Laguë, words cannot even begin to express my deep admiration, respect, and love for you. To Rupert Murdoch, for seeing and encouraging the potential in me that at times even I doubted that I had, and for believing in me and supporting me all these years at some of the most critical junctures. To Jorge Paulo Lemann, a Renaissance man, for sharing with me your supremely well-balanced outlook on life, your passion for sport, your wisdom, drive, and humor, as well as your dedication to knowledge. To Paul Tergat, you've entertained, fascinated, and inspired me for years with your athletic accomplishments. You are without a doubt one of Africa's most precious gifts to the world. To Howard Stevenson, for being a father to me; for always telling me the truth, even when it hurt; for pulling me out of more crises and cruxes than I care to enumerate; and for understanding, supporting, and encouraging me to dream big.

Special thanks to Marion Maneker, my esteemed editor at HarperCollins, without whose constant wisdom, guidance, encouragement, and insight this book would not have been. To the amazing Edwin Tan for his constant vigilance throughout the entire editorial process. Thanks as well to the entire creative, marketing, and support team at HarperCollins, with whom it is always a pleasure to work. Thanks to "Dr." Lisa Chase, the book physician, whose countless hours of painstaking surgery helped resuscitate the patient.

And last but certainly not least, to the Harvard Business School, Class of 1993, in particular the Slammin' "Ds," for two unforgettable years and for the unbreakble ties that continue to bind.

Endnotes

CHAPTER 2

1. Regrettably, shortly after we graduated in 1993 HBS dispensed with this wonderful Darwinian tradition and now preassigns seats instead.

2. Disclamer: I am frequently told that I look "different," I speak with an accent, and therefore I stand out. This means that when I speak it is easy for people to recall that I have spoken and not to confuse me with someone else. My comments, good ones and bad ones, were therefore more likely to be remembered by the professor and for a much longer time than usual. The impossibility of my simply blending in was indispensable to the success of my Cold Call Strategic Defense Initiative. Unfortunately, Grant Winfrey did not have that advantage.

CHAPTER 3

1. Even if one subscribes to a much broader geographic definition of "East Asia," the conclusions are the same.

CHAPTER 5

1. Modified from *Cultures of the World: Liberia*, by Patricia Levy, p. 90. Reference edition published 1999 by Marshall Cavendish Corporation, Tarrytown, NY, 10591.

2. From *Maiden Voyages and Infant Colonies: Two Women's Travel Narratives of the 1790s*. Edited by Dierdre Coleman Leicester, University Press.

CHAPTER 6

1. This was a game in which we would gather in the center of the gym and the coach would yell in random succession "port," "starboard," or "deck,"

and we would have to run either to the front, the middle, or the back—a very tedious and disorienting exercise that I detested but in which I excelled because of my speed and competitiveness.

CHAPTER 9

1. The Liberian government was in an economic depression at the end of King's term, and in 1926, while he was still in office, had obtained a loan from the United States, secured by Firestone. By 1931, it was clear that the government was unable to make payments on the loan and Firestone and the lending bank were unwilling to forgive it. The Council of the League of Nations had stepped in and offered to assist Liberia provided that the government give them carte blanche to run the administration. Eventually, King's successor, Edwin Barclay, accepted the assistance of the Council, but limited the scope of its mandate and the number of League delegates assigned to the Liberian government to two individuals.

CHAPTER 10

1. The latex is extracted or tapped from the rubber tree by means of making a small incision in the bark of the tree and collecting the milky white fluid, or sap, that drains out into little tin collection cups, tied around the tree for this purpose. We could always smell the distinctive scent of the rubber on those frequent trips between Yekepa and Monrovia as we drove along the road, both sides fenced by acres and acres of trees with the small tin cups tied around them.

2. Secretary of State Cyrus Vance resigned his post on Monday, April 21, 1980, over the Carter administration's decision to invade Iran to rescue the U.S. hostages that were being held there. The mass execution of the dignitaries in Liberia occurred one day later, on Tuesday, April 22, 1980. The failed U.S. hostage rescue mission to Tehran was launched two days later.

3. Once Doe had installed himself in office and demonstrated his version of a reformed government, Liberians facetiously referred to the PRC as "People Repeating Corruption."

CHAPTER 11

1. Abayomi is a Yoruba word meaning "I am satisfied." It is often the name given to the last child, as thanks to God and expressing one's gratitude and satisfaction. Pappi's last word was "I am satisfied."

CHAPTER 12

1. U.S. covert aid to Angola totaled about US$250 million between 1986 and

1991, making it the second largest U.S. covert program, exceeded only by aid to the Afghan *mujahedeen* (source: Human Rights Watch, *Angola Unravels,* 1999).

2. FAPLA: Forças Armadas Populares de Libertação de Angola (People's Armed Forces for the Liberation of Angola).

CHAPTER 13

1. In 2002 Valerie Giscard D'Estaing was elected chairman of the European Convention on the Future of Europe, the ultimate, though unlikely goal of which is to build a United States of Europe.

2. Bokassa returned to the Central African Republic in 1986 and was put on trial for treason, murder, embezzlement, and cannibalism. He was exonerated of the cannibalism charges, but found guilty of the rest. He was sentenced to death in 1987. The death sentence was later commuted to life in prison. In 1993 General André Kolingba, who himself had come to power in 1981 by a coup d'état against the former president David Dacko (who, with French support, had engineered the ousting of Bokassa), granted amnesty to Bokassa. Bokassa died in 1996 of a heart attack. He was 75 years old.

3. Huband, *The Liberian Civil War,* p. 174, as quoted from *The Liberian Civil War* by Mark Huband, copyright © 1998 by Mark Huband. Used by permission of Frank Cass Publishers, London.

4. Of course, by this, Swift is indicating that the inhabitants of Laputa have their heads in the clouds, although it must be said, in defense of half of the population of Laputa, and to Swift's credit, that apparently the women of Laputa, unlike the men, did not have their heads in the clouds, were not interested in these fancy theories, and longed to escape to terra firma, but for the fact that they needed the men's permission to do so, which was never granted.

5. *Gulliver's Travels: The Politics of Satire,* Ronald Knowles, London, Prentice-Hall International, p. 99, as quoted from *Gulliver's Travels* by Paul Turner, Oxford University Press.

EPILOGUE

1. "Pat Robertson's Gold Fever," December 2001, Bob Rury and Aram Roston, *GQ* Magazine, www.globalwitness, p.3.

2. Britain had sent troops into Sierra Leone in 2000 to help quell the rebel force and restore peace in the long-running civil war in their former colony. France sent troops to Côte d'Ivoire in 2002 to help stabilize the situation after rebels sought to overthrow the government there—both of these conflicts had strong links to the Taylor government of Liberia.

Index